Revealing Truth

Topical Insights and Revelations for a renewed life

Romans 15:18

by Linda Lange
Life Application Ministries

REVEALING TRUTH

First Edition published in Mt. Aukum, CA, February 2007
Second Edition published in Mt. Aukum, CA, May, 2008
Third Edition published and printed July 2008

4th Edition - Published and Printed 2015

5th Edition - Updated and Revised - 2018

Linda Lange Resources.
P.O. Box 165
Mt. Aukum, CA 95656
(530) 620-2712

e-mail: linda@truthfrees.org

www.truthfrees.org

Published by Life Application Ministries Publications (LAMP)

Book Cover Design: Barbara Hicks
Type design: Linda Lange, LAMP
Printer: Createspace.com

This book is a comprised edition of the teachings provided on the Life Application Ministries Web site.

All Scripture references are from the King James Version of the Bible

Dedicated to my husband Tom,
who patiently endured
while God was molding me and making me
into His image, and helping others.

Index

Preface

This is an condensed version of each topic that I teach in my conferences and seminars. Filled with personal experiences combined with scriptures and revelations that I have received from the Lord to share with others. Such as things I went through that caused me to change more in the Image of our Father in Heaven. Since God has given me the gift of teaching, I now share these insights and revelations with you in hopes you too will share and mentor others. We are all called to make disciples of all men. If you read that passage, we aren't to go about dragging people to church but to love on them and instruct them in the righteousness of God... then that causes them to turn to the Lord with their heart. *"The goodness of the Lord draws people to repentance"* (Romans 2:4).

This book/guide is to help us find health and healing for ourselves so we can be a witness and hope to others. If you go about teaching on healing and yet you are sick all the time, will they listen? Frankly, Christians are to be the happiest and healthiest people on this planet and if that is not the case, we need to see where we are missing something. This Christian life involves our participation. We are to be "doers of the word not hearers only being deceived." (James 1). The Scriptures say that we are to recover ourselves out of the snare of the devil (2 Timothy 2:24-26). We are to cleanse ourselves of the flesh and spirit (2 Corinthians 7:1).

This means, we have some things to do. If we are waiting on God to do everything, you will be waiting a long time. He came to "help" us, not do it for us. So as we walk in faith, it produces action. James says that our faith is demonstrated by how we live (James 2:18).

I have been given a commission of helping people become reconciled to God, thereby, manifesting truth within resulting in healing without. Before we begin, it's important we go to God and ask for His help and guidance during this time of teaching, learning, sharing and receiving. The Lord works on an individual basis so we need to begin by asking Him to teach you what is vital for your life, making things clear so you are equipped to teach others.

Revelation 12:13 says, *"We overcome him by the blood of the Lamb and the word of our testimony."* These teachings are comprised of my personal experiences on how the Lord applied His Word to my life. For over 20 years I have been sharing and teaching these principles and have helped countless thousands! I hope you will be counted with them.

Introduction

I've learned that complete restoration with our Heavenly Father is the main theme of this book. If we have any reservations about who God is, what He is doing, why we are here, why we aren't being blessed, doubt and unbelief toward Him, fear and worry, we are being separated from His blessings.

We cannot receive anything when we are not walking in fellowship with Him. Many people are angry with God for so many different things and they don't even know it. For example, when relationships don't work out, or when bad things happen, deep inside God is blamed. It's that "deep inside" stuff that is causing us to be separated from the blessings God wants us to have.

Relationship with the Father's love is the most important part of our healing and restoration. It isn't until we develop and understand the love of God in our lives that healing truly begins. When we have no worry, no doubt, no fear, but total trust—peace and joy in believing God for all things— then we can find complete deliverance.

Each situation in our lives, either physically or spiritually could be a direct result of the relationship we have with God our Father. Many cannot comprehend God as their LOVING Father because they've not known their own earthly father's love. Many have had poor examples of love and it has resulted in their dis-eases.

When we begin our quest for more of God it spills into our own relationship with ourselves. As we accept and receive God's love for us (which this book goes into details about) you are able to love yourselves easier. Until we know the love of God, we cannot love ourselves. When we aren't loving ourselves we cannot possibly love others, nor even God for that matter. When we have guilt, shame, self-hatred, self-rejection, and self-conflict we can't possibly love ourselves. We are separated from ourselves when we cannot love ourselves and accept who we are. This is telling God that He made a mistake creating us. But what does the Word say?

"Before you were ever conceived in the womb, I ordained you" (Jeremiah 1). *"We are fearfully and wonderfully made"* (Psalm 139:14). *"How precious are thy thoughts toward me"* (Psalm 139:17). These are the truths we need to feed ourselves so that it sinks deep into our spirit and becomes WHO we are— not just WHAT we know. Our head can be filled with so many truths, but until that truth becomes part of who we are and what we believe, we will still be in bondage.

This book is to help you discover if it's sin that could be preventing your blessings, or spiritual oppression, or if it's from your ancestors. This book will help you discover for yourself and teach you what to do about it so you can be made free, thus, being equipped to help others.

Many of the insights are speaking directly to you because you first have to get it before you can truly be effective to others. Romans 15:18 says that Paul only taught what the Lord wrought in him. In other words, we are to only teach what we received healing in. I know for a fact that it does more for a person who can see I am set free than someone who tells about it. It gives more hope!

A Few Reminders

1. As you access each session, it's important that you are "diligent" and complete each step to the fullest. A diligent person will make rich (Proverbs 10:24). Allow time after each session to reflect on what you have learned, not rush on to the next teaching before it has had time to really do a work in your heart. Head knowledge alone isn't going to make you free. We need to allow time for the seeds that have been planted to grow and take root into our hearts. We not only need the "knowledge" but the understanding as well. Understanding brings revelation, and revelation changes lives.

2. 1-2-3 punch! Enter into His courts with Thanksgiving. So #1 - Thank the Lord. Take a moment to really thank Him for who He is and what He has done in your life. This opens us up to God doing something in our lives. We get God's ear. #2 - Praise God. This brings Him into your environment. You may even FEEL His presence when we praise Him. He inhabits the praises of His people. #3 - Worship Him in Spirit and in Truth - This all about Him. Focusing on Him at this point tells God you really trust Him. That you reference and love Him. Nothing else is to be on your mind when you WORSHIP God. Him and Him alone. When we do these three things (every day) we are now positioning ourselves to RECEIVE all that we desire.

3. While reading these segments you may become overwhelmed or "heavy" spirited. That's the time to stop and take a breather. It reminds me of when rain comes down so hard that it causes flooding. If the waters come too quickly it doesn't have time to absorb into the soil, and all that water is wasted. But if the water comes softly and just enough that the ground absorbs it, then it does great good! This is like the information being imparted to you. If it comes too quickly, it will not absorb and much is lost and may even cause you to feel overwhelmed. So give yourself permission to read this book slowly. This is not a novel you can sit down and read in a few hours. It may take you a week or a month because you'll be "eating" a lot of truth and it has to have time to digest for it to be of any value. Remember, these are life-changing insights I went through over a 20-year span.

4. If you are using this book to teach others, be sure you have it clearly settled in your own heart first. If you need more help, you can contact me at any time at linda@truthfrees.org.

God bless you on your journey.

CHAPTER ONE

Salvation and Repentance

This session has to be the first one you go through because as a minister, my first order of business is to preach the gospel of salvation. It is the foundation for the Christian. By accepting Christ as your Savior, you are not only assured eternal life, but now have the power to live this in victory. I'm not saying that things won't be hard at times or you have to face some tough issues, but you will have the ability, power, and joy to endure all things!

So, if you go through these teachings without the power within to "do" what is taught, then it becomes a self-help book where you use your own power to accomplish. But when you have the power of the Holy Ghost within, then it will be easier to grasp and do.

Does any of these following statements pertain to you? If you are ministering to another, have them answer these questions.

- If you are saved but sometimes doubt you are saved.
- If you aren't saved, how to become saved and what it really means.
- If you believe you are a Christian because you go to church.
- If you think you keep loosing your salvation. (There are some who keep saying a sinner's prayer almost every week.)
- If you are not sure what repentance means.
- If you believe Jesus is Lord but don't believe He was raised from the dead.
- If you want clarity so you can help others come to know the Lord.

This session is to help you learn the truth about where you are in relationship to the Lord by helping you find your place in the Kingdom of God. I've had the opportunity to lead many to the Lord, some have even stated that they used to doubt their salvation but after reading this session, they are no longer in doubt. When we have this assurance, we will have what we need to be victorious believers.

For those who have not received Christ as Savior, it may be difficult to understand what I'll be sharing because it's the Holy Ghost within you that gives you the ability to understand what you are learning. So before going to the "meat" of the teachings, please go through this session thoroughly. This is also good information for those who are secure in their salvation to help others who aren't.

Before we can really start our journey to freedom, we have to get first things first—knowing without a doubt we have been bought and paid for by the Blood of the Lamb—Jesus Christ. If we are unsure, then we are in for a rocky relationship with our self, with others and with God, resulting in frustration, anger, hopelessness, accusations, fear, doubt and unbelief.

The Bible says that we need not keep going over the salvation plan or we'll never grow up (known as one of the doctrines of Christ - Hebrews 6:1). This has to be settled once and for all, and you have to believe it and never doubt it again. Some of you have been Christians for a long time, yet you battle daily in these very areas. I believe by the time you finish reading and praying through this you will have a certainty in your heart to live your life in Christ.

The first step is to go to the Word and see what it says:

- *"As it is written, there is none righteous, no not one"* (Romans 4:10).
- *"For all have sinned and come short of the Glory of God"* (Romans 4:23).
- *"For the wages of sin is death, but the gift of God is eternal life through Jesus Christ our Lord"* (Romans 6:23).
- *"If we say we have no sin then the truth is not in us"* (1 John 1:5-8).
- *"If we confess with our mouth the Lord Jesus Christ, and believe in our heart that God raised Him from the dead, we shall be saved"* (Romans 10:9).
- *"God so loved the world that He gave His only begotten Son, that whosoever believes in Him, shall not perish but have everlasting life"* (John 3:16).
- *"If we confess our sins, He is faithful and just to forgive us our sins, and cleanse us from all unrighteousness"* (1 John 1:9).
- *"Whosoever believes in Him shall not perish but have everlasting life"* (Romans 10:13).
- *"We are saved by grace through faith, not of yourselves, it is the gift of God, not of works, lest any man should boast"* (Ephesians 2:8).
- *"But the Comforter, which is the Holy Ghost, whom the Father will send in My name (Jesus), He shall teach you all things, and bring all things to your remembrance, whatsoever I have said to you. Peace I leave with you, My peace I give unto you; not as the world giveth, so let not your heart be troubled, neither let it be afraid"* (John 14:26-27).
- Acts 2:38 *"Then Peter said unto them, Repent, and be baptized every one of you in the name of Jesus Christ for the remission of sins, and ye shall receive the gift of the Holy Ghost."*

These scriptures clearly show us a main theme. If you believe! That is what you need to do to be saved and to continue growing in the things of the Lord. Being saved does not mean you have to go and prove to the world you are saved by starting some worldwide ministry, or "trying" to be perfect. Being saved comes from believing, and then from believing you will begin living accordingly. I discovered that I couldn't do anything from my heart if I didn't first believe it. If I began "doing" something without believing it to be true, it becomes works of the flesh and I can end up making a big mess! God looks upon our heart, not our works. Because our works reflect what is going on in our heart! So then as we "go" and "do" the Word then others will see our good works and that could lead to their conversion as well because it's from our heart. We win others by our example, not by our Words. (Except if you are preaching the Word... faith does come by hearing and hearing the Word of God - that isn't what I'm talking about here.) I'm talking about being living epistles.

Trying to be a good example is not what you are to do either to get God to love you and to accept you. If you believe that you are righteous, then you will live without judging others. If you believe you are holy, then you will love and forgive, yourself and others. If you believe you are forgiven, then you won't live under guilt and condemnation. If you live in God's mercy, you will be merciful. If you receive God's unconditional love for you, you will love yourself and others unconditionally.

Matthew 8:13 says, *As you have believed, let it be done unto you.* And when it's done unto you, you do it unto others, without effort! You cannot give to others what you don't have to give! It's who you are not what you do! I hope this is clear. It's not that we won't "do" things, it's when we "do" things, where is our heart?

However, IF... well I mean "When" we offend someone, we are to go to that person and be reconciled to them. This is what being a Christian is all about, loving and forgiving. But more about that in later sessions - I'm getting ahead of myself.

When you truly believe something, you will "live" it easily and naturally, without effort! This is the peace God speaks of in the Bible. If you start believing, the rest will follow. Believing is ONLY the beginning of a lifelong journey. If you don't believe something now, pray that God help you believe. Mark 9:24 is the story of a man who said to Jesus, I want to believe, so help me to believe.

The Bible is very clear that God puts in us the will and ability to do His good pleasure (Philippians 2:13). So get off that treadmill of "good works" and just believe what you believe and do what you know to do, because it's not you doing the "good" anyway. The Bible says we can do "nothing" apart from Him (John 15:5).

In other words, we can do nothing of "Heavenly value" without Him. This is where most people start to have problems. Once we are saved by believing, we are recruited to begin "doing" a bunch of stuff, either by others, our church or even ourselves. We jump in and begin "trying" to be a Christian! The same way you were saved is the same way you continue living, by believing (Galatians 3:1-3). We are only perfected in our Christian walk by faith (believing) and that comes in time, not over night! You do not need to be doing more than you believe right now!

What I mean is that you are okay right where you are, you don't have to "try" to do any more than you are doing, unless of course the Lord is leading you "by faith" to do something more.

I found that when I finally got the following things down in my life, my life took a radical change for the better:

- That I'm truly saved (I doubted it from time to time because of what I would do or think).

- To live my life simply believing (I wasn't doing this either, I was out "trying" to accomplish the Christian life instead of entering into God's rest to accomplish it for me!)

- And most of all that God loved me, just as I am, at all times, regardless of what I think, said or did.

If we believed we are truly saved, then we won't have any question about God's love for us. "For God so loved the world that He gave..." (John 3:16). This is the KEY to living the life of a believer. And I know that many of you "know" God loves you, but what you have to do is "believe" He loves you. That is evidenced if you can "receive" it personally right now for yourselves! When we truly believe something, it becomes part of us, not like "knowledge" that comes and goes. When we truly believe, it becomes a permanent fixture in our lives. We begin living what we believe! The Bible says that we should lay a firm foundation so we can begin building on it, but if we still have to keep going over and over the foundation points, we'll never grow. Ask God now to help you get this once and for all for yourself - even if you have been a Christian for many years like I was.

IMPORTANT! When we believe what I just shared, the next step is to receive. We believe AND receive to be complete. I can believe Jesus died on the cross for my sins, but until I receive that truth into my life, it's nothing. The devils even "believe" the difference is they cannot "receive." This is CRITICAL for you to be able to have the kind of relationship you want with God the Father, God the Son and God the Holy Ghost. We "receive" totally when we apply the sacrifice Jesus gave. So as we confess our sins, we then "receive" forgiveness of our sins by faith (believing our sins are forgiven). This is where people get tripped up. They may confess their sins, but can't believe they are forgiven. Again, if you don't believe you are forgiven, then you aren't. Remember, "Whatever you believe, let it be done unto you" (Matthew 8:13), it goes both ways.

Until we "receive" and "apply" (appropriate) that forgiveness to our sin, we will be under guilt and condemnation. People who are under guilt of any kind or feeling condemned for any reason have NOT applied the forgiveness and sacrifice to their lives.

So perhaps you "know" you are saved, but do you "believe" you are saved, that is the real question.

This is the foundation for us to grow up in Christ. Many are "trying" to be Christians but don't have the power behind it (the Holy Ghost within) to "be" a Christian. When we receive Christ (believe what I shared above), we are given the power to overcome sin. And truthfully, that is what being a believer means. Believing is the power to be victorious over all sin. If sin were not in the world, we would not need a Savior. After all, Jesus came to save us FROM our sin! It's all about "sin" (Matthew 1:21). Because it's sin that separated us from Him in the first place back with Adam and Eve.

Once we have been saved, now what do we do? As I shared moments ago, we are to continue our lives "believing" not "doing" as the scriptures say (Galatians 3:1-3). Doing comes after we truly believed AND received the salvation and forgiveness of sins. However, many are out doing a bunch of stuff thinking it's what they are supposed to be doing as part of their salvation. This is error and bondage. The scripture, "Faith without works is dead" (James 2:17) is really talking about the manifestation of faith. God looks at the heart and motive for whatever we do, and if it's not being done in faith, no matter what it is, it's counted as sin (Romans 14:23). But a person who truly has received a revelation on being forgiven and applying it daily to their lives, they will have "works" that are not dead. They will have fruit, and many will be touched by this person's life, because it's from faith.

Repentance:

Now that we understand a bit more about salvation, repentance follows. We need to understand what "repentance" means. We are to live a life in truth. (John 17:17) What is really awesome is that God has made a way for us to remain a Christian even when we do things wrong because of the price Jesus paid for our sins - we ARE forgiven. Forever! But we need to believe we are forgiven – that's what it means when Jesus told the disciples the work they were to do was "believe" (John 6:29). He knew that believing was going to be the most difficult thing we would do. But to only believe is the first part of repentance, then we need to receive. I can believe I'm forgiven, but it does me little good until I receive the forgiveness. If I go around "knowing" I can fall under guilt and condemnation. But once I "receive" it, I'm made free of all guilt and condemnation! We don't have to beg to be forgiven. We ARE forgiven.

A double minded man is unstable in all his ways and he shall receive nothing of the Lord (James 1:6-8). If we believe and then doubt, believe and then doubt, this is double-mindedness. We are not saved one day when we "think" we are good, and not saved the next when we "think" we are bad. When our children do this, does that make our children any less our children when they disobey? No, they are still your child. Same with us, we are still saved and children of God regardless!

As we go out into the world from conversion, we have opportunity to come up against so many obstacles. How deep our roots are from the first moment we believe is how we will weather these obstacles (Mark 4:3-8), Good roots are made deep when you truly "believe" what I've just shared. Paul said to be rooted and grounded in the love of God (believing in and receiving God's love). He knew this was foundation for living a victorious life in Christ.

When we receive Jesus Christ as our Savior, we have been given a desire to serve Him. We desire to turn from those things we used to serve to serve Him. We may not do such a good job, but we want to follow Him none-the-less. By turning from those things we used to follow, this is called repentance. Falling out of agreement with something we used to agree with – it's a choice. We may not do it perfectly all the time, but the desire is there, this is one indicator you are saved! Again, that is why Jesus came, so when we don't do things perfectly, we have a Savior to forgive us and help us go on.

I worked with someone recently who was seeking help from the Lord, people ministered to her, she even went to seminars and conferences, she knew the Bible was the help she needed but struggled terribly to live in victory. She shared with me that she realized she was never really saved! It wasn't until she "understood" what repentance meant that it "clicked" in her spirit. She has since found her assurance and hope and now is living serving the Lord and enjoying all the blessings promised. Before she kept wondering why she wasn't being blessed, she was "doing" all the things a Christian was supposed to do, but she only had half the truth. Salvation AND Repentance goes hand in hand.

Once we have recognized the need for a Savior and have received Him by confessing He is the Son of God and accepting all He did for us on the cross, we are SEALED by the power of the Holy Ghost (John 13). The Holy Ghost begins to shine the light on things inside of us that needs to go. As we see that thing, it's not time to get mad at ourselves, confused or fearful. It's time to say, "Thank you Lord for showing me what is in my heart, I want to be free from it." This is repentance. Recognizing the thing and then deciding in your heart you want no part of it. It doesn't mean you are going to be clean from it at that very moment because some things take time for God to work it OUT of us. Things like anger, fear, jealousy, etc. Some things take more time. Be thankful that God is taking His time with you and that you don't see all that junk at once!!

One area I find that could be a block to living in the Kingdom of God is that we live in our own kingdom. When we take on the robe Christ gave us, it's also saying we have enlisted in His army. 2 Timothy talks about being a "good soldier." Keeping our eyes on the "Commander and Chief" not on ourselves.

Recently the Lord showed me I had been living in my own kingdom. My husband would say things like, "The world as Linda knows it." What he was jokingly telling me was not everything was about me and for me. This is "self" kingdom living. It's something I had to see within myself and confess to God. As I did, it gave God permission to begin purging that part of me. It has been painful because it's an emotional pain of dying to self - but what I needed to focus on is the GAIN of it all! I'll be living in more peace, satisfaction, joy, love, and exercising the power of God in my life - because I'm dwelling in HIS Kingdom, not my own made up of wants and desires to make ME comfortable. I also know that my life will send out a beautiful scent of God, which will draw people instead of causing to run the other way when they see me coming. Jesus said if you lose your life for my sake you shall find it (Matthew 10:39 and Matthew 16:25). So by losing myself in His word He began teaching me how to find myself so that I can lose my life in Him. This is a process.

So where is God's Kingdom? It's inside of us (Luke 17:21). Because of this, it becomes a tug-of-war. How do I know when I'm living in my own kingdom? When I put my own interests, needs, desires before God and others. Repentance is described in 1 Thessalonians 1:9, as "Turning to God from idols." Remember the Holy Ghost says to believers, "Little children, guard yourselves from idols" (1 John.5:21). What are the idols talked about here? Anything that comes between you and your Heavenly Father is an idol. So how do you know if it's an idol? Whatever consumes you is an idol. We are to be consumed with God, praying without ceasing, acknowledging Him in all our ways, this clearly states we are to be consumed with Him. He's a consuming fire and wants to burn inside of you. But if you have one thing between Him and you it is an idol. See, God wants you to enjoy this life and have things, but not at the expense of losing Him.

He will give you what you want after you get first things first. Putting Him first is VITAL for your living then He can begin giving to you all your desires.

There have been times I've seen this happen. For example there was something I really wanted. I was so consumed in my thoughts about it. Then one day I said, Father, forgive me for being consumed with this desire. If I never get this thing, I will still love you, I release it to you now. I can't say it wasn't with tears and gut wrenching pain giving it up, but I gave it up. When I gave it willingly to Him, He removed the pain associated with that want. Then not too many days later the Lord gave it back to me in its fullness. This has happened many, many times in my life so I know this is true. But you have to truly be willing to dis-connect with that desire and if it's something God wants to restore to you, He will. This is what it means to lose your life and you shall find it.

God tested Abraham's devotion that day to check whether Isaac had become an idol in his life. God told him, as it were, that he had to turn from all idolatry if he was to serve the Lord. And so he had to place his son on the altar and give him up. God did not take Isaac away, because God was only detaching Abraham from his unnatural attachment to Isaac that would have hindered his walk with Him. God has to do the same with us. We have to give him that which is most precious to us.

Let me clarify something before we go on. When you are saved, you are saved. Repentance is what we do daily after we are saved that helps us to "serve" the Lord. Our main purpose on this planet is to serve Him and if you aren't doing that you'll never be completely happy.

Let's look at Isaac. He had to "turn from" idolatry if he was to "serve" the Lord. But the truth is, any person who claims to be a Christian gets a desire to "serve" the Lord, so that's why understanding repentance is important. If we don't get this, we may just go around in circles all our lives not understanding why God isn't using us while on this planet and why the blessings spoken of in the Word aren't happening in our lives.

In the rich young ruler's case it was his money. Just like God asked Abraham to give up Isaac, God asked the rich young ruler to give up his money. For all you know, if that rich man had only said "Yes, Lord, here it is all," God may have told him that he could keep his money, just like he told Abraham to keep Isaac. But he had to give it up first. As you know, this rich young man didn't give up his money and turned away sad. I believe that until we do what we were meant to do, we'll never be happy, there will always be sadness until it's fulfilled.

I ask that you take a moment to say: "Lord whatever Isaac's there are in my life, I lay them all on the altar and give them all up to you. I don't want any more idols in my life that come between you and me. I don't want to live for myself. I really want to live for you alone. I want to live for your glory. I don't want to live for myself or for my glory."

If you have wasted much time in profitless pursuits in the past, you can't do anything about that now. You can confess your sin of selfishness, etc., receive forgiveness now and start the day a-new. The Bible says His mercies are "new" every morning (Lamentations 3:23). Since you are reading this, I assume you are still alive and breathing so there is still time ahead for you. Salvation comes through faith in Jesus. There is nothing else you can do to receive it, earn it or pay for it. It's a free gift to all who believe. If you have problems believing then pray to God to "help your unbelief." 2 Timothy 3:15 says *"And that from a child thou has known the holy scriptures, which are able to make thee wise unto salvation through faith which is in Christ Jesus."*

On a final note, I need to bring to mind the story of the two thieves on the cross next to Jesus. The two thieves began having a conversation: One of the thieves questioned who Jesus was, but the other said, "This man has done nothing wrong." And admitted that his punishment fit his crime. Then he turned to Jesus and said, "Will you remember me in your kingdom?" And Jesus replied, "Today you shall be with me in paradise."

This is good news! The thief didn't have to get down off the cross to be baptized to be saved. He didn't have to say a sinner's prayer. All He did was acknowledge his sin, and believed that Jesus was the Son of God, and he was saved that day! We are making things more difficult than they need to be!

Romans 10:9 *"That if thou shalt confess with thy mouth the Lord Jesus, and shalt believe in thine heart that God hath raised him from the dead, thou shalt be saved."*

There are several prayers below that address each and every area we spoke of in this chapter. Be sure to go through them, or pray your own, the Lord is listening and waiting for you with open arms.

Prayer of Salvation: (For the unbeliever)

"Dear Heavenly Father, I recognize that I'm a sinner and in need of a Savior. I believe that Jesus is your Son and that you sent Him to die upon the cross to pay for my sins. I believe He died and rose again on the third day, and now sits at your right hand. I ask you to forgive me of all my sins and help me to know that Jesus paid for them all, there is nothing I can do to add to what Jesus already did at the cross. I ask Jesus to come into my heart and be my Lord and Savior and recognize that the Holy Ghost was deposited in me to be my comforter, teacher, guide and helper. Thank you for coming into my heart and saving me. In Jesus Name, Amen."

Prayer of Repentance: (For those who just prayed for salvation and believers needing to be refreshed in faith.)

"Lord I can't do anything about the years of my life that are past. But I want to live the rest of my life for you alone. Search my heart and see if there are any idols that I am worshipping. I want to turn from every idol in my life to worship and serve you alone. Lord Jesus I repent especially of the idolatry of living for myself. I ask you to come into my life, not only as my Savior, but as my Lord. I pray that you are Lord over my life, not me. I believe you have saved me and will not doubt that salvation again. Help me to believe this every day of my life Lord. I receive your Love, your forgiveness and choose to live for your glory every day. When I fail, I will come to you and confess, I will not fear or doubt or worry I've lost your love - I will only believe that you forgive and receive that love and forgiveness immediately. I pray all these things by faith, in Jesus precious name, Amen.

This is the best news in the world: We don't have to be slaves to our own ambitions and desires any more and thus waste our earthly lives, but can be free to live for the glory of God and thus live useful lives. To live for ourselves is to live in bondage and in chains. To live for the glory of God is to be like the eagles that fly in the sky. The good news of the gospel is that Jesus can break every chain and set you free—TODAY!!"

Prayer of Assurance of Salvation: (For Christians who think they keep losing their salvation.)

"Dear Heavenly Father. I accepted you as my Lord and Savior _____(when). And I have doubted it from time to time. I don't want to doubt it ever again, nor do I want to keep asking you into my heart every time I do something wrong. Help me to believe the complete work Jesus did on the cross. There is nothing I can add to what He has already done, I need to believe that. That Jesus died while we were yet sinners! It may be that I have not "received" so I receive into my life all that Jesus did. I receive the Holy Ghost that seals me and helps me while on this earth. There is nothing I can ever do or say that can take me out of your hands. When I do something wrong, I will not fear, but will run to you and confess all my sins to you, and "receive" forgiveness for my sins. I will not run in the bushes like Adam or blame someone else for my sin. I take responsibility, repent and confess them to you because you love me unconditionally. I receive your unconditional love now in Jesus name. When I do something wrong, I will simply confess my sin and receive forgiveness. I need to confess and receive, that's it Lord. Help me remember to do this. I thank you for your love, forgiveness and help. In Jesus name, Amen."

If you prayed one of these prayers, you'll want to share this with someone! Revelations 12:11 say that we overcome the devil by the blood of the lamb - which you just proclaimed by salvation, and the word of our testimony - which is sharing what you just did. Mark 5:19 says to go and share what the Lord has done for you. By doing this, you are solidifying your decision; you are making a proclamation to the world that you are no longer a puppet to the devil; you are even building faith within and helping others with their faith.

CHAPTER TWO

Baptisms

There are several baptisms named in the Bible, but I'm only going to cover two of them: Water Baptism and the Baptism of the Holy Ghost.

Water Baptism follows salvation and is a step of faith to those who believe. It's full immersion in water, not a sprinkle. It represents the death, burial and resurrection of Jesus Christ. We partake in His death and resurrection to new life by being Baptized, making a proclamation of our new birth in Christ. It's like going into the womb again and coming out anew. Water Baptism also ushers in the power of the Holy Ghost.

There are three instances of the Holy Ghost, and I share them below:

1. <u>Before Jesus, people were baptized</u>: Mark 1:4 *"John did baptize in the wilderness, and preach the baptism of repentance for the remission of sins."*

2. <u>At the time of Jesus, when Jesus was with them</u>: Matthew 3:11 *"I indeed baptize you with water unto repentance. But he that comes after me is mightier than I, whose shoes I am not worthy to bear: He shall baptize you with the Holy Ghost, and with fire."*

3. <u>After Jesus, when He left this earth in his ascension</u>: Acts 2:38 *"Then Peter said unto them, repent, and be baptized every one of you in the name of Jesus Christ for the remission of sins, and ye shall receive the gift of the Holy Ghost."*

Mark 1:4 talks about those who were baptized before Jesus came. And because of that, they would then need to "receive" the Holy Ghost.

Acts 19:2 *"He said unto them, have ye received the Holy Ghost since ye believed? And they said unto him, we have not so much as heard whether there be any Holy Ghost."*

This scripture is used widespread to indicate that a believer is to again receive the Holy Ghost. I believe this scripture refers to those who repented and were baptized BEFORE Jesus came. In the scriptures above, it says they were baptized in water for remission of sins, but Jesus had not yet ascended up into heaven nor was the Holy Ghost available. So when they were asked, "Have you received since you believed?" They needed to "receive" the Holy Ghost, which is done by confession of their faith in Jesus Christ and "receive" what He did on the cross. Again, He hadn't gone to the cross yet.

For us today, if you have received Jesus Christ as your Savior, you have the Holy Ghost because He bears witness in your heart that something took place

(Romans 8:16). We don't need to again receive the Holy Ghost, what you may need to do is be baptized in water to receive the "power" of the Holy Ghost.

Remember the Holy Ghost alighted on Jesus when He came out of the water (Luke 3:22) and after that was when He began His ministry.

Many people are out there doing a bunch of stuff and trying to work the works of God but have never been water baptized. It's not necessary for Salvation, because if we look at the cross, the thief next to Jesus went with Him to paradise the minute he died (Luke 24:43). He didn't need the "power" of the Holy Ghost to live out his life, because he didn't have a life to live out. He didn't have to get down off the cross and be water baptized to be saved. He was saved when he believed and received what Jesus represented! But for those who want to live in the power of the Holy Ghost, we need to be baptized in water.

Another scripture used in Christian circles to indicate the need to be Baptized "in" the Holy Ghost is when the disciples waited in the upper room for the Holy Ghost to come.

Acts 1:5-9 *"For John truly baptized with water; but ye shall be baptized with the Holy Ghost not many days hence. When they therefore were come together, they asked of him, saying, Lord, wilt thou at this time restore again the kingdom to Israel? And he said unto them, it is not for you to know the times or the seasons, which the Father has put in his own power. But ye shall receive power, after that the Holy Ghost is come upon you: and ye shall be witnesses unto me both in Jerusalem, and in all Judea, and in Samaria, and unto the uttermost part of the earth. And when he had spoken these things, while they beheld, he was taken up; and a cloud received him out of their sight."*

Acts 2:1-4 *"And when the day of Pentecost was fully come, they were all with one accord in one place. And suddenly there came a sound from heaven as of a rushing mighty wind, and it filled the house where they were sitting. And there appeared unto them cloven tongues like as of fire, and it sat upon each of them. And they were all filled with the Holy Ghost, and began to speak with other tongues, as the Spirit gave them utterance."*

Again, we need to see when this happened. They were with Jesus during His three years of ministry. They believed, and I bet they were baptized in water at some point. Jesus came with water baptism and with "fire." That fire is the power that He was leaving behind once He ascended into heaven. The disciples couldn't yet receive the Holy Ghost because Jesus hadn't left yet. Jesus said that He will send you the power AFTER He goes into heaven. So they waited in the upper room for that power to come. This is the Baptism of the Holy Ghost and with Fire. Again, this was after Jesus ascended into Heaven. When the spirit came upon them, they showed signs and wonders of that power, even talking in other languages which were understood by people in that native tongue. It wasn't gibberish, it was real words.

Acts 1:9 - part b - it says that when they received the Holy Ghost they will be given power to be a witness. Are you sharing your faith with others? Are you excited about reading the Bible and learning of God? Are you convicted when you sin? Then this is evidence you have the "power" of the Holy Ghost.

Acts 2:38 says that when we repent and are baptized, we shall receive the gift of the Holy Ghost." It doesn't say "gifts" - it says gift. The Holy Ghost Himself is the gift. So, it's very clear here that when you receive Jesus Christ - you are saved - and when you are baptized - you receive the power of the Holy Ghost. How else can you be led? It's the spirit within you leading and guiding you in all truth. You see very clearly when you sin, because the Holy Ghost is within you shining a light on that sin to help it be exposed so you can be cleansed. If that isn't happening in your life, then I would suspect salvation hasn't really occurred. I heard that there are hundreds of believers who don't believe Jesus Christ rose from the dead and many others believe that there is more than one way to Heaven. Even though they "think" they are saved, these individuals aren't and are struggling today "trying" to be a Christian but will never find peace because they don't have the power within to do it.

John 16:7 *"Nevertheless I tell you the truth; it is expedient for you that I go away: for if I go not away, the Comforter will not come unto you; but if I depart, I will send him unto you. And when he comes he will reprove the world of sin, and of righteousness, and of judgment: Of sin, because they believed not on me; of righteousness, because I go to my Father, and ye see me no more; of judgment, because the price of this world is judged."*

John 14:26 *"But the Comforter, which is the Holy Ghost, whom the Father will send in my name, he shall teach you all things, and bring all things to your remembrance, whatsoever I have said unto you."*

These individuals didn't have access to the Holy Spirit. They repented and were baptized, but there was no Holy Ghost to alight upon them, yet. "Have you received since you believed" should be asked for someone who never put their faith in Christ.

I have had several experiences where this was true and had the opportunity to lead them to Christ. They thought they were Christians. They attended church faithfully, they even sang in the choir, read their Bible and even helped in church services. They walked the walk, and talked the talk, but they knew something was missing. Inside they were confused and unsure and full of doubt and fear of many things, including salvation. So I simply asked, "Have you received the Holy Ghost since you believed?"

In one case, after ministering for some time I came to the conclusion that this person may not be saved, so I asked, "Have you received the Holy Ghost since you believed?" He wasn't sure what I meant. Then I asked, "Have you received Jesus Christ as your personal Savior?" He replied, "I've always been a Christian." Then I asked, "Can you tell me of your conversion experience?" He was unable to. But He said, "I believe that Jesus is the Son of God. I believe in God." I asked Him again, "But have you received the Holy Ghost since you believed?"

He paused for a moment and said, "No, I don't think so." After ministering to him along these lines he agreed to pray with me for salvation.

In these cases, after praying with me, they would tell me that they felt different. They knew something happened, yet all those years no one helped them come to Christ. They were given tasks and jobs and work to do but no one asked them, "Have you received the Holy Ghost since you believed?"

See, even the devils believe (James 2:19), but they can't receive!!!! We as humans can and have every opportunity to do so until we take our last breath on this earth.

Once we have received the Holy Ghost through salvation and water baptism, we are now able to baptize others. Yes, you! It doesn't have to be a preacher or a teacher or minister. It can be anyone who is a believer and has followed the Lord in full water immersion Baptism. How do I know this? Because the scriptures say that "we" are to baptize in the name of the Father, Son and Holy Ghost. Who are we? All of us.

Mark 16:15-19 *"And he (Jesus) said unto them, Go ye (all of us) into all the world, and preach the gospel to every creature. He that believes and is baptized shall be saved; but he that believes not shall be damned. And these signs shall follow them that believe; In my name shall they cast out devils; they shall speak with new tongues; They shall take up serpents; and if they drink any deadly thing, it shall not hurt them; they shall lay hands on the sick, and they shall recover. So then after the Lord had spoken unto them, he was received up into heaven, and sat on the right hand of God."*

I am greatly disturbed by religious beliefs that evidence of having the Holy Ghost is that you have to speak in tongues. This is totally false and puts so many in doubt, fear and unbelief because they think they are missing something. This can cause them to think God has held something back, which can result in more problems in their walk. They think that God has some how left out of this part for them and so they begin wondering if God really loves them as much as they love those who do speak in tongues. I would like to put that to rest and say, speaking in tongues is one gift, but not the only gift. And it's evidence that you have the Holy Ghost in power when you have a desire to follow the Lord. When you want to share your faith. When you want to live for God. See, I know many who speak in tongues but their lives are a wreck. I know many who don't speak in tongues, and they have peace. But the problem is, those that speak in tongues make those feel bad who don't, and it's a form of manipulation and pride. We need to stop all that and just love.

If you feel that you don't have the "power" to live as a believer, perhaps you have not received since you believed. If you want to be water baptized, find someone who is a believer and has been baptized in water to baptize you. Simply have them say, "I baptize you in the name of the Father, the Son and the Holy Ghost - Amen." Then dunk you. As you are put under remember that this signifies Jesus' death, burial and resurrection. Acknowledge that as you go down, and when you come up, open your heart up to receiving the fire of the Holy Ghost. When you do this, you are now equipped to lay hands on the sick so that they recover, to cast out devils, to speak with new tongues. And by the way, it's not just speaking in so called "tongues" it's speaking with authority in words of faith and hope. You begin speaking through the power of the Holy Ghost. You will understand what it means when the Lord said "Don't take thought of what you are going to say, the Holy Ghost will say it through you" (Matthew 10:19).

But there are also Christians who have believed, received and have been water Baptized yet don't live in power. That power doesn't take over, you don't become a puppet. Even with accessing this power, you have to be determined and willing to allow that power to indwell in you. And during this book, you will see perhaps what is blocking this power from dwelling richly in you. Not just power to "do" a bunch of stuff, but the power to just live in righteousness, peace and joy every day of your life so that no matter what comes your way you remain stable and secure.

After having gone through everything I have shared with you in this book, I can say that I am on the other side of things. I am living in a peaceful calm state of mind. It was all that "junk" that had to go in order for me to dwell in this environment 24 hours a day. It can happen for you too. Just press on and press in with God, do your part, but above all, let Him do His.

CHAPTER THREE

Image of God

A father's presence is so critical to the environment of the home environment. I had been told that the woman is the one who holds the family together, but that isn't true. It's the man who sets the tone in the home. Because if a man loved the wife as Christ loved the church, the woman would be at peace, then the children would be at peace. We put too much on the mother, when it's the father's responsibility. You may even see that for yourself in your own family. A father that is demanding and unyielding is a father who breeds fear in the wife, which then passes on to the children. This is a woman who doesn't feel loved by her husband and will treat the children as she is being treated. It's the man's responsibility not the woman's to hold the family together. The anointing doesn't flow up, it flows down from the head, God, to Jesus, Jesus to the man, the man to the woman, etc..

As we look at the relationship we have had with our earthly father and mother, it will determine how much intimacy you will have, how much you can trust, how much you can believe and affects your image of God.

When we fail and know we deserve judgment are we fearful of God? If we are, then we'll treat others the way we believe God treats us when we fail. This too is incorrect.

God wants to inhabit us (abide in) and be comfortable with Him, be ourselves, feeling accepted, and full of peace. He doesn't want to be a visitor or a fare weather friend. He wants to move in to our home, which is our heart. When we entertain visitors we put on an "act" and we can't really be ourselves most of the time. God is not looking for a visitation, He's looking for habitation.

We need to believe God loves us the way we are, not the way we should be. And as taught in previous sessions, the Holy Spirit will lead, guide and direct you in all truth so that you can confess anything that is in you that is not of God, thereby, being purged and cleansed bringing you into more holiness.

God will not rest until we rest in Him. Isaiah 66:1 (Where is there a house I may rest?) He will not cease in His labors until he finds rest in you. He will never give up on you! And as long as we feel unworthy, stinky, we can't love ourselves, nor find rest in God, He will be there wooing us into His arms.

John 1:18 (Jesus proceeded from the bosom Father) John 8:14 (Jesus then went back to where he came) Verse 21: Disclose -I will make known to you by all your 5 senses; 25 - I will make a home in you.

We can't rest when we think we have to be perfect and do everything right. If our image of God is that we're loved when we do everything right, we will never be at peace.

When the world is pressing in on you, when you are made to feel shame, what do you begin to think? If it's anything other than: "The Father Loves me the way I am now, not what I should be" then you'll look for comfort in all the wrong places.

When you feel like you have let people down, fallen short in your Christian walk, what is your image of God? Do you feel ashamed and unworthy? Or will you go to God and find comfort from Him?

It all comes down to the image of God when we fall.

There are two reasons why we feel this way: 1) A misrepresentation of the earthly father, and we look at God through the lens of that relationship; 2) We develop a false image of God through false religion and fear. (Religion based on performance or fear is built on hidden lies that say we must perform to receive God's love, it plays on feelings and emotions.)

When we are busy "doing" we will get tired and not have enough to give to those who "need" it, which is our families.

Here is a personal account of what I'm talking about.

One night I was in the kitchen looking for something to eat. I wasn't hungry, I just "needed" something. I always attribute everything to food, shopping, or another type of enjoyment. But then after thinking about what I've been sharing, I decided to go to my husband. I asked him to hold me. And much to my surprise, the "need" for food had disappeared. What I "needed" was love, feeling safe, being touched and held in a comforting and caring way. I also know that not everyone has that, that is why it's so important to go to our Heavenly Father. Even though I'm married, there are times when my husband isn't available, especially if he's out of town. I have found myself lying in bed, feeling alone, and in "need." I then reach out to my Heavenly Father and say, "Lord wrap your arms around me and hold me, I need to feel your love." And that's exactly what happens. I fall asleep in His arms!

Now let's see what Jesus said about His Father: John 14: 1-3 (Matthew 20:18-19 - Jesus told his disciples he will be condemned and killed.) The disciples believed Jesus was going to be set on a throne in this world, but that's not what was going to happen. Total panic and anxiety hit them, and not only that He's going to leave them. They knew that when a leader was killed, the followers were killed as well, and they began thinking they were going to die too. This was not a happy moment. The disciples were in fear and disappointment.

Let you heart not be troubled, believe in God, believe also in me.... I go to prepare a place for you. (John 1:18 John 8:14 - From the bosom of father, back to bosom of father) Jesus went to prepare a place. And you know the way where I'm going? Thomas said, how do we get there? Jesus said, "I am the way, the truth and the life, no man comes to the Father BUT by me." Which is God's love - His bosom. This verse is all about intimacy and all about our relationship with Him.

The "way" has no meaning if it doesn't get you someplace. What is the final destination? The Father. We are not taking anything away from what Jesus did, His finished work on the cross gave us access to the Father.

John 14:7 - He who has known me, knows the Father.

John 14:8 - 10 "Jesus show us the Father and it will be enough. Then Jesus said, John, He that hath seen me has seen the Father also. The Father that dwells in me, He does the work." In other words, show me our Father in Heaven and I'll finally be content. We have had a relationship with Jesus, and not with God. We had an unhealthy fear of God. But Jesus died to bring us a deep loving relationship with the Father. Jesus was the man He was because of the Father He had. He wasn't the man He was because He was God, but because of His Father. Jesus gave to us what He himself got from His Father. (John 14:24).

John 8:28 - I do nothing but what I've seen my Father do, and speak only the things I've heard my Father do. (Before Jesus could do anything, Jesus copied the Father.)

What did Jesus do? (Remember, whatever Jesus did, He first saw His father do.)

Jesus was motivated by need - He sees the "need" that the people were hungry? Were there thieves, tax collectors, defiled, (gentiles) in that crowd? Yes, He met ALL needs. He came for the unrighteous, those that were needy, and He fed every one of them. Keeping in mind, He only did what He saw His Father do. When Jesus sees a need, He wants to fill it.

God's desire to bless us is not based on our behavior - but on our need. This helps us understand why others seem to be blessed who you "think" doesn't deserve it. It's because God sees their need.

We think that by giving, fasting, reading the word that we are earning God's approval. We need to understand that God lives to supply all our needs according to His riches in Glory.

Let's talk a look at Rebellion. Rebellion comes because of having laws without intimacy (love). When you see someone in rebellion, you'll see someone who is under some sort of law by a person they don't feel loved and accepted by. It could be a parent, a boss, etc., but always has something to do with relationship. If we do not have a loving relationship with someone and we ask them to do something, it will become hard pressing and seem like a law. But if we love the person we are wanting to do something, and they are feeling that love from you, that law is no longer hard and pressing, but a joy to do. It's the same with God. We will obey God and not fight Him when we truly have an intimate relationship with Him.

Intimacy with God and family all begins with your image of HIm. If you believe God has caused a lot of your problems such as gave you a disease, caused you to be where you are right now, you need a new image of God.

How can we believe God is the angry God, and Jesus is the loving God? But they are one in the same. If you believe that God is an angry God but Jesus is loving, then you have separated the two... they are ONE. We think that Jesus is protecting us from an angry God. You need a new image of God because remember, they are one!

Hebrews 1:3 - Jesus represents the nature of God

Col. 1:15 - Jesus is the image of the invisible God.

Our Image of God - Do we want to spend time because of who He is in Love, or do we have relationship with Him to get what we can get from Him?

Below is the nature that Jesus showed us that reflects the same nature of God. Jesus said, when you see me, you see the Father, I and my Father are one. (John 10:30)

Nature of God the Father; (Jesus showed us who the Father is)

Meek and Lowly (Gentle and Humble spirit)

Servant

Generous (Jesus fed the 5000)

Doesn't Judge

He loves me the way I am, not the way I should be

Not the way others tell me to be

Come to me when you are in tribulation

Loving

Forgiving

Calm the storm in my life

Cares about every need

Everything I see in Jesus, is GOD.

Compassionate

Empathy - discern needs of others

Childlike

Father

How did Jesus treat Lepers? In the Old Testament, lepers had to shout out "I am unclean". But what did Jesus do? He touched them. A desperate need they had was to be touched, because law forbade them to be touched. But Jesus touched them, the unclean, and since Jesus can only do what He saw His father do, God then touches the unclean to heal.

Let's look at the Prodigal Son: In the Old Testament, It was a law that anyone who was unclean had to go through a ritualistic cleansing before they could enter into the house. But in this story, knowing that his son was unclean (living with pigs), he ran to the son, in his filth, and hugged him and loved him, covered him with a clean robe, put shoes on his feet (slaves don't wear shoes) and gave him a ring. He was welcomed into the home just as he was. Before he took a bath! God is running toward you to ready to restore you to his love even in your mess.

- Hebrews 2:11- Jesus is not ashamed to be your brother.

- Hebrews 11:16 - God is not ashamed to be your God. No one is too unclean to be touched.

- Luke 15:31 - God is always with us, to give all that he has.

- Hebrews 13:5 - I'll never leave you nor forsake you.

- How can we have intimacy with an angry God? We can't. We have to get our heart right with God in confession, become restored to God which will result in a healthy image of Him.

- John 8: (Adulterous woman) Jesus took His time to respond - we need to stop and ask God how we are to respond to those who come at us? He said to her, woman where are thy accusers? "There are none" "Neither do I accuse you." (Before Jesus spoke these words, He heard his father say it) A loving father gives us what we need - regardless of our obedience.

- John 5:22 - The Father judges no one!!!! We keep thinking God is judging us, that is not true. But He who the father loves he disciplines, but he doesn't judge. So as soon as we misrepresent the father's love to our family, What's the first thing we think? Blame or feeling of unworthy and we have a hard time going to God.

- John 5:24 - He who hears my words, does not come into judgment.

- John 3:17 - God (father) did not send the son into the world to judge the world, but to save them. Those who believe in Jesus is not judged or condemned, does not accuse.

- John 12:47 - Jesus spoke - "if anyone hears my sayings and does not keep them - I will not even judge you, I didn't come to judge, but to save the world. He who rejects me, does not receive my sayings, and the words I spoke will judge him at the last day. And it says judging those who did not receive Jesus!!! Believers wont' be judged even at the last day.

- Hebrews 9:27 - It is appointed for us once to die, and then the judgment. So why do we judge each other if God doesn't judge until the end?

80% of Christians thoughts are negative - Why? Because we are tied into accusatory, negative thoughts, judgmental negative thoughts because we have a wrong image of God. We need to know He constantly loves us and accepts us.

John 16: How many have never been hurt by another Christian? Have you wondered why many can be so cruel? How many people hurt us in church using the Word even - they think they are doing God service. They do these things because they don't know "The Father." If you don't have a good image of God, you don't' have a Good image of Jesus and visa versa.

V23 - 24 So in "that day" all about pain coming to our life .... What are we to do? Jesus said, go to the Father in my name. We are to go to the Father through Jesus! Jesus said "don't ask me but ask the Father". If we pray to Jesus, we stop short, because we need to pray to God.

Every ones need is to have a place in the Father's heart. If we stop at Jesus, we will miss out, and we will still be in need. Casting all our cares to God for He cares for us. The "Jesus Only" churches are really missing out! Yes, Jesus is God, but Jesus was very clear that we are to go to the Father not to Him.

Where do we want to run in crises? To the Father! When we know we are loved and accepted by God it doesn't matter what anyone says because what matters more is what God thinks of you than what others think of you.

Do we feel more like a servant trying to please a master, or are you feeling like a son or daughter in the father's love? That will determine the image of the Father you have.

Jesus' last two hours on this earth He spoke of His Father in Heaven. John 14-15-16 spoke of the Father 51 times saying we need to know our Heavenly Father. (John 3:16) - my Father Loves.

- John 14:28 - I go to the father for the Father is greater than I. There is one in heaven greater than I.

- Matthew 18:4 - whoever humbles himself as a child, is greatest in the kingdom of heaven.

Remember, Jesus is humble and gentle in heart. There has to be a childlike innocence in the father. Jesus portrayed this childlike innocence.

Matthew 23:11 - the greatest among you shall be your servant. Whoever exalts himself shall be humbled.

Whoever wishes to be greatest among you shall be your servant, and whoever exalts self shall be abased. (Matthew 20:26-28). Whoever is to be first, will be slave. Jesus came not to be served, but to serve. He only does what He sees His father do.. so God is servant to all!!

John 13:1 - "Having loved His own He now expressed His full extent to the love of His disciples." This was said when Jesus washed their feet. This act was reserved for the lowliest slave to do, and if that house didn't have slaves, it was reserved for the youngest child. Feet had to be washed before coming into a house because of the filth in the streets (animal stuff, etc.) So what did Jesus do? No one washed anyone's feet at the Passover so Jesus stepped in to fulfill the need. The fullness of love is expressed through serving.

Jesus cleaned and washed the disciples feet taking on the form of a servant and said, "I only do what I see my Father do. The greatest will be servant of all, the greatest will be as a little child. There is one greater than I."

Our Father is going to kneel at our feet at the gates of heaven, and He's going to wash me from all the filth of the world; pain, hurt, or whatever. He's going to remove all the filth that I had so I can enter into His house clean. He's going to wipe away every hurting tear. I do believe that I won't be singing and shouting, I will be in awe that day because of His love for me and finally understanding my Father's love.

We haven't expressed the fullness of love to others until we are willing to meet another's needs (serve) at our own expense. Foot washing is a spiritual express of our love and service to another. I want to wash my husband's feet to wipe away all the hurt I have caused him, I want do this as a service to him.

God is not the cop in the sky, He's a father who is ready to lay down his life and serve us. Who shall serve the wedding supper of the lamb? Not us, we are the bride... The greatest in heaven will be servant of all.

Do we feel like a slave? We haven't realized the love of the Father.

Love covers a multitude of sins. When God loves us, it covers all our sins. We can also do this with others. As we love others, and they love us, all our sins are forgotten.

What is your happy thought? That My Father Loves me like I am, not like I should be.

Peter Pan flew when he would think his happy thought. His happy thought was to be a daddy.

We are God's happy thoughts. I Corinthians 13:5 - love thinks no evil. He can't think negatively about you, He doesn't judge you, He's not ashamed of you... And when we believe we are His happy thought, we start living it, our childlikeness has been restored, and we are being restored in our heart so that all pain goes - now we can fly and rescue others.

- God loves me the way I am, not the way I used to be.

- Which God would you have honor and have respect for?

- Angry God or a Compassionate God

- Which God would your children like you to be more like?

- Which God would you love to spend all eternity with?

- Which God is more likely to cause you to love Him?

- Which God makes you more likely to increase the fear and failure in your life?

- There are two God's - Father of Love and Father of Lies.

- Which one do you serve. Which one do you represent to others as a parent?

People are more important than a ministry. My husband, my family, and those in my church family are more important than running a ministry. But the truth is, we are all ministers to each other, and ministry is simply the office of love.

Let me end with a story:

There was a young man who grew up without a father. He was made fun of all his life people always asking him who his daddy was. He never felt complete, always under something. Never at peace. He even asked himself that same question. So not only did others reject him, but he rejected himself. One day, there was commotion down the street and he wanted to know what it was. So he popped in and sat in the back row. It happened to be a revival meeting. He had planned to leave before it ended but got so caught up, that he stayed for the whole thing, finding himself leaving with the crowd. The traveling preacher was at the exit greeting people as they left. He saw that young man, obviously alone, and reached out to him. He said to him, "Son... who is your father?" With that, he saw the young man's face look to the ground and so obviously he knew he hit a chord. Then immediately said, "I know who your father is, you look just like him! He is your Heavenly Father.!"

This story is one we can take personally for ourselves. YOU are the IMAGE of your FATHER in heaven. If you can get a hold of that one statement, it can change the way you see yourself and how you see God. You will find yourself within His arms of love daily. When you look in the mirror, you will see a reflection of the Father. Now, not everything we DO reflects our Father, that is what forgiveness is for, but what we LOOK LIKE does! You are the chip off the ole' block!

Ministry

If you want to develop a right image of God and receive from Him the truth of who He really is, then pray with me:

"Dear Heavenly Father, I recognize that I have had a poor image of who you are. I can say that I know you love me, but I have had a hard time believing it for myself and feeling it in my heart. I always thought that what I did caused you to bless me or not bless me, love me or not love me. I had an ungodly belief toward you, and I'm asking you to set me straight. As I see Jesus' life, He showed me who you are. Jesus isn't to run interference between us, He's to be the "way" to you. He represented you in His life, and I want that to be my image of you. You aren't an angry God ready to judge me and condemn me. You sent Jesus so He would cover all my sins, I'm not to pay for anything. You love me, always have and always will. Your blessings are ever before me. Help me to see you clearly Lord. I demand every lie to leave my mind and thoughts that are not right toward you Lord. Teach me who you are, help me to discover you the way you intend me to see you. Forgive me for fearing you in a wrong way, but let me come to you no matter what at all times without fear of rejection or retaliation, because that is not you. I cast out every evil thought that is not true about who you are. Help me to learn more of you by learning more of Jesus. I thank you for this truth. Help me to abide in you every single day, and find you as my "safe place", being covered and hidden under the shadow of your wings. I ask you to forgive me for blaming you for what not giving me what I think I needed to be okay. But you have been giving, I haven't been receiving. Help me to learn how to receive from you Father so that I have it to give away. Help me to be the Mother or Father you intended me to be from the foundation of the world. Help me to accept all your love for me, loving me just as I am, not as I should be, so that I can love my family the same. Heal my broken heart Lord, and heal all those around me whom I've hurt. Restore my heart and restore theirs as well. I thank you for your love toward me, and I receive it now, as it's all I need. In Jesus name, Amen."

CHAPTER FOUR

Relationship With the Godhead

Relationship with God the Father:

The main theme is having our relationships restored with God, ourselves and with the people around us (Matthew 22:38-40). I will repeat this over and over but there is a reason for it. We need to hear it over and over! Because I know for a fact that If we aren't in fellowship (relationship) with God, how can He give us anything? We prevent Him from moving in our lives. Can you trust your possessions to someone you don't know? Would you hand over your billfold to a stranger to hold while you ran an errand? No, of course not. But that's how we treat God, like a stranger. This is evidenced in the way we live our lives. Do we trust God with our life, finances, or our family?

Until we understand the Love of God, we cannot receive anything from Him in the amount He wants us to have. So if we haven't received His love for us personally, we certainly can't love ourselves, let alone love others. Are you trying to forgive and love? Did you know that all your "trying" will only cause you to be frustrated?" Wouldn't it be nice if you can simply "forgive and love?" Did you know that forgiveness and love brings health?

As we enter into this teaching, it is important that you take your time going through it. Give it time to absorb. I've had people say that there is a lot of knowledge being imparted and it's very over-whelming to take in all at once. But be "diligent" and don't give up because a diligent person will obtain righteousness and honor (Proverbs 21:21). These insights and teachings didn't come to me over night, these were things taught to me over time that I've compiled in this book. It took almost ten years to put this all together, so give yourself time as well.

What Do Relationships Have to Do with Blessings?

This ministry believes in the Godhead: God the Father, God the Son and God the Holy Ghost. We need to understand these three characters of God in their entirety in order to understand who God is for us. (Ephesians Chapter 4) We will be identifying each of the Godhead separately for complete understanding and knowledge. Many don't know Jesus personally, God personally or the Holy Ghost personally. It's important to see all their attributes and characteristics so we can "know" Him fully.

Our bodies are balanced in perfect homeostasis when our hearts are balanced in relationship with the Lord, with ourselves and with others. I was in bondage to fear until I understood and received a relationship with the Godhead fully. It opened the door for me to love myself and to love others. This is one of the most important teachings offered to help in your restoration and blessing. The book of Jeremiah talks about relationship with God, others and with ourselves, explaining the results of not abiding in truth! Take the time to read through Jeremiah for further understanding. You can also read the "truth" scriptures found at the back of this book.

The following teaching describes the relationship we are to have with God, Jesus, the Holy Ghost, ourselves and with others. Hopefully this will help you discern your own life. We need to know ourselves, where we are, and what we believe before we can really move forward. And I would suspect that many reading this don't know themselves very well, some avoid seeing within their own hearts, and some refuse to admit their own failings. We have to get past all that, and face ourselves in truth. But we can only do this when we get a revelation on God's love for us. Because it's His love that will help us see within more clearly without guilt, shame, condemnation or fear. And if we do feel those things, we will know what to do because we have a revelation on the love of God.

This is a KEY scripture and a very important for foundation:

"Thou shalt love the Lord thy God (relationship) with all thine heart (spirit man), soul (battle ground) and mind (flesh) and you shall love your neighbor as yourself. Upon this, the law and the prophets hang." (Matthew 22:37-40, Mark 12:29-31.) You can't love yourself and have self-hatred and guilt. You can't love your neighbor with unforgiveness. You can't love God, because scripture teaches, how can you hate your brother whom you have seen and love God whom you have not seen?

By breaking down this key passage of scripture, it will help us gain KNOWLEDGE necessary to IMPACT our lives to change our mind, body and soul.

We are to Love the Lord God with all our heart, soul and mind..." So how do we Love God? First we need to know Him. How can you love someone you don't know?

You'd be surprised how many people see God as a tyrant waiting to pounce on them when they do something wrong. They don't see Him as a loving Father wanting to help His children. They only have their own fathers to compare God with and don't understand the Love of God. They may fear their fathers to the point of avoiding them. Many people transfer this kind of fear to God. God wants us to come to Him any time, day or night, about anything! So, what have you believed about God?

Proverbs 2:1-5 says, *"My son if thou wilt receive my words, and hide my commandments with thee, so that thou incline thine ear unto wisdom, and apply thine heart to understanding, Yea, if thou cry after knowledge, and lift up thy voice for understanding, if thou seek for her as silver, and search for her as for hid treasures, THEN shalt thou understand the fear of the Lord, and find the knowledge of God."* When we understand the "fear of the Lord" that's when we'll find what we are looking for.

Fearing the Lord or Fear of the Lord?

Let's stop for a moment and do a quick study on "the fear of the Lord." Many are truly afraid of God and what He could do to them. Others say it's giving respect to God. I believe these are both correct to some degree, but that is not what this passage is saying. I wanted us to look at is that little word "of." See, it's not YOUR fear that He is talking about, it's God's fear! If we had God's fear, then we would know what it means to have the Fear OF the Lord. How does God fear? It says in Proverbs that the fear of the Lord is to hate evil. Does God hate evil? Yes, He does. So can we. But hating evil doesn't mean hating one another, it means to hate the "evil in the world" the devil. We can even hate the sin in us, but we are not to hate ourselves. And when we understand that we are on the same side as God, and can hate those things He hates, now you are understanding how you can walk IN the fear OF the Lord.

Relationship with God the Father

It's time to begin (or continue) participating in your "sanctification" process. We have to see the truth in our own heart before we can get the freedom we desire. John 17:19 *And for their sakes I sanctify myself, that they also might be sanctified through the truth.*

Get your tablet of paper out and begin to answer these questions.

1. Do you see God as a tyrant? If so, why?

2. Do you feel you cannot come to Him for everything? If so, why not?

3. Are you fearing Him to the point of not talking to Him? If so, why?

4. Are you mad at God for your life or current situation? If so, name the situation.

5. Are you unhappy with how He created you? If so, what is it you don't like about yourself?

6. Do you see God as your Heavenly Father? If so, how?

We need to identify where we are RIGHT NOW so that we have a starting place! The first step in healing and freedom is "acknowledging" some things.

Compare your notes to these truths about who God is: (If there are scripture references, please take the time to open up the Bible and read for yourself – remember, God's Word heals and delivers. What we say, doesn't! "The horse is prepared for the day of battle, but deliverance and victory are of the Lord" (Proverbs 21:31).

- God is our loving Father
- He created you with His hands
- God is Love. (1 John 4:16) (Jesus is not love. God sent Jesus to SHOW us His love)
- God is a Friend (Luke 11:5-11). Abraham was the friend of God. Moses

was the friend of God. Enoch was a friend of God. Adam was a friend of God. Can you go boldly to God at any time for any reason? (Genesis 18:22-23)

- God is sovereign (Patient and Kind when dealing with us.)
- God so loved the world that He gave us His Son (John 3:16)
- God is omnipotent. He sits on the throne in Heaven
- We need to draw close to the throne (Hebrews 4:16)
- God gives mercy and grace (Psalm 23)
- God exalts us (Hebrews 5:5)
- God is good
- God is the Godhead
- God never changes
- God is Holy
- God answers prayers
- God blesses
- God longs to visit with us. We were created for fellowship with Him
- God promotes us God Honors us God lifts us up. (Hebrews 4:10)
- God is my Shepherd (Psalm 23:1)
- God is with me always (Psalm 23:4)
- You are precious in His sight because He loves you (Isaiah 43:4)
- God is my hiding place IF I let Him hide me

If we knew how much God loved us, we wouldn't be acting the way we do. Do you have kids that are disobedient and disrespectful? Are they struggling with their lives, with relationship with you and others and themselves? It's simply because they don't know how much you love them. It's not that you don't love them, it's that they don't know how to receive your love. This is the same with our relationship with God. We don't know how to receive His love. There are a number of reasons why we can't receive His love and this portion of teaching will hopefully help you to see where you are right now in your relationship with Him, yourself and others, which will begin your healing process. As you continue in the following sessions, we will cover more on this area. But for now, recognizing what your relationship is like with God is the first step.

Question: Whom do you serve?

We need to come into the intimate presence of the one true God. A place of safety, a place in the Father's heart knowing that when we do it will produce peace which can impact our health. So what has this to do with the image of God? Everything. Because if your image of God is not a safe place, then you are serving the wrong God. Below lists two scenarios, which one do you believe?

- One that judges and punishes or one that is forgiving and loving?

- One that produces fear or one of love and acceptance?
- One that rewards failure with pain or one that rewards failure with forgiveness and comfort?
- One that keeps track of all your failures and sins and brings them up over and over, or one that forgives and forgets?
- One that is angry or one that is compassionate?

Questions:

1. Which one would you have honor and have respect for?

2. Which one would your children like you to be more like?

3. Which one would you love to spend all eternity with?

4. Which one is more likely to cause you to love Him?

You can't have intimacy with a person that you feel is angry with you, yet, religion teaches of an angry God. It misrepresents Jesus. Jesus died so we can have intimacy with the Father through His life.

That's the reason Jesus came, to show us the Father's love so we can come into an intimate relationship with Him, religion teaches contrary.

A father's presence is so critical to the environment of the home. I had been told that the woman is the one who holds the family together, but that isn't true. It's the man who sets the tone in the home. Because if a man loved his wife as Christ loved the church, the woman would be at peace, then the children would be at peace. We put too much on the mother, when it's the father's responsibility. You may even see that for yourself in your own family. A father that is demanding and unyielding is a father who breeds fear in the wife, which then passes on to the children and the home is not at rest. This is a woman who doesn't feel loved by her husband and will treat the children and her husband, as she is being treated. It's the man's responsibility not the woman's to hold the family together. The anointing doesn't flow up, it flows down from the head, God, to Jesus, Jesus to the man, the man to the woman.

As we look at the relationship we have had with our earthly father and mother, it will determine how much intimacy you will have, how much you can trust, how much you can believe and affects your image of God.

When we fail and know we deserve judgment are we fearful of God? If we are, then we'll treat others the way we believe God treats us when we fail. This too is incorrect.

God wants to inhabit us (abide in) and be comfortable with Him, be ourselves, feeling accepted, and full of peace. He doesn't want to be a visitor or a fair weather friend. He wants to move in to our home, which is our heart. When we entertain visitors we put on an "act" and we can't really be ourselves most of the time. God is not looking for a visitation, He's looking for habitation, he wants you to be yourself.

We need to believe God loves us the way we are, not the way we should be. And as taught in previous sessions, the Holy Ghost will lead, guide and direct you in all truth so that you can confess anything that is in you that is not of God, thereby, being purged and cleansed bringing you into more holiness.

God will not rest until we rest in Him. Isaiah 66:1 (Where is there a house I may rest?) He will not cease in His labors until he finds rest in you. He will never give up on you! And as long as we feel unworthy, stinky, we can't love ourselves, nor find rest in God, He will be there wooing us into His arms. John 1:18 (Jesus proceeded from the bosom Father) John 8:14 (Jesus then went back to where he came).

We can't rest when we think we have to be perfect and do everything right. If our image of God is that we're loved when we do everything right, we will never be at peace.

When the world is pressing in on you, when you are made to feel shame, what do you begin to think? If it's anything other than: "The Father Loves me the way I am now, not what I should be" then you'll look for comfort in all the wrong places.

When you feel like you have let people down, fallen short in your Christian walk, what is your image of God? Do you feel ashamed and unworthy? Or will you go to God and find comfort from Him?

It all comes down to the image of God when we fall. There are two reasons why we feel this way: 1) A misrepresentation of the earthly father, and we look at God through the lens of that relationship; 2) We develop a false image of God through false religion and fear. (Religion based on performance or fear is built on hidden lies that say we must perform to receive God's love, it plays on feelings and emotions.)

When we are busy "doing" we will get tired and not have enough to give to those who "need" it, which is our families.

Here is a personal account of what I'm talking about.

One night I was in the kitchen looking for something to eat. I wasn't hungry, I just "needed" something. I always attribute everything to food, shopping, or another type of enjoyment. But then after thinking about what I've been sharing, I decided to go to my husband. I asked him to hold me. And much to my surprise, the "need" for food had disappeared. What I "needed" was love, feeling safe, being touched and held in a comforting and caring way. I also know that not everyone has that, and that is why it's so important to go to our Heavenly Father. Even though I'm married, there are times when my husband isn't available, especially if he's out of town. I have found myself lying in bed, feeling alone, and in "need." I then reach out to my Heavenly Father and say, "Lord wrap your arms around me and hold me, I need to feel your love." And that's exactly what happens. I fall asleep in His arms!

Now let's see what Jesus said about His Father.

John 14:1-3 *"Let not your heart not be troubled, believe in God, believe also in me... I go to prepare a place for you."* He came from the bosom of the Father and is returning back to the bosom of the Father (John 1:18) Jesus said, *"I am the way, the truth and the life, no man comes to the Father by me"* (John 14:6) Which is God's love—His bosom. This verse is all about intimacy.

The "way" has no meaning if it doesn't get you someplace. What is the final destination? The Father. We are not taking anything away from what Jesus did, His finished work on the cross made the way possible to access the Father.

- John 14:7 - *"He who has known me, knows the Father."*
- John 14:8-10 *"Philip said, Jesus show us the Father and it will be enough."* Then Jesus said, *"Philip, He that hath seen me has seen the Father also. The Father that dwells in me, He does the work."* In other words, show me our Father in Heaven and I'll finally be content. We have had a relationship with Jesus, and not with God. We had an unhealthy fear of God. But Jesus died to bring us a deep loving relationship with the Father. Jesus was the man He was because of the Father He had. He wasn't the man He was because He was God, but because of His Father. Jesus gave to us what He himself got from His Father. (John 14:24).
- John 8:28 - "I do nothing but what I've seen my Father do, and speak only the things I've heard my Father do." (Before Jesus could do anything, Jesus copied the Father.)
- What did Jesus do? (Remember, whatever Jesus did, He first saw His Father do.)

Jesus was motivated by need the needs of others. Were there thieves, tax collectors, defiled, (gentiles) in that crowd? Yes, and He fed them all. He met ALL needs. He came for the unrighteous, those that were needy, and He fed every one of them. Keeping in mind, He only did what He saw His Father do. When Jesus sees a need, He wants to fill it. Jesus said He didn't come to those who needed a physician, He came to those who had a need. Interesting that He calls himself a physician.

God's desire to bless us is not based on our behavior - but on our need. This helps us understand why others seem to be blessed whom you "think" don't deserve it. It's because God sees their need.

We think that by giving, fasting, reading the word that we are earning God's approval. We need to understand that God lives to supply all our needs according to His riches in Glory.

A person in need often falls into rebellion. Rebellion comes because of having laws without intimacy (love). When you see someone in rebellion, you'll see someone who is under some sort of law by a person they don't feel loved and accepted by. It could be a parent, a boss, etc., but always has something to do with relationship. If we do not have a loving relationship with someone and we ask them to do something, it will become hard pressing and seem like a law. But when we ask someone to do something who we love and they also "feel" your love, their request isn't a law but a pleasure to do. It's the same with God. We will obey God and not fight Him when we truly have an intimate relationship with Him.

Image of God

Whom do we serve? Or in other words, "Who's your daddy?"

We need to come into the intimate presence of the one true God. A place of safety, a place in the Father's heart knowing that when we do it will produce peace which produces balanced chemicals in the body resulting in a healthy body. So what has this to do with the image of God? Everything. Because if your image of God is not a safe place, then you are serving the wrong God. Below lists two types, which one do you serve?

- A God of Love or a God of Fear? (1 John 4:18)
- A God that judges and punishes or a God that is forgiving and loving?
- A God that produces fear or a God of love and acceptance?
- A God that rewards failure with pain or a God that rewards failure with forgiveness and comfort?
- A God that keeps track of all your failures and sins and brings them up over and over, or a God that forgives and forgets?
- An angry God or a compassion God?

We can't have intimacy with a person you feel is angry with you. Yet religion teaches of an angry God. It misrepresented Jesus. Jesus died so we can have intimacy with the Father through His life. That's the reason Jesus came. To show us the Father's Love to bring us into an intimate relationship with Him.

You don't know how valuable you are, accepted and loved... if you battle this, you will be filled with anxiety and fear.

Intimacy with God and family all begins with your image of Him. If you believe God has caused you a lot of your problems such as gave you a disease, or allowed things to happen to you that weren't good, then you need a new image of God.

How can we believe God is an angry God, and Jesus is a loving God? But they are one and the same. If you believe that God is an angry God but Jesus is loving, then you have separated the two... they are ONE. We think that Jesus is protecting us from an angry God. You need a new image of God because remember, they are one!

Hebrews 1:3 - Jesus represents the nature of God. Jesus is the image of the invisible God (Colossians 1:15).

Do we want to spend time with Him because of who He is, or do we have a relationship with Him to get what we want?

Below is the nature that Jesus showed us that reflects the same nature of God. Jesus said, when you see me, you see the Father because I and my Father are one (John 10:30).

- Nature of God the Father; (Jesus showed us who the Father is)
- Meek and Lowly (Gentle and Humble spirit)
- Servant
- Generous (Jesus fed the 5000)
- Loving and Kind
- Forgiving
- Calms the storms in my life
- Cares about every need
- Compassionate
- Empathy - discern needs of others
- Childlike

How did Jesus treat Lepers? In the Old Testament, lepers had to shout out "I am unclean" (Leviticus 13:45). But what did Jesus do? He touched them. A desperate need they had was to be touched, because law forbade them to be touched. But Jesus touched them, the unclean, and since Jesus can only do what He saw His father do, God then touches the unclean too.

Let's look at the Prodigal Son: In the Old Testament, It was a law that anyone who was unclean had to go through a ritualistic cleansing before they could enter into the house. But in this story, knowing that his son was unclean (living with pigs), he ran to the son, in his filth, and hugged him and loved him, covered him with a clean robe, put shoes on his feet (slaves don't wear shoes) and gave him a ring. He was welcomed into the home just as he was. Before he took a bath! God is running toward you ready to restore you to His love even in your mess.

- Hebrews 2:11- Jesus is not ashamed to be your brother.
- Hebrews 11:16 - God is not ashamed to be your God. No one is too unclean to be touched.
- Luke 15:31 - God is always with us, to give us all that He has.
- Hebrews 13:5 - He'll never leave us nor forsake us.
- How can we have intimacy with an angry God? We can't. We have to get our heart right with God in confession, become restored to God which will result in a healthy image of Him.
- John 8:10 In the story of the adulterous woman, Jesus took His time to respond when she was being accused. We need to stop and ask God how we are to respond to those who come at us? He said to her, *"Woman where are thy accusers?" "There are none"* she answered. And Jesus replied, *"Neither do I accuse you."* So if Jesus only said and did what His Father said and did, then God also doesn't accuse.

- John 5:22 - The Father accuses and judges no one!!!! We keep thinking God is judging us, that is not true. But He who the Father loves He disciplines. This isn't judgement. However, many of us have been brought up believing God is always judging and ready to "get us" when we do something wrong. This has to be changed in our thoughts. So as soon as we misrepresent God's love to our family, we are causing them to have wrong thoughts toward Him.

- John 5:24 - *"He who hears my words, does not come into judgment."* He is judging, but not His children! As this scripture points out. You have to know that you are separate from the world. You aren't judged at all, you are accepted in the beloved.

- John 3:17 - *"God (Father) did not send the son into the world to judge the world, but to save it."* Those who believe in Jesus is not judged or condemned.

- John 12:47 - Jesus spoke - *"If anyone hears my sayings and does not keep them - I will not even judge you, I didn't come to judge, but to save the world. He who rejects me, does not receive my sayings, and the words I spoke will judge him at the last day."* And it says judging those who did not receive Jesus!!! Believers wont' be judged even at the last day. At the last day we will be given rewards, it may be a small crown or a large crown, but you aren't going to be judged. Those being judged are those that did not receive Jesus Christ as Savior and they will be judged and cast out into outer darkness.

  Hebrews 9:27 - *"It is appointed for man once to die, and then the judgment."* So why do we judge each other if God doesn't judge until the end? But again, the judgment is reserved for those who didn't profess Jesus as Lord and Savior.

Why are Christian's thoughts negative? Because we are tied into accusatory, negative, judgmental thoughts because we have a wrong image of God. We need to know He constantly loves us and accepts us.

How many have never been hurt by another Christian? Have you wondered why many can be so cruel? How many people hurt us in church using the Bible? They do these things because they don't know "the Father." If you don't have a good image of God, you don't' have a Good image of Jesus and vise-versa.

John 16:23-24 says in "that day" what are we to do? Jesus said, go to the Father in my name. We are to go to the Father through Jesus! Jesus said, "Don't ask me but ask the Father." If we pray to Jesus, we stop short, because when making petition we need to pray to God. What day does He talk about? The day we need help.

Everyone's need is to have a place in the Father's heart. If we stop at Jesus, we will miss out, and we will still be in need. Casting all our cares to God for He cares for us. The "Jesus Only" churches are really missing out! Yes, Jesus is God, but Jesus was very clear that we are to go to the Father not to Him.

Where do we want to run in a crises? To the Father! When we know we are loved and accepted by God it doesn't matter what anyone says because what matters more is what God thinks of you than what others think of you.

Do we feel more like a slave trying to please a master, or are you feeling like a son or daughter in the father's love? That will determine the image of the Father you have.

During Jesus' last two hours on this earth He spoke of His Father in Heaven. John 14-15-16 spoke of the Father fifty-one times saying we need to know our Heavenly Father (John 3:16).

John 14:28 - *"I go to the Father for the Father is greater than I. There is one in heaven greater than I."* As I was sharing this with my husband he said, "Jesus is the car but God has the car keys!"

Matthew 18:4 - *"Whoever humbles himself as a child, is greatest in the kingdom of heaven."*

Remember, Jesus is humble and gentle in heart. There has to be a childlike innocence in the father too for Jesus to portray this.

Matthew 23:11 - *"The greatest among you shall be your servant. Whoever exalts himself shall be humbled."*

Whoever wishes to be greatest among you shall be your servant, and whoever exalts himself shall be abased (Matthew 20:26-28). Whoever is to be first, will be slave. Jesus came not to be served, but to serve. He only did what He saw His Father do so if Jesus served then it's also true that God is a servant.

John 13:1 - *"Having loved His own He now expressed His full extent to the love of His disciples."* This was said when Jesus washed their feet. This act was reserved for the lowliest slave to do, and if that house didn't have slaves, it was reserved for the youngest child. Feet had to be washed before coming into a house because of the filth in the streets (animal stuff, etc.) So what did Jesus do? No one washed anyone's feet at the Passover, so Jesus stepped in to fill the need; the fullness of love is expressed through serving. Jesus cleaned and washed the disciples feet taking on the form of a servant and said, "I only do what I see my Father do. The greatest will be servant of all, the greatest will be as a little child. There is one greater than I."*

Our Father is going to kneel at our feet at the gates of heaven, and He's going to wash me from all the filth of the world; pain, hurt, or whatever. He's going to remove all the filth that I had so I can enter into His house clean. He's going to wipe away every hurting tear. I do believe that I won't be singing and shouting, I will be in awe that day because of His love for me and finally understanding my Father's love.

We haven't expressed the fullness of love to others until we are willing to meet another's needs (serve) at our own expense. Foot washing is a spiritual expression of our love and service to another.

I want to wash my husband's feet to wipe away all the hurt I have caused him, I want do this as a service to him.

God is not the cop in the sky, He's a father who is ready to lay down his life and serve us. Who shall serve the wedding supper of the lamb? Not us, we are the bride. The greatest in heaven will be servant of all.

Love covers all sins (Proverbs 10:12). We can also do this with ourself and with others. As we love others and they love us, all our sins are forgiven and removed. Matthew 5 says that when we forgive others, so will God forgive us. This all has to do with love.

In the movie "Hook" when Peter Pan flew it was because He would think his happy thought. His happy thought was being a daddy.

We are God's happy thoughts. 1 Corinthians 13:5 says that love thinks no evil. He can't think negatively about you, He doesn't judge you nor is He ashamed of you. And when we believe we are His happy thought, we start living it, our childlikeness has been restored, and we are being restored in our heart so that all pain goes—now we can fly and rescue others.

Ministry

If you want to develop a right image of God and receive from Him the truth of who He really is, then pray with me:

"Dear Heavenly Father, I recognize that I have had a poor image of who you are. I can say that I know you love me, but I have had a hard time believing it for myself and feeling it in my heart. I always thought that what I did caused you to bless me or not bless me, love me or not love me. I had an ungodly belief toward you, and I'm asking you to set me straight. As I see Jesus' life, He showed me who you are. Jesus isn't to run interference between us, He's to be the "way" to you. He represented you in His life, and I want that to be my image of you. You aren't an angry God ready to judge me and condemn me. You sent Jesus so He would cover all my sins, I'm not to pay for anything. You love me, always have and always will. Your blessings are ever before me. Help me to see you clearly Lord. I command every lie to leave my mind and thoughts that do not depict a good image of You.

Teach me who you are, help me to discover you the way you intend me to see you. Forgive me for fearing you in a wrong way, but let me come to you no matter what at all times without fear of rejection or retaliation, because that is not you. I cast out every evil thought that is not true about who you are. Help me to learn more of you by learning more of Jesus. I thank you for this truth. Help me to abide in you every single day, and find you as my "safe place," being covered and hidden under the shadow of your wings. I ask you to forgive me for blaming you for not giving me what I think I needed to be okay. You have been giving but I haven't been receiving. I take responsibility and I will no longer blame you for me not receiving. Help me to learn how to receive from you Father so that I have it to give away. Help me to be the Mother or Father you intended me to be from the foundation of the world. Help me to be the wife/husband you created me to be. Help me to be me. Help me to accept all your love for me, loving me just as I am, not as I should be, so that I can love my family the same. Heal my broken heart Lord, and heal all those around me whom I've hurt. Restore my heart and restore theirs as well. I thank you for your love toward me, and I receive it now, as it's all I need. In Jesus name, Amen."

Loving God

As you go through this section, it may seem that I'm repeating myself, well, I am. Because God's love is the most important issue that has to be established IN you once and for all. However, as a minister, I'm here to help you find the truth about God's love that will result in you living in peace and freedom.

I will not play God in your life, and I will not tell you what to do for your situation. I will lead you to our Father who has all your answers, and help you to develop the kind of relationship you need with Him so you can hear from Him for yourself. So with that understood, I'll begin sharing what the Lord has laid on my heart.

We start by building a proper foundation. I shared some already in this chapter but need to reiterate it. Some of you may have been Christians for a long time now, yet you still find that something is missing in your life. It could be your foundation has a crack in it, or you've built your house upon the sand. We need our house built upon the Rock. Jesus is the Rock. It's okay to admit you have a shaky foundation, no one needs to know but you and God. Remember, recognizing truth about your own life is going to help make you free.

I've seen foundations built from old religious traditions passed down in the family that amount to only half-truths by the time it got to you. We then also build our foundation on what we "want" to believe, therefore, making it unsound and shaky.

How do you know if your foundation is flawed?
- If you feel like something is missing from your life.
- If you have hard time hearing God speak to you
- If you feel your prayers aren't really being heard
- If you have doubt, confusion, anxiety and stress, frustration, worry, anger, unbelief, rejection, not feeling loved
- If you are living in fear
- If you have a hard time reading your Bible
- If you are bored with Christianity

If any of these ring true for you, it's time to face what has made that crack in your foundation and allow God to repair it. Can I say that the crack I'm talking about is really a breach in relationship with someone in your life? Your parents? Your Spouse? Even God? Fear comes when we are not made perfect in love. I've often said it this way, "Fear is the absence of Love." I teach in later sessions that when Satan was cast to the earth, not only was he stripped of any authority he had in heaven, but was also stripped of God's love. What is left? Fear and torment. That is all he is and that's all he gives. But we as humans have a choice. We can receive God's love, which casts out all fear and torment. So if you are experiencing fear and anxiety, then this session is a must for you!! By obtaining love fear will have to go.

Let's start by identifying what your foundation is with your biological father. Let me explain. If you believe you had a great relationship with your father and he provided all the love, encouragement and care you needed as you were growing up, then you can skip this paragraph. However, if you never heard your father say "I love you", "I'm proud of you", "I'm glad you were born," and "I'm glad you are my child," then your foundation was never laid properly for you to go out into the world and live a stable and secure life. Some of you will never hear these words from a parents, even as adults because some of your parents are long gone, but I'm here to tell you that even though you never heard these words, you can hear these words today from your true Father, your Heavenly Father.

The first thing you need to learn and get a deep understanding in is that God is your true Father. Our earthly father is our biological father who was instrumental in bringing you into the world, but you need to know who your true Father is and what your true inheritance is. Do not continue with the mind set that your earthly father is your father—truthfully, your father, in reality, is your brother. Why? Because we are all brothers and sisters in the Lord, and when we go to be with the Lord in Heaven, for all those who have received Christ as Savior, they will be our equal. There won't be any differences, so if we have that mind set now, it will help us understand that our parents are children like us too.

Let me reiterate something: You need to understand that your earthly father is not your true father. God is your true father. You may have had a father who abused you, lied to you, or said hurtful things to you. Perhaps your father simply ignored you or abandoned you. Perhaps you never knew your father and you are continually wondering about him. You don't need to wonder any longer, because you need to realize God is your REAL Father. You need to separate the things your father on this earth said to you from the things God says to you now. God is your true inheritance! Ask God to help you get a revelation on Him as your Father.

Our Father has something to say to you right now:

"My child, I am sorry that your earthly father didn't love you like you needed to be loved. I'm sorry he spoke to you in wrong ways or hurt you. I'm sorry that he ignored you, and was silent to you. But you have to know that I'm not that father. I am your real Father! You need to know that I love you with unconditional love. There is nothing you have done or ever will do that will separate you from my love. (Romans 8:38-39).

You need to know how proud I am of you, yes, you! I want you to know that I am so glad you were born, I created you just like you are, there are no mistakes in my design. And I want you to know how very pleased I am with you. Yes you! You may wonder how I can be pleased with you because of all your "stuff" but I am. Don't try to figure me out, just receive my love, for I love you always and forever."

These are the true thoughts of God your Father toward you. Meditate on them, ask God to help you receive these words into your heart and allow Him to love you as you always hoped a Father would.

In order to develop a solid foundation on this kind of love, built on solid truth, because it's the truth that makes us free (John 8:32), we need to go back and re-build our proper foundation. (You have already begun re-building by having received the love prayer just spoke to you by your Father in Heaven.) I say to go back and rebuild because many of you are adults now and the foundation you have may have been compromised or never been built in the first place, or you don't even know where it is!

I believe what I'm going to share with you is what you need to learn to get your life back. The Bible says in 2 Timothy 2:25 "... If God peradventure would give them the repentance of the truth, that they (you) may recover themselves (you) from the snare of the devil who is able to take him (you) captive at his (the devil's) will." I'm going to help you get "unstuck," and free from whatever prevents you from being free and allows you to be taken captive because all of that comes right from the pit of hell. God's purpose for your life is that you live as His child, filled with love, peace, righteousness and joy. But truthfully, if you are reading this teaching, that may not be the case in your life. You may have been a Christian for years yet you know something is still missing.

There is Hope!

I have found that there are two beliefs that have to be established for creating a firm foundation in a person's life before really living a full and victorious life. They are: Believe that God loves you, right now, no matter what you think about yourself, and always, at all times, unconditionally, 24 hours-a-day, whether you are doing some great thing for Him or not! This is first and foremost. Because how can we receive something from someone we may not feel truly loves us? We may "know" He loves us, but we have difficulty receiving it for ourselves. By receiving God's perfect love, He removes the fear and torment. "Perfect love casts out all fear and torment" (1 John 4:18). This is the first step toward freedom and peace.

That your sins are truly forgiven. If you live in shame, guilt and condemnation, there may be a problem in this area. If you truly believed you are forgiven, you wouldn't have guilt and condemnation in your life. I have found in ministry that guilt comes from some sort of sin we haven't confessed, and I have found these sins to be shame based so we don't even want to tell God! (More covered in Guilt and Condemnation teaching.) But remember, He sees everything, He knows everything, it's up to you to believe He will "still" love you even when you tell Him your most deepest secrets. These kinds of sins can also come from "thinking" we are supposed to do more. We "feel" guilty because we didn't say this or do that. Go to God and tell him why you feel guilty, then receive forgiveness and then forgive yourself! Guilt always comes mainly from unconfessed sin about something.

This is the foundation I am speaking of. Many walk around in life, especially as believers, under guilt and condemnation, bitterness and fear, jealousy and envy, not thinking they are loved and accepted, confused and unstable, and have all kinds of diseases, yet think they are okay with God. A person cannot be okay with God and have any of these things I just listed. As you continue reading the rest of this you may discover truths for yourself that you have not seen before.

Let's look at God's love. I bet if I were to ask you if you loved God, you would think that was a silly question, because of course you do. But let me shed some truth on that, because if you truly loved God, you wouldn't need ministry. The Bible says in Matthew 22:38-40, *"We are to love the Lord our God with all our heart, with all our soul and with all our mind. And the second is like it, we are to love our neighbors as ourselves, upon these hang all the law and the prophets."*

I believe and know without a doubt, that if we understood what this scripture meant, and lived it; we wouldn't be in the mess we are in today. Not that we would become perfect, or everything would be perfect around us, but our hearts would be right to the wrongs in the world and will set us and keep us free from the pain of this world.

See it's not necessarily the person or circumstances that cause us our grief, it's how we have responded to it and how we have allowed it to affect us, emotionally. It's what we have allowed to come into our lives that have caused these affects in our lives. Jeremiah 5:25 say that "Your iniquities have turned away these things, and your sins have withheld good things from you."

Somewhere along the course of your life, you have permitted things in your lives that has caused the result of your life today. Proverbs 26:2 says it this way *"... the curse causeless shall not come"*, and Galatians 6:7, *"Whatsoever a man sows, that shall he also reap."* Not everything comes from our sowing, it could be coming from our ancestors. I have found that most of our problems start from what we think! And when we think something long enough, it becomes who we are, then goes into our actions, and then if never dealt with, can develop into emotional or physical complications. Did you know that dis-ease is just a chemical imbalance? Our bodies either block chemicals or produce too much, all from our thinking. In the medical society, there is a drug that is called a beta-blocker. It does just that, it "blocks" off some chemicals that is producing ailments. So what does this have to do with God's love? It's His love living in us and through us that will balance out our chemicals. It's His love that causes us to be at peace, and when we are at peace, our bodies are at peace and our chemicals balance.

In a nutshell: We first need to Love God. However, the truth is, we can't truly love God until we "know" He loves us first! 1 John says that, "We love Him because He first loved us." And we can't really "know" He loves us until we "know" Him. Isn't it true that we don't' trust just anyone? We trust those whom we "know" and "know" loves and cares for us. It's no different with God. Here you are, all of a sudden, His child through conversion, and now you are told to obey. Yet the reason you struggle with obedience is because you haven't gotten to "know" your Heavenly Father. You need to KNOW Him first. By searching the scriptures and speaking with Him, you'll begin to experience Him in your life. You will get to know His character, the truth of who He is in your life, and all those things you have lived without for so long. I too had to do the same thing. And when I started my "love quest" with God, and asked Him to reveal this love in my life, EVERYTHING began changing! My heart was becoming lighter; my circumstances began changing for the better, I was happier, healthier, and continue enjoying the presence of God twenty-four hours a day. I hear Him when He spoke to me, I don't fall under guilt or condemnation any more when I mess up, my prayers are being answered even before I finish the last word! Because I "know" He loves me, I know how to "receive" His love and forgiveness and because of that things come effortlessly.

But what happens is because our earthly father didn't demonstrate this kind of love, we transfer all our thoughts to God, our Heavenly Father. Our Father in Heaven is nothing like our earthly father, we need to get to know Him from the love Jesus displayed by reading the scriptures - then you'll get the true picture of your Heavenly Father. One who loves, gave His son to die so we wouldn't ever have to die, heals us, delivers us, helps us, keeps us, and on and on. That is our "real" Father. So today, cast down any thoughts that think otherwise (2 Corinthians 10:5) because they are ungodly.

See, I had been under fear most of my life. 18 of those years I was a Christian! And it was all because I wasn't "receiving" God's love. I didn't know how. I didn't know that's what I was missing! In talking about foundation, this is the number one building block for a firm foundation. Now I know, and now you know. We need to be able to receive God's love even in the state we are in. Even though you don't think you deserve to be loved. You have to get a revelation that those things do not matter to God. God loved us while we were yet sinners (Romans 5:8). This is the love that equips you to defeat the enemy!

The Bible says, *"Perfect Love casteth out fear"* (1 John 4:18). He loves you anyway and always. This love quest is a forever thing. The Bible describes God's love as huge. I believe it's so huge that no one in this lifetime can ever attain all of the Love of God. And that is a good thing, because if we think we have obtained all of God's love, then we'll stop seeking what we think we have, but this way we will keep seeking Him on a daily basis. I have been seeking and receiving and getting revelations every single day on God's love for me, and I've been doing this for several years now and will continue for the rest of my life. The Lord told me one day that, even with all this seeking I have done, I haven't even skimmed the tip of the ice burg! In other words, I have only begun to truly understand His love for me. And boy, if there is more, I'm really excited about it, because my life is so blessed now.

You need to become honest with God by identifying where your heart is with Him. If any of these statements ring true with you, note them and we'll get back to them momentarily.

- I have doubt and unbelief toward God.
- I believe God can help others, but have a hard time believing He can help me.
- I don't think God really loves me like He loves others because I haven't seen much happen in my life like I think should be happening.
- I don't think God hears my prayers.
- I think God is mad at me or disappointed in me.
- I am mad at God.
- I'm not happy how God has allowed things to happen in my life.
- I have a hard time truly believing God even exists.
- I have doubts that I'm really saved.
- I don't think God will heal me, I know He can, but He has chosen not to.
- I think God gave me this disease.
- I am not happy with my life, I have had so many let downs and disappointments, there's no use even trying any more.

If any one of these statements reflects your thoughts, then what I'm sharing with you will be your "lifeline."

We have to get a revelation on the Love of God in our lives - I've said this before, and I say it again. That is the FIRST and FOREMOST thing you can do to find your answers. It sounds simple, but it's the hardest thing to do. Because we come up against walls when we are supposed to believe God loves us, because you know yourself all too well and wonder how anyone can love you, especially God. But the truth is, He does, and you have to get past all that stuff you "think" of yourself and allow God's thinking to penetrate into your life.

Every one of those statements started with a thought. Where did that thought come from? From you? From what your parents taught you? Passed on from your ancestors? But regardless where they came from, you are responsible for what is going on today. So then if you dwell on those thoughts year after year, you not only begin to "believe" them as truths, your body begins to respond as well. You can act out irrationally or you can end up with physical ailments such as panic attacks, heart problems, digestion problems, autoimmune diseases, emotional illnesses, and relationship problems including isolation, and so much more.

The reason all these thoughts are there is because the truth is not there; the truth of God's love. Because if you truly "believed and received God's love for you personally, you wouldn't be thinking any of these thoughts at all because you would know they are lies! It's not that a thought won't come again contrary to God's Word, it's that when it does come you don't entertain it, once you begin to entertain it you will begin to believe it! What are you to keep your mind on? What does Philippians 4:13 say? Truth. God's thoughts are only truth, and as you begin to receive God's love, His thoughts become your thoughts! Remember, you have the mind of Christ! Choose today whom you will serve. Will you serve truth or lies? If you don't choose truth, you will serve the other. When we lie the Bible says we serve our father the devil. That's pretty strong words coming from a loving Jesus. That means this is critical to your life.

Study these scriptures below by reading them from the Bible in complete context. That means, read the scriptures before and after it for the complete thought.

- 1 John 4:8, *"He that knows not love, knows Not God."*
- 1 John 4:18, *"There is no fear in love; but perfect love (God's love in you) casts out all fear, because fear has torment. He that fears is not made perfect in love."*

We need to "know" God and how we get to know God is we get to know (believe) Jesus. Your job as a believer is to believe. John 6:29 *"...Jesus answered and said unto them, this is the work of God, that ye believe on Him who He has sent."* In other words, to believe the Word. To believe you have been forgiven. To believe God loves you. Jesus came to us to bring us two things, Love, showing us how much God loves us, and forgiveness so we can be restored to fellowship with God.

But again, in order to believe anything, we need to KNOW Him. They work together. As you begin to read the Word, ask for the Lord to help you understand and believe. This is helping you re-build your relationship with your Heavenly Father and building your faith because faith comes by hearing the Word of God. You are restoring the crumpled foundation you've been trying to live on. The cracks in your life will begin to be filled in. The Bible says that when we know Jesus we also know the Father (John 8:19). A good way to really get a revelation on "knowing" your Heavenly Father is to get a concordance and look up the word Father. Then go to all the scriptures that are in red (the words that Jesus spoke), and this will truly help you get to "know" your Heavenly Father.

As you get to "know" Him, believing and receiving comes so much easier. Then as you believed, so it will become part of your life. You can only "do" what you "believe." Otherwise your "doing" is all works of the flesh could result in frustration and backsliding! Matthew 8:13 says, "... as you have believed, so let it be done unto you."

I've addressed in length what the first part of Matthew 22:38-40 is saying. "We are to love the Lord our God with all our heart, soul and mind." There is so much more you can read into that, and as you do your study, you will get a revelation on what this scripture is saying. And as we get to know Jesus, we get to know the Father, and we also get to know the Holy Ghost. You need to look up references on all three to get a clear picture of God. We have some misconceptions of Him and all those lies have to be blasted out of our minds, and only the truth of God reside.

What I have just shared with you I have shared in my conferences, seminars, and individually with people. But it's the same story. The foundation of love was never established in a person's life.

When you get love rooted and grounded in your life, you will see changes!!!

Paul says, "That Christ may dwell in your hearts by faith; that ye, being rooted and grounded in love, may be able to comprehend with all saints what is the breadth, and length and depth and height; and to know the love of Christ which passes knowledge, that he (you) might be filled with ALL the fullness of God" (Ephesians 3:17).

**Everything begins AND ends with Love. That is why God said He is the "Alpha AND Omega" beginning and the end
(And I will add, everything in between!)**

Ministry Prayer for You:

"Father, your love is big and can cover anything we have going on in our lives. I pray this dear Saint gets a revelation on your love, and begins applying forgiveness to their life daily. In order to truly receive your love, we need to deal with the spirit of fear. You have said that you have not given us the spirit of fear, but you have given us Power, Love and a Sound Mind. You also said that "perfect love" casts out all fear and torment. This individual needs your perfect love flowing in them. I break the power of fear off this individual now and cast it out in Jesus name. I ask for your love Father to flood this person's heart with your perfect love. Give them a revelation of your love. I pray that the power of the Holy Ghost, Your love, and the Word who is Jesus become clearer to them. I pray you fill them up right now with your love, compassion, joy and truth. I pray that every lie that has made a home in their thoughts be cast out in Jesus name. Fill them with all that you are. Help them seek out your love, get to "know" you, and begin loving themselves.

I believe that it is Your love and Your love alone that is the cure for all that ails them. So help my dear friend believe You. Help them to receive Your love in new and marvelous ways. I ask for You to touch their life for healing in their bones, body and mind. I pray that the chemicals balance out in their brain, resulting in balanced chemicals in the body. I pray they recognize the thoughts that have caused the imbalance and cast those thoughts down as 2 Corinthians 10:5 tells us to. I ask for Your truth and love to replace every lie. I pray Your relationship with them is restored to fullness, that there is a sweet communion and fellowship from this day on. I ask You to help them to believe You love them right now, no matter how they feel or what they think. You ARE love Father. I pray that anything else that is distorting who You are in their thinking be cast out in Jesus name. As they receive your love, fear cannot reside. Help them be completely set free from fearful thoughts and doubts and unbelief, and when they do have these thoughts to remember to take them captive and cast them out!

I thank You for my dear friend Lord, and ask that what I have shared with them becomes reality in their life. I know this is what we all need. I know this is what will impact every life forever. Help us to realize that love IS the answer. I praise You Father for what You have done so far in my friend's life, even if they think You have abandoned them, You are working things out in their life, even as we speak. I look forward to the day my friend can walk in complete peace, fearlessness, love and sound mind. Help us to remember in order to get to that place with You, we need to recognize what we are to do as believers. It's our job to recognize and know the truth, but it is Your job to make us free, heal, restore and deliver. Help my friend to trust You and your love for them. Help them to wait patiently for You. Help them to continually seek Your love and fear will have no place in them. I thank You for your truth that makes us free. In Jesus' name. Amen."

The only way you are going to be truly free from whatever ails you is for you to come into a tight relationship with God. I know what I am speaking about. I was very ill, and truly messed up in my thinking about God and His love. Now that I've been seeking Him for several years, every day I get freer, even in areas I didn't even know I was in bondage to! That is how cunning the enemy is. But as God helps me expose the enemy in my life, the freer I become. Don't be afraid of "seeing" the truth in your heart. God sees it anyway; you might as well come clean before Him, no matter how ugly or embarrassing it may be - even though you are a Christian! Because truthfully, the people I minister to ARE and have been Christians for years... but somewhere along the way something happened that caused a disconnection.

What I taught you is more precious that silver and gold. It is all you need at this point to find your freedom. This is true deliverance. Being delivered out of the snare of the devil because this leads to being set free and healed in many areas of your life (2 Timothy 21:24-26).

Heart After God

Let's take a close look at Psalm 51. Within this passage are the keys to living with a clean heart toward God and man. This is a psalm written by David, the chief Musician, when Nathan the prophet came unto him, after he had been with Bath–she'ba.

David was known as a man after God's own heart yet he sinned terribly. Not only did he steal another man's wife, but also had him killed in battle. So how can this be possible? Is it possible for you to be known as a man or woman after God's own heart even after all you have done? Yes!

This teaching will help you discover for yourself how you too can be known as a man or woman after God's own heart by understanding how David addressed his sin before God. I will go through Psalm 51 and identify key aspects for you to take to the Lord.

Verse 1 - *Have mercy upon me, Oh God.*

David knew that God was the one he need to go to. He believed God was real and his answer for whatever was happening in his life. He didn't run from God, he ran to Him, even when he did some really ugly things.

Verse 2 - *Wash me thoroughly from mine iniquity, and cleanse me from my sin.*

He knew there was nothing he could do about it but take his transgressions and sins to God for Him to cleanse him.

Verse 3 - *For I acknowledge my transgressions.*

David looked inside his heart and saw what was in there.

Verse 4 - *Against thee, thee only, have I sinned, and done this evil in thy sight: that thou mightest be justified when thou speakest, and be clear when thou judges.*

David acknowledged His own heart condition and realized it was against God that he sinned, even though it was against another human being. He knew God was the only one who could forgive, heal and restore.

Verse 5 - *Behold, I was shapen in iniquity; and in sin did my mother conceive me.*

David knew that iniquity was in his family line! If you recall, Solomon, his father, had hundreds of wives and concubines... So that spirit of lust passed on to David. In this passage he actually blamed his family for his sin!

Verse 6 - *Behold, thou desires truth in the inward parts: and in the hidden part thou shalt make me to know wisdom.*

David had to see all that was in his heart so he could repent. These were the things that were keeping him bound. And only God could show him when it was him or when it came from his ancestors. That hidden part could be iniquities from his generations, or it could be something he's blocked out. In this case, the action was his to own up to, but the reason for doing it could have come down through his generations. If you remember, his father had hundreds of wives and hundreds of concubines. So as David did, we also need to open our heart and allow God to expose everything that is not of Him for purging.

Verse 7 - *Purge me with hyssop, and I shall be clean: wash me, and I shall be whiter than snow.*

Once we see what is in there, its God who purges us and makes us whiter than snow!

Verse 8 - *Make me to hear joy and gladness.*

David lost his joy and was not at peace since he committed this sin. He knew that only God could restore him.

Verse 9 - *Hide thy face from my sins, and blot out all mine iniquities.*

He knew that he would have peace restored if only God would hide from David's sins and blot out all his evil deeds.

Verse 10 - *Create in me a clean heart, Oh God; and renew a right spirit within me.*

He knew by confessing and being humbled before God that He would create in him a clean heart.

Verse 11 - *Cast me not away from thy presence; and take not thy Holy Spirit from me.*

David knew that the Holy Ghost was given to him because of his love and holiness in the Lord. And he knew that by sinning, he was jeopardizing that. He knew that without the Holy Ghost he wouldn't have that joy.

Verse 12 - *Restore unto me the joy of thy salvation; and uphold me with thy free Spirit.*

So he was asking for mercy and he got it. Ask and you shall receive! And he also knew that he couldn't do it, it had to come from the power of God in his life.

Verse 13 - *Then will I teach transgressors thy ways; and sinners shall be converted unto thee.*

Because of his experience, he has the compassion and understanding to minister to others and restore them to the Lord.

Verse 14 - *Deliver me from blood guiltiness, O God, thou God of my salvation: and my tongue shall sing aloud of thy righteousness.*

I see two scenarios - being delivered from the sin of murder that produced blood being spilled AND from curses from his ancestors who spilled blood. He wanted deliverance for murdering and without guilt! He knew that he wouldn't be able to live with the guilt for what he had done and knew God was the only one who could deliver him from it.

Verse15 - *Oh Lord, open thou my lips; and my mouth shall show forth thy praise.*

David began thanking God even before God delivered him. And during his praise he was set free. David was thankful! He praised God to everyone he could. Telling others how God's love and forgiveness is greater than anything he could ever have done. He shared this for the rest of his life. He wrote Psalms and praised God in every breath. I know personally that we praise God more when we are delivered from much! David's fire was re-kindled. Yes, it was going out, but it was still a little ember that was sparked because of truth and his desire to be clean.

Verse16 - *For thou desirest not sacrifice; else would I give it: thou delightest not in burnt offering. Verse 17 - The sacrifices of God are a broken spirit: a broken and a contrite heart, Oh God, thou wilt not despise.*

David knew it wasn't what he did, but was a matter of his heart.

Verse 18 - *Do good in thy good pleasure unto Zion: build thou the walls of Jerusalem.*

Though David confessed he also knew that whatever happened to him was due to God's righteousness and justice concerning him. And if it pleased God to build Jerusalem using him, then so be it.

Verse 19 - *Then shalt thou be pleased with the sacrifices of righteousness, with burnt offering and whole burnt offering: then shall they offer bullocks upon thine altar.*

Then after confession is made and the heart surrenders, God will happily receive the offerings. I believe this is what happens to people who tithe and are still in want. They tithe without a pure heart, and God doesn't accept their gift. The book of Matthew says if you come to the altar and offer your gift but you know someone is mad at you, go and be reconciled to that brother then come and offer your gift.

What is this passage instructing us to do?

1. Look to God. Don't run away from Him but run to Him. That is faith, believing God loves us no matter what!!!

2. Acknowledge our sin before Him. Even though we may be mad at a neighbor it's God that we are sinning against.

3. Be accountable for our actions and take responsibility for them before God.

4. Confess our sins to God as it is He who then cleanses, heals, purges and restores us.

5. Receive forgiveness and with that forgiveness, we can forgive others.

6. He puts back in us His joy which becomes our strength.

7. Then we can help others. We are excited to share with others what God did in our lives so that they are restored as well.

8. As we offer our tithes and offerings He will be pleased because we are doing it from a clean heart. Then we'll understand the fullness of His glory.

9. Then we will enter into His rest. When we come to the Lord we are received with gladness and our praise and worship toward Him is heard! We find peace there, we find acceptance and joy. Having the "rest" of God means we take Him at His Word in everything! Remember, Jesus taught that if we come to the alter with unforgiveness in our hearts toward another, to leave our gift at the alter and be reconciled to our brother, then come and offer the gift (Matthew 5). In the book of Geneses, Cain's sacrifice was rejected - why? I believe it's because

God knew his heart and contempt toward his brother - and of course you know the story, Cain killed his brother later. I don't believe Cain got jealous of his brother because his offering was rejected, I believe he hated his brother all along but this was the last straw that brought him to that murderous act.

Ministry Prayer for You:

"Father in Heaven, I pray that this individual sees that they may have done some terrible things, but you are bigger than anything they could have ever done. As demonstrated in David's life, we too can be restored in the joy you so desire us to have. Help us to come clean before you, confess our hearts to you, believe you are the one who is able to deliver, and help us receive the forgiveness you give. Restore them Lord to your heart, so that they are known as a man or woman after Your heart. Bless them as they seek you more each and every day. In Jesus' name, Amen."

Relationship with Jesus - The Son

As you will notice, we spoke in depth on our relationship with God the Father. There is a reason for it. That's whom Jesus came to represent. When we see Jesus we see the Father and vise-versa. So as we continue looking into the life of His Son, we will see more of God.

Take the time to answer the following questions. This will help pin point where you are in relationship with Him.

1. Who is Jesus?

2. Is He your personal Savior?

3. Is He the center of your thoughts?

4. Do you accept the total redemption He paid for you or do you think you have to earn it somehow?

5. Do you have to pay penitence for your sins?

6. Do you love Him to the degree you trust Him completely with everything in your life?

These are good questions to ask yourself to see where you stand in your relationship with Jesus. As you go through the list below of Jesus' characteristics and attributes, be sure to locate the scripture that references them. Some scriptures are there, but there are some that aren't. Be a good Bible student and find them. By doing this you are "seeking" Him.

Below lists some of the attributes and characteristics of Jesus:

- Jesus is our Lord and Savior.
- Jesus was the Lamb of God who came to take away the sins of the world.
- Jesus is our provider.
- Jesus is the Way, the Truth and the Life.
- Jesus is our brother
- Jesus is our friend.
- We are heirs with Him.
- He is God's only begotten Son.
- He came to show us the Love of God our Father.
- We are also children of God because of what Jesus did.
- We do not pray to Jesus, but we pray to the father IN THE NAME of Jesus. Jesus tore the wall down so we had free access to God ourselves. (John 16:25-27). Jesus is the author and finisher of our faith (Hebrews 12:12)
- Jesus was a carpenter. He's building a mansion for us in heaven.
- Jesus was the Word made flesh. (Jesus is the Godhead bodily.)

- Jesus helped God build the earth. He was there when all was being created.
- We were made in His image.
- Jesus experienced what it was like to live in this fallen world.
- Jesus was tempted yet didn't sin.
- Jesus rose from the dead and is alive forever more. (If you do not believe Jesus rose from the dead that is the key ingredient for salvation.)
- Jesus has the power over death (Hebrews 2:14).
- Jesus is the great high priest (Hebrews 4:14).
- Jesus is there in the time of need (Hebrews 2:18 and Hebrews 4:15).
- Jesus sets people free.
- Jesus is faithful (Hebrews 3:1)
- Jesus is my teacher, master, Rabbi.
- Jesus is the great physician.
- He has all things under his feet (Hebrews 2:8)
- Jesus sits at the right hand of God, making intercession for us.
- Jesus is the sole expression of God's glory.
- Jesus is the very imprint of God's nature.
- He is higher than the angels.
- Jesus is the light of the world.
- Jesus gives abundant life.
- Jesus is light and in Him is no darkness.
- Jesus' prayers were heard because He reverenced God his Father.
- Jesus was obedient.
- Jesus sits on the right hand of God in Heaven (Hebrews 12:2).
- Jesus is the author and finisher of our faith (Hebrews 12:2).
- Jesus is the same yesterday, today and forever (Hebrews 13:8).

As you seek out Jesus, you are seeking out the Father. Because as you know, most of the teachings so far has been focused on God the Father. Because that is who is at the bottom of everything we need! Jesus made the way "to" the Father.

Relationship with the Holy Ghost – The Power of God

Once we have begun understanding our relationship with God the Father and Jesus the Word, it's now time to get intimately acquainted with the Holy Ghost.

Write down the answers to the following questions:

1. What do you think about the Holy Ghost? Or have you even given Him thought?

2. Do you know what power He has given you? (For those who are in Christ.)

3. Do you know His attributes?

4. Do you believe you have been equipped to do all things?

5. How do you see the Holy Ghost?

6. Have you ever received gifts of the Holy Ghost? If so, what are they?

7. Do you believe in eternal salvation?

8. How does the Holy Ghost speak to us?

9. Did you know He brings to our minds things we need to get through trials and tribulations?

The following scriptures describe the Holy Ghost and His function. In order to obtain and understand the power given you as a believer, you must know the One whom distributes it to you. Look up these scriptures and write down what you find.

John 16 –(Describes the attributes of the Holy Ghost. I've listed some of His attributes below. But write down others you find as you study.)

- Holy Ghost is our Comforter.
- He is our helper
- He is our intercessor
- He is our advocate
- He is our strengthener, standby
- He is our remembrancer
- He is the Truth bearer
- He convicts of sin
- He guides us
- He give us Power.

- He reveals secrets of God to you.

- Holy Ghost speaks to us (Hebrews 3:7 and 12).

John 15:26-27 *But when the Comforter is come, whom I will send unto you from the Father, even the Spirit of truth, which proceedeth from the Father, he shall testify of me: And ye also shall bear witness, because ye have been with me from the beginning.*

John 14:26-27 *But the Comforter, which is the Holy Ghost, whom the Father will send in my name, he shall teach you all things, and bring all things to your remembrance, whatsoever I have said unto you. Peace I leave with you, my peace I give unto you: not as the world giveth, give I unto you. Let not your heart be troubled, neither let it be afraid.*

By seeking God in all three persons, you are coming into the fullness of His glory. You are building a solid foundation for your life. You are developing your relationship with Him as He has desired of you. After all, the reason He created you was to worship and serve Him. But more than that, to call you sons and daughters so that when the winds of life blow over you, you will not be moved or fall into fear. You will be a testimony of His greatness toward you.

Ministry:

By acknowledging our need for MORE of the Godhead in our lives, we are putting ourself in position to receive. So pray this prayer:

"Dear Heavenly Father. I see from this study that I could receive MORE from You, Jesus, and the Holy Ghost. Thank you for teaching me the differences of each of your nature, so that I can have a relationship with You, Jesus, and the Holy Ghost. I realize now that I need all three strong in my life. Help me to seek you every day, and gain more knowledge and understanding in my relationship with the Godhead. Help me to believe. In Jesus name, Amen."

CHAPTER FIVE

Relationships with Ourselves and Others

Relationship with Ourselves

Before we can have a good healthy relationship with others we need to have a good and healthy relationship with ourselves. Building our relationship with God the Father, the Son and Holy Ghost will equip you to love yourself.

In the following sessions, we deal specifically with loving and forgiving ourselves. I know that perhaps many of you struggle in this area. But we have to realize that if God loves and forgives us, who are we to think any different. If we don't take Him at His word, we are making our thoughts higher than His and that is sin. Because of our wrong mind sets, we put ourselves in our own predicament and then blame God.

We can see what's wrong in other people, we may even have a 7-step plan for their breakthrough, but we just don't see inside ourselves as clearly. (We think we do, but we really don't.) If you really want to know what is inside you, really want to know, ask one of your family members or closest friend. Believe me, they know. We can see clearly in other people's lives, but we just can't see clearly in our own.

One day I was talking to a friend at work. She said to me that she felt uneasiness from me. She had thought I was mad at her or something. I sat her down and said, "let's investigate." See I know from experience that others see me better than I see myself. So after we talked for a bit, I confessed to her that I was going through some personal issues and was hurting and that's what she sensed. I didn't even know what I was going through that caused my demeanor to change. So after we talked a bit more I asked her to pray for me. She prayed for me and I had a heart to heart with my Heavenly Father and was restored. See I had not realized how I was being, but then through someone else's eyes, I saw it. I was set free! I could have brushed this off and said, "Oh, there's nothing wrong." But then we would have both still "felt " the dis-ease. This way, we were both set free.

See, God will use others to help us see stuff in ourselves as well. Once we recognize (which is the first step to freedom) what is in us, then we can cooperate with God as He begins purging those things from our lives.

We need to be open to get to know ourselves. It could be a bit unnerving at first because you may not like what you see. But it is so rewarding. I remember when the Lord introduced me to me, I cried for three days and never wanted to show my face in public again. I saw selfishness, bitterness, anger, fear, resentment, self-hatred, pride, arrogance, self-righteousness, greed, jealousy and envy, distrust, frustration, control and manipulation, self-pity, self-centered, and on and on. Believe me, it wasn't pretty. But after I had my screaming fit about it, God closed up my heart and put a zipper on it. He said He wanted to show me what He sees (because He knows the heart and all that is in it - Psalm 44:21; Psalm 51:6) and to know that He still loves me and that I need to love me too.

His mercy keeps those things covered until we are ready to see it so we can be set free. Because of the call on my life to help others, we had to begin working right away and didn't have a lot of time to mess around. So I got to see all this stuff at one time. I do remember saying, "But God, everyone sees all that in me." He said, no they don't, I have protected you from that and only showed you what was there so we can work on these things together without you falling apart as we begin the purging process.

Believe me, this is a process, but the best road you can be on. As you begin getting purged from within, your life improves in your relationship with your Heavenly Father, relationship with yourself and relationship with others. I found myself in the store one day just talking away with myself. And yes, I answered. I heard the Holy Ghost say, "It's nice to see you enjoying yourself, you are becoming your own best friend now."

Loving and Forgiving Ourselves

It's a known fact that we need to have a good healthy relationship with ourselves. This is one of the most important things we are to do in order to have good relationships with others. However, it's the one area that we fall short in and that's why we have so many problems. I'm not talking of self-conceit or self-righteousness. I'm talking about accepting oneself, loving self, and forgiving self every single day. The same compassion you may have toward a lost puppy on the road, or a child crying, or even one of your own children who lost their way, is the same compassion you need for yourself. I recall a lady saying that she really has lots of great friends, and treats them well but she really doesn't like herself all that much. I had to tell her the truth, because how we treat and feel about ourselves is really how we treat others.

We can be self-deceived thinking we are doing good, but truthfully if we don't love ourselves and accept ourselves, how can we really love our neighbor? And we can take that one step further and say, how can we really love God? As indicated in the previous sessions, we have been using Matthew 22:38-40 as our reference scripture. "We are to love the Lord God with all our heart, with all our soul and with all our mind, and the second is like it, we are to love our neighbor as we love ourselves..."

Before we can have a good healthy relationship with others we need to have a good and healthy relationship with ourselves.

I noticed that we can see what's wrong in other people, we may even have a 7-step plan for their breakthrough, but we just don't see inside ourselves as clearly. (We think we do, but we really don't.) If you really want to know what is inside you, really want to know, ask one of your family members or closest friend to tell you. Believe me, they know. If someone says to you, "Gee, weren't you a bit hard on that person?" And you reply, "I don't think I was hard, as a matter of fact, that was the nicest I've ever been." Then you need to go back and ask God if you were hard on that person. Don't let yourselves be deceived any longer – start listening to what others say to you and take it to God. If it's something God agrees with, He will let you know, because not everything people say is correct either.

Matthew 5:25 says to agree with your adversary quickly, while you are in the way with him; lest at any time the adversary deliver you to the judge, and the judge deliver you to the officer, and you be cast into prison. How many of us have been judged and cast into a prison? I'm not talking about bars... This scripture says that if someone says something to you that you may not believe or agree with, just take it to the Lord in your quiet time to see if it's true or not.

I remember working for a Jewish boss many years ago. He didn't like the fact that I was sharing the gospel and leaving tracks around the office. So one day he had each person I worked with write down what they didn't like about me. He met with me and had me read it. As I read through the list, tears welled up in my eyes as they said horrible things about me. I didn't get defensive because I was too stunned and crushed to. So I excused myself and went into the bathroom to recompose myself. While I was in there, I knew this wasn't the place for me to be working, but I wasn't going to leave on a sour note with hurt and bitterness in my heart. So the next day I marched into his office and said, "Bob, thank you for sharing that information with me." He was stunned! It wasn't what he expected from me. But the truth was, I did take all those things to the Lord and almost every one of them were true!!! So this was the beginning when God began working these things out of me. I thank God for this because what the enemy meant for evil, God meant for good.

There is stuff in us that God wants us to see, and now is the time to see it all. It's the truth about what we see in ourselves that helps make us free. Once we recognize (which is the first step to freedom) what is in us, then we can cooperate with God as He begins purging those things from our lives. He needs us to see so that we He does begin purging us, we won't freak out and wonder what is happening to us.

In order to see what is in us, we need to stop and turn around and face ourselves. So take a minute and look inside your heart. What is in there? Do you have fear, anger, jealousy, envy, feelings of being unworthy, feeling rejected, sad, depressed and the like? Write those things down, and by the way, these are your sins. It may be that as you begin writing, you had no idea you had so many! I had over 50 when I started my list, but it grew as the Lord revealed more. There was a lady I shared this with and after making her list came running toward me saying, "I have 145 sins on my list" and then stopped in her tracks to write something else down, "No I have 146 sins on my list." Once we stop and reflect on what is in us without any fear of what we see, that is the first step to our healing.

We need to get cleaned out before we can truly live clean lives. We are to clean out what is inside the cup so the outside will be clean (Matthew 23:25-26). Another scripture we hear so often is, "Remove the beam that is in thine own eye before removing the mote in your brother's" (Luke 6:41-42). I learned by personal experience, that when I finally get the beam out of my own eye (purging from sin and iniquities), I don't even see the mote in my brother's eye. It's not even an issue! What I realized is that the beam I had was what I "filtered" through. That beam is gone, there really isn't anything to see because if we are cleaned up in those areas all that is left is love and forgiveness, compassion and mercy toward others.

We need to get our lives right with God, and we do that by confessing ALL our junk and allowing Him the freedom to clean every bit of it out. It doesn't mean we are perfect. It means that we are willing to "see" everything inside us and cooperate with Him to clean us up!

What about the fact that we are forgiven of all our sins already? Why do we have to do this?" Look at it this way, do you like the way you are? Are you living free from guilt, shame, anger, fear, etc.? If you are free, then why are you reading these teachings? The truth is we all carry around stuff, what makes a big difference is facing each one and committing them to the Lord... THEN they are forgiven. We have to know what we are being forgiven for before we can be forgiven. God already knows your sins, but He wants you to know. He doesn't just say, "Okay, I've removed all your sins and now go and be free." He won't do anything we have not agreed to doing. Otherwise we would be robots. He gave us free will. It's like when you discipline your kids, don't you want them to know what they are being disciplined for? God can purge us, but if we don't know what he's purging us from, how do we "resist" it when it tries to come back if we don't know what it is. So to make a long story short, we need to know what God has forgiven in our lives, and when we confess them to Him, we are giving Him the approval to remove them.

So now take your "rap" sheet to the Lord and confess your sins, then receive forgiveness. 1 John 1: 9, says that if we confess our sins, God is faithful and JUST to forgive us our sins and cleanse us from all unrighteousness. This is a New Testament scripture, and written after Jesus rose from the grave. So even John knew we still needed to confess.

Once the sin is recognized and confessed, God purges. Now the work of God in your life has begun in the areas you confessed. Until we see what is in us, God cannot deal with these individual things. He doesn't force anything on us, but has to wait until we are ready to see.

This is how God works: Let's say we received forgiveness of our anger. But within minutes you find yourself angry again. Instead of getting mad at yourself, or wonder why you are still angry when you just confessed it, stop right there and confess your sin of anger. Ask God to show you where the anger is coming from so you can get to the root. See anger (and many others) are a manifestation of another deeper issue. In the instance of anger, fear and pride is behind it. By confessing to God, we give Him permission to work it out of us.

The anger can be there in layers. Once you confess your sin of anger, now you'll need to confess the sin of anger in every area of your life. It may be that I have anger when I drive my car, when I talk with a co-worker, when I have to make a decision, when I see something horrible happen, etc. These are "layers" of anger that has to be removed. The same way the anger came, is the same way it may have to go to be removed, one at a time.

Many times the anger (or thing we are dealing with) will get worse and worse before it is completely out. I find that when God starts working in an area, the sin intensifies! It's not time to fear, doubt, or run, it's time to buckle your seat belt, hold on with both hands and go for the ride. I no longer fall into fear, guilt and condemnation, or despair, when I feel like things are getting worse, I start rejoicing now because these are signs God is doing a work! I am "cooperating" with God by not fighting the process of purging. Yes, I'm forgiven, but now it has to be worked out of us because my mind habitually followed after that sin. The "work out" is working it out of us, and all the residue it left behind in our thinking.

The lady that told me she had 146 sins had a problem with a co-worker who was a teacher. She just couldn't get along with her and didn't know why. It's not that this person did anything to her; she just didn't like her. While ministering, we began talking about her husband. It appears that when we dealt with the issues of her husband (who was a teacher also) and forgave him from her heart as I describe in the forgiveness chapter, her feelings toward her co-worker changed. She no longer had a grudge against her, and all within minutes of forgiving her husband! It was because her relationship with this woman was filtering through the issues with her husband, and whatever was in that woman reminded her of her husband, so it transferred to this woman, hiding the real issue.

We may think that someone in particular is a problem to us, but the truth may be they may just be the "scape goat" or the representation of the real problem at hand. Remember, it's not flesh and blood we wrestle against, it's spiritual, all of it! That's why it's so important to ask God to show us clearly what is in us because some things may be hiding the real things that need to be dealt with.

Believe me, this is a process, but the best road you can be on. As you begin getting purged from within, your life improves in your relationship with your Heavenly Father, relationship with yourself and relationship with others. I found myself in the store one day just talking away with myself. And yes, I answered. I heard the Holy Ghost say, "It's nice to see you enjoying yourself, you are becoming your own best friend now."

Even David wrote, "Search me, Oh God, and know my heart; try me, and know my thoughts; and see if there be any wicked way in me and lead me in the way everlasting." I think this is something we should pray to the Lord often. This is giving God permission to continue working and cleansing us. Yes, we are forgiven, but now we need to appropriate that to our individual lives.

The reason I know this to be true is that I have been on this path of being purged and cleansed since 1998. I can say that I am not easily moved or pushed from side to side because of sin. It no longer has a hold on me because it's being exposed. Once it's exposed and brought into the light, it looses it's power. The only way it has power is if we hide from it. So as I repent, and fall out of agreement with it, I actually have a peace that passes all understanding! I enjoy my life now without feeling guilty all the time. My mind is no longer racing with thoughts every time I lay down to go to bed. I'm getting along better with people and if someone rejects me, I don't fall to pieces. I forgive them and move on. It's an awesome existence... This is what it means to be free. Yes, at first it may seem a bit grueling because your mind needs to be renewed, but give yourself time, it took time to get you into this mess, give yourself time to get out. You will see a huge difference in your life as you come before God each and every time you recognize something in you that is not of His nature and character, take responsibility for it and repent, and allow God to purge it. How awesome is that!

Ministry:

"Father, I have to admit that I may have been deceived in many areas of my life. I didn't see myself clearly and I pray that you help me see within my own heart so that I can become free of those things that don't belong there. Even David prayed for you to reveal any evil in him, because he too knew he could be self-deceived. Thank you for forgiving me of the sins I recognized, and if there are any others, please let me know. I want to be clean before you Father. I desire to be used of you to help others and I know if I am full of "junk" then I'll only give junk. I can only give to others what I have, but if you purify me, and fill me with your love every single minute of every single day, then I'll have what I need to love you properly, love myself and love others. Guide me and direct me in this Lord, remind me that when I do sin, I simply confess them, receive forgiveness and by faith, release them to you no matter how large or small.

Let me experience the peace that is being taught here, I want that. Help me to trust you more and more and to know you to the depths of my soul. I want to know you more and more Lord, to understand your ways so that I can choose wisely for my own life and direction. Let me be free from all fear of making wrong choices, and that whatever choice I make, you will be there to work things out for good. I love you Father, and thank you for loving me. In Jesus name, Amen."

Relationship with Others

Once we have begun this journey of relationship, it naturally flows out to others. It no longer is a burden to love, it's a pleasure, because you now have what it takes to love others. It's when we understand that sins is what causes us to have problems loving others, but the scriptures say that love covers ALL sin (Proverbs 10:12). So what is our problem? It's because we don't really understand how to forgive.

Did you know that if someone hurts your feelings, or does something to hurt you, that you are supposed to love them anyway? How can we? By the Love God has imparted to us when we receive His love.

Let's identify where we are in our relationship with others:

Write down your answers to the following questions:

❑   Are you easily offended?

❑   Do you get hurt feelings easily? If you do, then you get offended easily. Offense brings all kinds of sins into a person's life. Such as jealousy, envy, strife, hatred, judgment, and murder. Offense builds up lots of hurts. If you are hard and callous, it is probably because of broken relationships with people.

❑   Do you think people are always talking about you?

❑   Are you suspicious of people's intentions?

❑   Do people have to walk on egg shells around you and be careful what they say? It's time to be honest with yourself.

❑   Do people irritate you?

❑   Would you rather live on a mountain top all alone?

❑   Is there anyone you hate?

❑   Is there anyone you will never be able to forgive?

❑   Do you love your next door neighbor?

For total healing in mind, body and spirit, we are to obey the Word of Truth. Obedience comes when we understand God's love and have received it. Here is something the Lord showed me:

"Desire leads to seeking which leads to knowing which leads to believing which leads to receiving which leads to trusting which leads to love which leads to obedience which leads to peace. And if you are like I was, my whole desire was to have PEACE!"

Our obedience comes easily when we know the one we are to obey loves us. Sure, we can just obey, but both you and I know it is very hard to do at times. We even say, "Why can't I just obey?" It's because you don't know the One intimately with whom you want to obey. We will trust someone we know intimately. I submit to my husband without question because I "know" he loves me and I don't have any fear in our love. I'm saddened when I hear that there are women who have a hard time in this area because they don't think their husband's love them. But when we know God loves us, we can submit to Him in obedience because of that love. But if you don't believe God loves you, then you will remain stuck.

In Matthew Chapter 5 Jesus tells us to handle people like this: If someone hits you on one cheek, turn the other also. If someone wants your shirt, give him your coat also. If someone wants you to walk a mile, walk with him two miles. If someone wants to borrow something, let him have it. These are instructions on how NOT to get offended! You overcome evil with GOOD! But again, we have to have that "good" planted in us to be able to do it, right? I'm not saying you are to stand there and be a punching bag, but the principle here is that we look upon what others need before we look upon our own needs.

Here is an example: Let's say you have a problem and you went to a close friend for their advice. Their suggestion was to "just forget it, it's not worth it." So you take that advice and you try forgetting it. It's hard to do, sometimes it takes a very long time to forget. But the truth of the matter is you really haven't forgotten it at all. What you have done was pushed it down inside to the point it's simply avoided. But it's inside you still! It's in there to torment you when it wants to come up in the future. It's also used as a "filter" toward other people and that's why you act the way you do. You may treat someone badly and not even know why. It's because of the "junk" you still have in your heart toward a past relationship that comes up when someone is a reminder of that past situation. You don't even have to recall the past issue; the devil does it for you through your emotions. God wants this "junk" out of you so you won't be tormented with it any more. Keeping this stuff distorts your perception toward everything. When the junk is removed, the bitterness is gone, the offence is gone and then you can see clearly and respond positively in any given situation.

Ministry:

"Father, I offer a prayer for my dear friend. I ask for Your complete restoration in their relationship with You, with themselves and with others. We give you all the praise and glory. In Jesus' name, Amen."

Loving and Forgiving Others

In this section, we are addressing forgiving others, which includes receiving God's forgiveness. These, working together with the "Love of God" will help you gain understanding, which produces freedom. Freedom is being free from sin, and in this session, we will be coming into truth about our own heart condition.

The heart was made to love, nothing else. When we forgive, we ARE loving. Love IS forgiveness. Jesus showed us the ultimate love by dying on the cross for us, and did it to bring us forgiveness. The first part of Matthew 22:38-40 was described when I spoke of the Love of God. As we read on in Matthew 22:38-40 it says, "...and the second one is like unto it, we are to love others as we love ourselves." Simply put, as we get to "know" God and how much He loves us and is able to receive that love for us personally, we are to do the same with others! We are to get to "know" people, so that a trust will build and that love begins flowing freely and honestly between each other. We need to forgive each other (including ourselves) and receive forgiveness (from God and each other).

In order to love others though, we need to love ourselves. How do we do that? While on your love quest with God, His love begins to take root into your life. Then you are able to love yourself, in spite of yourself because it's His love in you loving you. As you "receive" God's love more and more, more of the impurities surface. Your sins are being exposed so you can confess them. When you confess them, God purges you and brings you even closer to Him. When you finally get that going with God, then loving others is a piece of cake (John 4:19).

We get stuck though at the loving ourselves part! It's because we know ourselves all too well, all the hidden junk, all the past mistakes, that we don't even want to make friends in fear they'll find all this stuff out. But the truth is, God already knows it anyway. We might as well come clean before Him, let Him sort things out from then on. When we isolate ourselves from people, we are living in fear. We are not being made perfect in love because we put our focus more on what others may think than what God thinks.

I have discovered something that rings true for every person who has difficulty with what I've been talking about so far. And that is, we are not living IN forgiveness. What I mean is that we are not applying the forgiveness Jesus came to give us every single day of our lives. When we make a mistake (sin), we get mad at ourselves. We think we have to "pay" for them in some way, and stay miserable for days. But, if we truly believed we are forgiven, we would boldly go to the Lord the minute we sinned, thereby staying free FROM sin, as Jesus promised. It's not that there won't be sin any longer, it's that when we do sin, we will recognize it, and apply the forgiveness of sins to our lives immediately.

I don't believe people are doing this. If they were, no one would be offended, hurt, or angry. We are only offended, hurt or angry when we "think" someone has done us wrong and we've taken it and did not forgive them for what we "think" they have done to us. But we wouldn't take it if we understood what forgiveness truly meant. I heard something the other day at church, "A humble man cannot be offended." As I thought about that, it is very true. A humble person understands God's love and has applied forgiveness to their lives, thereby, exercising compassion and love to others. I think that's a pretty good place to be.

David said in Psalm 51, "Only against YOU Lord have I sinned." He knew that any time we sin against anyone, it's really sinning against God. Matthew 25:40 say that whatever you do (or not do) to others, including forgiveness, you do it unto Him!

Your job as a believer is to believe, right? Then begin to believe you are forgiven, for all past sins, current sins, and future sins. And begin to receive God's love, so you can love yourself, and so you can forgive others.

This is the foundation I speak of. Everything, and I mean everything, has to start here if you want to see change in your life.

So what about all those people who caused you hurt, people you think you have forgiven or those you just don't want to forgive? The Bible is clear when it says, "If you do not forgive others, neither will your Father in Heaven forgive you." (Mark 11:26). And we all know that forgiveness from God is the only way we can have fellowship with Him. He demands holiness. And when we take what Jesus has given us, we are made righteous and holy! So then we can have sweet fellowship with God.

If you have difficulty hearing from God, it's because you are blocking your reception. God is talking but it's our "receiving" that is the problem - again, because of our thinking. But when all our "junk" is out in the open and transparent and we receive the forgiveness He sent to give us, THEN your relationship with God will greatly improve! Yes, even with all your junk you just confessed and that which is still in there.

The Bible says that what we do to others, we do unto Him. So if we don't forgive our brother, we are causing a breach with our Father. Remember, Jeremiah 5:25 says that we withhold good things from us. When we don't forgive, we block all blessings! Isaiah 59:1-2 says, God can heal us, but our sins and iniquities prevent Him from choosing to do so. He cannot move against our will nor does He move against His own words. The Bible is filled with condition - the condition is always about love and forgiveness! So what are our sins here? Our sins are unforgiveness and not receiving God's love. Yes, not receiving God's love is also sin.

Here is a way you can know for sure if you have forgiven from your heart. When you think of them you are at peace. There is no pain associated with that person, and even the memory has faded. The pain that is in you is a result of unforgiveness.

So how do we forgive from our hearts? Not only are we to forgive with words, but we are to forgive from our heart. In the love chapter in Corinthians, it says that love doesn't keep a record of wrongs done. So how big is your basket of "wrongs done" to you that you are carrying around?

We need to forgive as God forgives us and casts that sin out completely, as though it never happened!

See, if you truly applied the law of forgiveness to your life immediately to those who hurt you those many years ago or when you made a mistake, you would be a completely different person and in a complete different place! But over the years the memory grows and grows which begins manifesting in our relationships with others. We start living through those painful filters. Let's say you were betrayed by someone or they lied about you. So you are now on your guard with others and being suspicious of just about everybody - and you may not even know why you have a hard time trusting. It's not anything they have done, it's because you are still filtering through those past hurts. It's just that the junk is rooted deep and more junk has been added on top of that junk that you can't see it any more. We are a BIG stinky onion! Layers and layers of pain!

Every pain in your life is a result of unforgiveness. Either you did not receive the forgiveness immediately from God, or you didn't forgive someone else.

So how do you forgive from your heart?

Decide today to do something about it. Get a journal and write down every person's name that you can think of that you "believe" you have forgiven but you still have discomfort when you think of them, or those who you have not. Ask God to help you.

Then take one name at a time and place it at the top of a blank page. Draw a line down the center of the paper making two columns.

On the left column, write down all the "offenses" this person did that hurt you. Many of you may have done this in the past through help by a counselor or even an AA meeting, but this is only the first part. Many are still stewing in their juices as they are brought up over and over and many are stuck, reliving the pain all over again. But this teaching is to help get rid of the pain once and for all.

So now write down all the things you became BECAUSE of that person. For example: angry, jealous, fearful, unwanted, unloved, bitter, confused, ashamed, embarrassed, rejected, abandoned, depressed, etc. Go ahead and write down as much as you can think of. If you can write things down, then you have NOT forgiven the person, otherwise these things would not be there. These things that you have "become" are YOUR sins that you retained from that relationship.

John 20:23 says, *"Whosoever sins you remit shall be remitted unto them, and whosoever sins you retain shall be retained."* This scripture clearly points out that when you do NOT forgive others, you get their sins! In other words, when you forgive, you do not take on their offenses (sins) but when you don't forgive, you GET their sins. So you are not only carrying around your own sins, but theirs as well. Isn't it a wonder why people don't want to be like the very person that hurt them, yet they turn out to be just like them? It's because the sins of the perpetrator becomes theirs. I find that as I minister to people, when listing this column of sins, these are the very things the other person is experiencing too! Then to take it even further, now we are living through these painful filters, and doing the very things to others that were done to us. What a horrible cycle. We can only give away to others what we have.

It's important to identify any and all sins as it pertains to the person you are forgiving so you can become totally clean. See, it's not what the person did to you that is the issue; it's what you have retained from that person that is the issue. When we come before the Lord and confess these sins, we then are forgiven. Now we are "free" and clean to forgive the person from our heart! Not just with lip service, and not with a "but". What I mean is that you can tell if you truly forgave someone if 1) you have love and compassion for them 2) You don't feel the pain of that memory; and 3) there is no I love you "but." If you have a "but" this is a sign that you may not be forgiving from your heart.

Why is this so important. Do you want your sins forgiven? Then you need for forgive others. Matthew 5: "If you do not forgive others of their trespasses and sins, neither will your Father in Heaven forgive you yours." This is pretty serious stuff. But the good news is that as long as you are willing to forgive, and follow the example I shared, you will find yourself forgiving from your heart without struggle!

Now I'm not saying that you stay in an abusive relationship. But when we forgive from our heart, we see clearly to make sound decisions for our life. AND... one of the greatest benefits of forgiving is that it releases all wrong soul-ties and codependent characteristics. What a bonus is that. We talk more in later sessions on soul-ties and codependency, but this is a start!

So what is your part in all this? Confessing the sins that you retained out of that relationship and receive forgiveness so you can be free. These sins bind you to that person and neither are you are free. If some of the individuals are still in your life, you will see that they can control and manipulate you with a look! This means that you still haven't forgiven them from your heart. When we do, we are no longer tied to them emotionally, and that my dear is freedom!

Now take your list to God - those sins on the right column. And by the way, they aren't emotions - they are sins. I John 1:9 says that if we confess our sins, He is faithful and just to forgive us our sins and cleanse us from all unrighteousness. The reason we have to recognize our sins now is because we never did it back when they happened. So take this list to God and talk with Him.

Sample prayer:

"Father, I come before you with these unresolved and un-confessed sins. I did not receive forgiveness for these things when they happened, so I've been carrying them around all this time. I receive forgiveness for them right now, applying the sacrifice Jesus came to bring me. He paid for all my sins, and I accept that and receive that right now. I ask for forgiveness and thank you for forgiving me for (name off each sin on your list). I receive forgiveness for each and every one, right now. Cleanse me and restore me Lord. I believe by faith that you have cleansed and purged me from all sin. Now I am free to forgive (the person's name), and I thank you for restoring me to (name of person). I also forgive myself. I ask you to put a new heart in me toward (name of person). I ask you to bless them Lord. Love them Lord and let them know you love them too. I also ask you to forgive me for blaming you and restore our relationship. Help me to receive your love right now and fill those areas where the sins were. Help me to "know" you more. In Jesus name, Amen."

As you have confessed and received forgiveness for your sins, you are now "free" to forgive the person who hurt you. The reason people aren't set free when they forgive, is because they didn't know they "took on" sins that had to be confessed too. Did you know a victim has also sinned? Even those who were raped and abused need to confess their sins. Why? Because when you don't forgive the perpetrator, you take on their sins too! Yikes! I know, I was one such person. I had gone through several abusive relationships along with being raped more than once, but I had to forgive. But I really couldn't forgive them. All that would come up is that shame and feeling dirty. But when I realized that my sins retained were keeping me in pain, that's when I decided to take God at His word. So I wrote down what I became. Not because I did something wrong but because they did something wrong and I "retained" their sins. For example, what I retained was this: Shame, anger, guilt, hate, distrust, feeling dirty, fear, suspicious, isolated, feeling unsafe, etc. See how even a victim can be filled with sin that has to be confessed?

So now that you have dealt with one person, it's time to continue this same process with the rest. Not in groups, unless it was a group thing, but each person individually. And you just can't say, "I forgive everyone." This is a good place to start, but then facing one by one is the only way you are going to find your peace. I found that the same way it went in is the same way it has to go, one at a time. I had to do this over 200 times. After awhile, I didn't need to write them down, I just went through this process in my mind whenever things came up.

Then as you do this with all those who have hurt you from childhood, the layers of pain are removed! Your onion that you had been becomes smaller and smaller (I teach more on the onion principle in a later session). Then to stop having painful things added from this day on, you forgive at the moment you "feel" pain by an offense. If someone does something today to hurt you or offend you, you just need to say, "I forgive you" and do it quickly; right at the time it happened so that their sins won't jump on you and become you! You are not only keeping yourself free, but you are helping the other person become free too.

This is how that works. When you forgive someone, you are releasing him/her to God. If you don't forgive them, you are still connected to them by way of a soul-tie. This prevents God from moving in both of your lives.

By forgiving quickly, you are making them free game for God to do His will in their lives as much as in your life. Try it, you'll see.

During my seminars, I teach this principle. Each and every person experienced a lighter feeling because layers of hurt were being removed from their lives, right before their eyes! Some have reported back that when they saw that person again, there were no ill feelings at all, only love and compassion! I know that when we forgive from our heart not only are we set free, but others are too.

Scriptures to reflect on:

❑ John 15:10-11 - "This is my commandment that ye love one another that your joy may be filled" (To love is a condition for joy).

❑ Proverbs 18:19 - "A brother offended is harder to be won than a strong city" (When we offend, it may take a lot to get it restored).

❑ Proverbs 18:24 – "A man who has friends must show himself friendly" (If you don't have friends, it doesn't start with them!).

❑ Jeremiah 22:3 and 13 - Life is not mere substance, but doing justice and justice involves people. (There is no room for selfishness in our relationship with others.)

Prayer:

"Father, I ask that you help us to gain the knowledge and understanding and wisdom to know when we need to take action for our lives. Having a good relationship with ourselves is critical in having a good relationship with others. I now know this is key to receiving healing, wholeness, wellness, joy and peace. Thank you for this truth that makes me free. In Jesus name, Amen."

CHAPTER SIX

Faith

There are three types of faith that I discovered, there could be more but this is what I know so far that has helped me grow in faith.

    1) Romans 12:13 says that God has dealt to every man the measure of faith. Even non-believers have faith. Faith to believe the chair won't break when they sit in it, things like that.

    2) The Gift of Faith. It is one of the gifts of the spirit. Some have the gift of faith, some have prophecies, or are teachers, etc. This is not the same as faith to believe. We won't be talking much about this one in this session.

    3) So since there is faith to believe before salvation it means we also have the faith to believe for salvation. The Spirit of God draws us to believe, that is faith stirred up inside. This is the faith we need to receive Jesus Christ as Savior and to live our lives as Christians. This is the faith that I'll be discussing in this session.

If I were to ask you if you needed more faith, would you raise your hand? I'm thinking that perhaps you would. But I would like to submit to you that perhaps it's not more faith that you need, but more love. Why? Because we have all been given a measure of faith (Romans 12:13). Even a drop of faith can move mountains (Matthew 17:20). Ephesians 2:8 says, *"For by grace are ye saved, through faith, and that not of yourselves it is the gift of God, not of works lest any man should boast."*

It is very clear to me that faith is a conduit to receiving grace. It's more of God's love that we need to ask for and the ability to receive it. I noticed that the more grace I believe for AND receive, my faith increases. Everything, again, boils down to God's unconditional love in our lives.

Let me share an illustration the Holy Ghost taught me. Take a minute and find a drinking straw, it could be any length. If you look at Romans 12:13 again, it says, "a measure of faith." This tells me that it is like a ruler and so faith represents a length. As a matter of fact the straw can be short or very long, it doesn't matter because if you look inside the straw, no matter the length, the space inside is still the same. How big that opening is however, is how much grace you are allowing in your life! So as you begin to receive more of God's love for you, and continue pressing in to seek Him out with all your heart, soul, mind and strength (Mark 12:30) that space will enlarge! The larger that space the more grace. Some of you are only receiving drops of God's love. It's not that He isn't loving, you it's that you aren't able to receive very much. You may feel Him loving you from time to time but what if you can experience His love day in and day out! Wouldn't you think your faith would increase? And you wouldn't be doing it... the love of God would be doing it. The Bible says that God will expand our borders (Exodus 24:34 and Deuteronomy 12:20). I believe this is also talking about expanding our faith.

James 2:18 *"Yea, a man may say, Thou hast faith, and I have works: show me thy faith without thy works, and I will show thee my faith by my works." James 2:20 "But wilt thou know, O vain man, that faith without works is dead?"*

These two verses are the manifestation when someone has faith. So many are out doing a bunch of stuff thinking it's faith, but it is not. When we have faith, the kind we are talking about, it becomes who we are. We begin to live what we believe, and then our works follow! I am doing more in my life as a Christian than I ever dreamed possible because as I step out "in faith" and do what I believe, my works show you my faith.

Then we know we have faith because of our works. The enemy wants us to be so busy with doing, doing, doing, and not getting God's love deep inside of us so that the love produces fruit. Sure, doing a bunch of stuff can produce fruit, but you have to keep on doing, doing, doing, to keep it producing. But if we produce fruit from God's love, it's God's love doing the work and that's when we find rest. Mark 4:20 says *"And these are they which are sown on good ground; such as hear the word, and receive it, and bring forth fruit, some thirty fold, some sixty, and some an hundred."*

It's very clear that in order to produce fruit you first must "Hear the word, believe it to receive it." So simply put, believe God loves you, so you can receive it. His love will cause your faith to increase.

I have been sharing the Lord with a waitress at a nearby restaurant. So as we were talking, she told me that she wanted to meet Jesus. She was actually looking for God to see if He was really there. Someone told her to pray. So she began praying for a home for her and her daughter and within one week she had a 3 bedroom 2-bath home for $300 a month. She said, "Is that a sign He is there?" I smiled and said, it's God loving you. She said, "This will help me have more faith, won't it?" See the goodness of God opened her to believe God loves her and cares for her. It will help her believe God, even in difficult times, because of the provision He made for her already. Her faith boundaries are already being expanded because she is receiving God's love. It will expand even more as she walks out her newfound faith in Jesus.

Now that we understand that what we really need is more of God's love in our lives and from that our faith will increase and works will follow, it's time to look at "why" we have problems doing this.

All your questions about faith are answered in Hebrews 11:6, *"But without faith it is impossible to please him: for he that cometh to God must believe that He is, and rewards them that diligently seek Him."*

When the Lord showed me what I'm about to share with you, I was changed almost instantaneously to the point my faith increased immeasurably. I pray the same for you.

So lets dissect this scripture.

"But without faith it is impossible to please Him." Okay, we understand this. It's very clear that faith is what we need to please God. Does it say you have to be perfect? No. Does it say you have to lead a worldwide ministry? No. Does it say your kids have to be perfect? Does it say you need to be wealthy? No. It says *faith* will please God. Okay, we have that one down. We know we need faith, as a matter of fact, we already addressed the real need, and that is being able to receive His love in our lives.

Now let's go on to the next part of that verse which is the key:

"For he that cometh to God must believe that He is..." Let's stop there because this is where the problems start. It says that when we come to God, we must believe that He is. Can I submit to you that it backs up the first part of this verse? That without faith it is impossible to please Him? So I noticed that the faith God is talking about here believes that He is... Let me say it again. We are looking at getting "more faith" but dear saint, we have the measure of faith God has given already, and scriptures say that even faith as large as a small seed is enough for us to do mighty things. What we need to understand is that "faith" IS "believing" God "is."

God Is or God Isn't?

The Bible tells us to "Believe that He is..." as found in Hebrews 11:7. But do we? Have we trusted God in every area of our lives? Do we have doubt and unbelief still? Are we battling with frustration and anger still? Do you still feel "under" rather than "over?" If you have done all you know and still feel "stuck" in areas of your life, then this insight will truly help you.

We must believe that He is. But before it says that it says, "For without faith it's impossible to please Him, for we must first believe that He is..." I believe this scripture describes faith. Yes, faith is believing, but believing what? Believing that He exists. When you do that, you please Him. So many of you are saying I do believe He exists. I would like to submit to you the possibility that in some areas of your life you believe He is there, and in other areas you do not believe He is there. How do you know which areas?

Exercise:

Get a piece of paper and draw a line down the center making two columns. On the left top column write, "God is" and on the right top column write "God isn't." Then begin to write down all the areas you believe about God in the left column. Things like believing He loves you, He's loving and kind, He cares about your situation, etc. Now if you have any doubt at all about any area of your life, then write it on the right hand column. I believe you'll write more down on the right side than on the left especially if you are still struggling in your life as a Christian. But this is NOT to condemn you, it's to help you see so you can go to God in these areas of your life for Him to help you resolve. Because when there is any doubt toward God in any area of your life, that very thing could be the block preventing you from receiving blessings.

For example on the right side it may be that you don't trust Him completely in your finances. How do you know that? If you are worried about them all the time, especially when bills come or it's payday. How about when you need car repairs, home repairs, etc. Are you in fear about how you will meet those needs. If you are, then write it down on the right column. In order to be free, you have to see what has you bound.

Many times in the Word of God it says what things are not before it says what it is. For example, "The Kingdom of God is NOT meat and drink, but righteousness, peace and joy in the Holy Ghost" (Matthew). So it says here what it's not before it lists what it is. So we need to recognize what the "isn't's" are before so we can see how to be free. We need to recognize what is in our heart first!!!

Now once you have a made a list of things, start with the first thing and take it to the Lord. Be specific too. If you have a hard time talking with someone because you are afraid of their response, then tell that to God. Be specific in going to God. It's those little hidden things that could be keeping you stuck!

This teaching is critical in seeing the Word of God at work in your own life. If you don't have a close personal relationship with God, and trust Him in every area of your life, you will struggle. You may even feel like you aren't progressing in your life as you think you should be. It could be these little foxes, things that may seem insignificant but causes great problems. Like the leaven in bread, one drop can leaven the whole lump, so can a "little" sin.

God only wants you to live in peace. He doesn't say everything will be perfect around you because He does rain on the just and the unjust. But when those rains come you will not be moved! That's where he's getting you. And in order to get there, you really need to know Him intimately in every area of your life. I know when someone is in fear and worrying about a family member, there is a possible problem with control. God is in control and the only one - so we need to rest in knowing that. We cannot change anyone, nor can we ultimately keep them safe, only God can do that.

I pray you get a deep revelation in this area of your life that before you can really see all the blessings come to you, you need to "know" the blessing giver and that He is in every area of your life, and that Blessing giver is God, the Father of Jesus Christ.

Are You Receiving?

Many struggle with "receiving" God's love. You can believe He loves others but you may have a hard time believing He loves you. Why? Because you don't really believe He exists. Think about it. I know in my own life that I believed God for waking me up in the morning, but then would doubt Him when I needed provision or healing. If we have any doubt and unbelief toward God, then we "don't believe that He is!" That He is "doing" something!!!! We must FIRST, FIRST, FIRST believe that He is. If you were like me and I was stuck in doubt and unbelief for so long, I simply confessed this to God saying, "God, I don't believe you exist. I believe Jesus is there, and yet I don't believe you are there for me. I ask you to forgive me and help my unbelief." After I confessed this, things began changing. We have to admit the truth in our heart.

You may have been a Christian for 18 years like I was; yet there was doubt and unbelief toward God. Be honest with Him right now. Stop right now from reading this and go to your loving Heavenly Father. It may be hard because you see all the "undone" things in your life, but go anyway. He is right now ready to receive you! Yes, now.

You may have mountains in your life that you have to face, huge things that you don't think you can overcome. It's because you didn't have the faith, this faith that I talked about. The faith to believe that God's love in you will give you what you need to believe your situation is in God's care.

Mountains can be moved without any effort. We'll watch God plow over and through things we never dreamed possible. When I see a mountain ahead of me, I look at is as an opportunity to grow in more faith because I finally believe - without one drop of doubt - that God loves me and wants the best for me and will do everything in my life that He can to see me succeed. Sure, we may have to go through some hardships, those are the times my faith is being developed.

James 1, *"the trying of my faith works patience..."* We need to have our faith tried to see how far it will bend and where the breaking point is. Because that breaking point is where we are the weakest. So God will keep bending us until there is no breaking point just flexibility!! And that's when you will get your peace because when patience comes, it brings us peace.

I believe that on the top of each person's prayer list is the desire for more "peace." Well, without even focusing on that, that's what we accomplished here. So in a nutshell: By receiving God's unconditional love, our faith is increased; by believing that He is; my faith is increased; by being tried; patience is increased which brings peace. It all works together.

James 1:2-8 *"My brethren, count it all joy when ye fall into divers temptations; Knowing this, that the trying of your faith worketh patience. But let patience have her perfect work, that ye may be perfect and entire, wanting nothing. If any of you lack wisdom, let him ask of God, that giveth to all men liberally, and upbraideth not; and it shall be given him. But let him ask in **faith**, nothing wavering. For he that wavereth is like a wave of the sea driven with the wind and tossed. For let not that man think that he shall receive any thing of the Lord. A double minded man is unstable in all his ways."*

This scripture clearly tells us that when we believe God is, when we believe and receive His love for us, we will be able to ask for anything and it will be given because we are stable and sure and secure in Him.

John 15:5 *"I am the vine, ye are the branches: He that abideth in me (receives His love), and I in him, the same bringeth forth much fruit: for without me ye can do nothing.* (It's God's love in you that gives you the ability to do this or that.)

Acts 17:28 *"In him we move, and live and have our being."*

Again, it's God in us doing great and mighty things. We give Him all the glory. Remember, we are vessels, but what are we filled with? Love of God that produces good fruit, or doubt and unbelief that produces dead fruit.

Ministry Prayer for You:

"Our Father in Heaven. I come before you with this dear saint. Perhaps they have doubted you for some time, perhaps they believe you care for others but have a hard time believing You care for them. It's good they see that Lord, thank you for helping them see the truth in their own heart toward you, this is their first step toward peace. I ask your love to penetrate their hearts and minds Lord, removing all fear. Help them to believe Lord. Increase their borders so that as they begin to truly "believe" and "receive" all of your love and goodness, they will have the faith necessary to move mountains. Thank you for changing them already, and giving them peace. In Jesus' Name, Amen."

A prayer you can pray if you desire more faith.

"Dear Heavenly Father, everything that I was taught in this session applies to me. I have been wavering in faith. No wonder I've not been given things I've asked for, I haven't really believed you exist - for me. Oh, I may see you blessing and loving others but I had a hard time believing for myself. But I confess that to you now. I've been in doubt and unbelief and unstable in my thoughts toward you. I ask for your forgiveness and I ask you to help my unbelief. Help me to believe you are... that you love me... that you exist in every area of my life... and even when things aren't going so good, that I still believe. I know it's those times you are stretching my faith to believe more. Help me not to break and fall into doubt again, but to hold on and believe even more. I thank you for this teaching Lord, and ask you to help me receive all you have for me. In Jesus' Name, Amen."

Habakkuk 3:17 *"Although the fig tree shall not blossom, neither shall fruit be in the vines; the labor of the olive shall fail, and the fields shall yield no meat; the flock shall be cut off from the fold, and there shall be no herd in the stalls: Yet I will rejoice in the LORD, I will joy in the God of my salvation. The LORD God is my strength, and he will make my feet like hinds' feet, and he will make me to walk upon mine high places..."*

Closing Comment:

This teaching is to bring you into a relationship with your Heavenly Father. Give yourself time to reflect and to acknowledge your whole heart before Him. He will take all you bring to Him and make it into something beautiful in His time (Ecclesiastes 3:11). Don't be afraid to tell Him everything. If you fear God in a wrong way, you may need to go over the "image of God teaching again. Because we are to be excited with joy to come to Him with all our junk! Just as a child does when he has a broken toy. If the child is fearful that he broke the toy and afraid to go to his father, then this child is in fear because he doesn't feel loved by him. But if a child runs to the father and says, "fix it." This child trusts his father and knows he will do everything in his power to fix it because he's loved. You are God's child and He will never forsake you or cast you off. Nothing can separate you from His love... nothing!

CHAPTER SEVEN

Accusations

In the 12th Chapter of Revelations it says [9] *And the great dragon was cast out, that old serpent, called the Devil, and Satan, which deceives the whole world; he was cast out into the earth, and his angels were cast out with him. [10] And I heard a loud voice saying in heaven. Now is come salvation, and strength, and the kingdom of our God, and the power of his Christ; for the accuser of our brethren is cast down, which accused them before our God day and night."*

From this passage, it looks like Satan is no longer accusing us to God because He was cast out from before God, never to return. So where is he and what is he doing now? He's on this planet accusing us and causing us to accuse each other.

When we accuse, we are acting out the devil's character. When we believe a lie, we are "receiving" what the enemy is dishing out. We become the "accuser" - We need to confess our sin of accusation toward God.

This teaching is desperately needed, especially for those who feel God has abandoned them in some way. What I mean is that many people have been living their lives "thinking" God is not going to answer their prayers, so secretly may be mad at God.

The truth behind all this thinking is because some of our prayers are not answered or perhaps we've had disappointments in our life, or dreams and wishes that have never come true.

Because of this, way back in our mind we "think" God has somehow left us. Maybe He really doesn't love us? Maybe we aren't good enough to have our dreams, and prayers answered.

These thoughts are all lies! John 8:44 say that Satan is the father of lies. And if we believe these lies we are calling God a liar! We are accusing God of lying to us about His love, His care, His provision, His help, His healing, His peace, and all that He is. And when we do that, we are causing our own block from His blessings. The truth is He has never left us or abandoned us. God IS love - He can do nothing else. In Him is no darkness at all. The Bible says, "Let God be found true, and every man a liar" (Romans 3:4).

We think things like: "If God really loved me, this never would have happened. Or if God is love, why are all the children dying? After all, He could have prevented things from happening, but didn't." The truth is, this is true in part. God can stop things from happening, but He allows it to bring us to a place to trust Him all the more. Many of the things that have happened are because He wants to get to some of our own heart issues. When things happen it's a test to see what is truly in our heart whether we are going to fall to pieces or trust Him.

For example: Let's say you have been doing your job for years, and doing it well. Then one day you get a new boss who doesn't think you have the skills to be doing what you are doing. They don't see it and they don't want to see it. This person is making life difficult for you, and even causing you "grief." But the truth is, God is smack dab in the middle of it. He has allowed that situation to come into your life because there is a deeper work to be done in your heart. Yes, God can stop these things, but then we wouldn't grow! In this particular case, it could be God is wanting to remove pride... and learn to submit when you don't want to. Only you will know what God is doing, it's different for each one of us.

The bottom line of living as a believer is to love; give love and receive love without fear. Not to worry what people think, or doubt God's love ever again. This is the place He is taking us. If you can get past what things "look" like, and begin to see the bigger picture, and you are only a piece of that puzzle, believing God is intricately immersed in your situation and is orchestrating things for your good, we wouldn't accuse God any longer. We would begin to thank Him for "meddling" in our lives, knowing that it's causing us to become the person we have desired to be.

The only one in this universe that can truly give us the desire of our heart, or bless us beyond anything we hoped, asked or dreamed of is God. And as long as we "think" wrongly about Him, we are blocking our blessings. I've quoted Jeremiah 5:25 several times already, but it says it all. We prevent good things from happening to us because of our sins and iniquities.

We need to be forgiven of that doubt (sin) and ask God to help us believe even more. Be determined to push pass what we are "feeling" and begin to believe the truth. When we do that, our feelings catch up with the "right" thinking, and PEACE comes. If you do this each time something like this happens, provoked by you or for some other reason, peace comes easier and easier. You begin to trust God more so that you can say as Job said, "Though He slay me, yet will I trust Him." That is true freedom.

2 Corinthians 2:5-11 explains what forgiveness is, how to do it, and why it's important. And by receiving forgiveness, giving forgiveness and walking in love with everyone we KEEP THE ENEMY AWAY! We don't' even have to fight with him at all when we truly walk in love.

Let me ask you a question. Can you receive something from someone you are mad at? Not really. This is what is happening with God. When we "think" God doesn't love us, or feel like He's really not there for us, yet at the same time make prayer requests, we are not going to receive anything. James 1 says that a double minded man is unstable in all his ways and let not him think he shall receive anything from the Lord. Hebrews says we must believe that He is... (i.e. That He is going to hear our prayer. That He is who He said He is. That He is the provider. That He does exist. That He is our portion! That He is all in all. That He has finished everything and everything is available to us who believe that He is. (Hebrews 11:6) One area in my life that caused a huge transformation for me was when I finally believed that God Is!

Out of the heart flows the issues of life. What is in our heart? Paul said it's not what goes into the mouth that defiles the man, but what goes out of the mouth, that defiles him (Mark 7). Whatever we begin to "believe" as truth is coming out of our heart! If what is in our heart is fear (which is why people think the way they do) then that's what we will live. Fear is the opposite of God's love. As long as we fear, we are not receiving God's love.

These "thoughts" come from fear. Satan's faith!

A scripture comes to mind found in Psalm 89:30-32, "If my children forsake my law, and walk not in my judgments; if they break my statues, and keep not my commandments; then will I visit their transgressions with the rod and their iniquity with stripes."

When I read this, I understand why for so many years (even as a Christian) I imagined God was sitting on a throne somewhere up in the sky with a big stick (rod) and ready to bop me on the head when I broke one of His laws. But if you read further, it goes on to say, "Nevertheless, my loving kindness will I not utterly take from him, nor suffer my faithfulness to fall."

So regardless of our own sin, His love is there. And, if you look closely at that scripture, the penalty for sin is being hit with a rod and lashed with a whip (stripes). But guess who did that for us so we won't have to experience it? **Jesus**.

Yes, we deserve to be bopped on the head, but Jesus took all that for us. We need to understand Jesus paid it all, we do not need to pay the penalty for sin any longer, as some of you are still trying to do by staying under guilt and shame.

And what has all this to do with accusations? Because until we get a revelation on what Jesus represents, we'll continue playing the blame game. Even though most of the disappointments in life have to do with people and situations, the bottom line is that we have bitterness (accusation and blame) toward God because we think that God could have fixed these situations. We are secretly angry and/or disappointed with Him. Oh, we can go to church, praise Him and do all that, but our hearts are far from Him. The Bible talks about that. "Outside they worship me but inside their hearts are far from me." (Isaiah 29:13)

Our accusing God blocks our blessings. God looks at the heart, and gives according to the heart. Look at Abraham, his believing heart was counted to him for righteousness. (Romans 4:3) It's not what he did that earned him that status its what was in his heart and then from the heart his works followed.

So how do we get that part in our heart right?

The first thing to do is acknowledge what is in your heart. Take the time to see if you have any bitterness or unforgiveness in your heart toward God. I know that if we accuse God, we are unable to receive forgiveness. We remain in guilt, feeling unloved, unworthy, depressed, angry, fearful, confused, condemned, betrayed, rejected and abandoned. These things come when we don't "receive" forgiveness of our sins and iniquities, which block the flow of God into our lives. He is ever flowing, don't think any different, it's that we prevent Him from coming into our lives.

Identify what is truly in your heart. If you have any prayers unanswered, dreams unfulfilled, wishes that have never come true, then it is most likely you have accusations toward God. In other words, you are blaming Him for not being the God you think He is supposed to be in your life. Not giving you what you "think" you need to be OK. Blaming Him for not making things happen than you felt should have happened. Oh, you may not say this out with your mouth, but whenever we have any unfulfilled dreams, etc., it stems down to accusing God of not being there. The truth is, He's been there all along!

When you identify what is in your heart, confess them to God and receive forgiveness at the moment of confession. And then when you sin again or begin to feel guilty for anything, make confession to the Lord and receive forgiveness immediately. This way you stay clean before God like David did. He was a man after God's own heart. It wasn't that he was sinless, you and I both know he committed murder and adultery, but it was because he confessed these things to God and was restored. When we do our part, God does His part. He heals, sets free, delivers, and restores.

By staying IN forgiveness you are walking IN love. You are open to God's love more and more. "There is now no condemnation for those who are IN Christ Jesus" (Romans 8:1). If you are feeling unloved, guilty, sad, separated, etc., you are not IN Christ. We need to "put on" or "receive" what Christ did for us 2000 years ago. That's how you are "in" Christ. Begin to receive NOW what Christ did and stop trying to pay for things or figure them out.

In my research, I found that Jesus came and brought two main things:

- ❑ Love (which includes forgiveness and restoration and relationship with God).

- ❑ Peace. When Jesus ascended to heaven Jesus said, "I leave you my peace."

These are the two areas we as Christians have problems with - Love and Peace.

Well, no longer. Now that you know where the breach lies, you can stay in relationship with God by going to Him with ALL your stuff - even if it's something that you want to blame Him for. Go to Him with it immediately, confess your sin of accusations, and receive forgiveness, then watch God move in that area. He will either move in the situation or He'll change your heart about the situation.

So when something happens that causes you to wonder where God is, you won't. Because the truth is, whatever happens He is in it, He has even orchestrated it to bring something out of you that has to be revealed so He can purge you. But whatever it is, it is ALWAYS for our good and purpose in mind. That's why we have to stay in fellowship with Him. To know how He thinks. To truly "know" His heart, so that when something unforeseen happens, we aren't tossed to and fro (meaning having doubt and unbelief toward God).

James 1: 6-7 *"For he that wavereth is like a wave of the sea driven with the wind and tossed. And let not that man think he shall receive anything from the Lord for a double minded man is unstable in all his ways."*

Not only do we accuse God, but we also accuse others. If we were doing it to others, know assuredly that you are doing it to God. "Whatever you don't do to the least of these, you also don't do it to me" (Matthew 25:40). It goes on to talk about if we see others in need and don't give it that we are not one of His. This may be a strong statement, but it's there just the same. We have to believe the whole Bible, not just the parts we like. It's time we get reconciled to God, to ourselves and to our brethren!

And for those who don't "think" they are mad at God or accusing Him, who are you mad at and accusing? Remember, what we do to others, we do to God. And if you go on to read verse 41 it says, "Then shall he say also unto them on the left hand, depart from me, ye cursed, into everlasting fire prepared for the devil and his angels."

He's talking to the person whose heart is not right. Not that they do everything right, but that they have not confessed the junk in their heart, received forgiveness for their sins by applying what Jesus did on the cross. That is the only way we can have a true relationship with God. Remember our relationship comes through believing, not a bunch of works.

In order to get our hearts restored with God, it needs to be clean of all offense. Such as unforgiveness toward others, anger, hurt, bitterness, fear, rejection, etc. We do that by confessing what we see in our heart. If we don't see things, ask God to help us see. As we confess, God cleanses as long as we "believe" we have received forgiveness. (We will teach forgiveness in a later session.)

If you stay in guilt and condemnation for anything, you are NOT receiving forgiveness and you are NOT receiving God's love.

Now don't go into fear because you see a lot of stuff you have to deal with in your heart. Be thankful that God allowed it to be revealed so it can be removed. God will cover your sins and have mercy on you to keep you until you have completed your journey. And not only that 2 Corinthians 2:11 says that when we do this Satan won't get an advantage over us! And my dear friend, we will continue this walk until the trumpet blows. Because even though we have dealt with past junk, we get opportunity to deal with new junk. But remember, the new junk won't be added, if we forgive quickly. We were created for love; anything else is of the devil.

Let me tell you a story that happened to me. I decided to cut my hair. There were two reasons why I cut my hair. One was because I wanted to look more professional and two was because my hair was damaged and needed help. I've had a deep desire to have long hair. I remember as a child I would bobby pin toilet paper lengths to my head so I could feel the long flow down my back. My mother realized I was serious about having long hair so she bought me a play wig. I grew up with five sisters and she kept all our hair short for easy maintenance. It appears from writing this that I need some ministry there... Hmm... well anyway, one morning while I was writing in my journal, I began looking at the intent behind cutting my hair. Then I grew sad. I wanted long hair. Then as quoted in my journal, "For some reason I feel out of sorts this morning. It could be my hair, yep! That's what it was. I don't feel bad that I cut my hair, just SAD that I can't have long hair." It seems when it would grow to a certain length it would begin breaking.

I secretly blamed God for not giving me what I wanted, nice hair. I asked Him for over 10 years why I had hair problems and why it won't grow and if there is anything I could do to help prevent it from happening. But the answer never came. So I realized that deep down I blamed God, after all, He could wave his hand over my head and fix it. And yes, my hair is still the same, but I will not blame God for it. It was an idol!! I was consumed with it and as long as it was an idol, it wouldn't be fixed because God doesn't "fix" idols, he removes them. Oh my, I'm getting delivered right now! My hair was being "removed" from my head because it was an idol! Yikes! "I repent right now Lord. I confess this to you now and ask you to forgive me for placing so much importance on my hair. I believe You for complete restoration in my heart and will trust You with my hair. After all, you know the number of hairs on my head." But before this revelation came I had to just trust Him. It still bothered me but I still had to trust Him. When I did that, He brought peace. My hair didn't change much, but I had peace.

So regardless if I was going to get what I wanted or not, I chose not to blame God, nor blame Him for not telling me why. Also, by trying to get God to do something in our lives out of vainglory is bordering on control and manipulation on our part. There is a happy ending to this story though. After 20 years - yes 20 years - I still have my hair and it's even looking very nice! But I had to get rid of my secret blame toward God before my blessings would come...

So even though things are "real" that you have disappointments or sadness in, we are to keep our relationship blameless before God. Job said, *"Though He slay me, yet will I trust Him."*

If you are "thinking" that's not fair... you best think again, and confess your wrong thoughts toward God because God is just and fair and good. If we say anything else, we call Him a liar. And we are back in the same "accusing" mentality as when we first started. See how cunning the enemy is?

Be blessed now and always, keep in mind that God is good, and in Him is no darkness at all (1 John 1:5).

The accusing spirit wants to separate you from God, yourself and others, isolating you, causing division, and causing you not to be a part of the body of Christ. When you accuse yourself, you are allowing the spirit to separate you from yourself. We are playing right into the enemy's hand by allowing Him to use us to accuse one another. We need to repent for this and allow God to purge us from all unrighteousness, replacing it with God's love, compassion, tolerance and forgiveness. This is the only way we are going to defeat the enemy.

The accuser likes to use the Word but twists it for his own purpose. Turning the truth of God into a lie (Romans 1:25).

He uses our own mistakes to accuse us too. It's important that we identify.

Read the passages below to get a clear understanding of what is going on. Do not skip this step... it's the Word that heals, not my words... so be sure to read them for yourself allowing the Holy Ghost to teach you what you need to know so you can keep yourself from the snare of the devil (2 Timothy 2:26).

Accusing **Scriptures**:

2 Peter 2:7;

Acts 23:30;

Matthew 27:37;

Rev. 12:10-11;

John 8:10;

Job 2:3-6;

Genesis 3:13 (where accusing first came into the world);

Isaiah 53:1-12;

1 Corinthians 3:20;

Matthew 12:34;

Ephesians 3:17-19;

1 John 3:20;

Luke 6:7;

Matthew 15:19

What is the antidote?

2 Corinthians 10:5; Hebrews 5:12-14; 1 Peter 2:1; 1 John 1:7;

Romans 2:1-2; 1 John 1:9; Galatians 6:1; Luke 19:5-8.

Our mind brings up things that accuse us! We have to take those thoughts captive, and cast them down as 2 Corinthians 10:5 tells us. We need to clean out our conscience so that the truth remains. So when we listen to our conscience, we don't hear any lies or old thoughts of accusing. Because as long as they are there, the enemy will use them against us. Especially if they are things that are true. The enemy, in most cases, uses those things we have actually done to accuse us. He wouldn't be able to if we went to the Lord with those things in the first place.

We need to be cleaned out of all sin that could lead to accusing so that the enemy won't have anything to torment us with, or used to torment others with.

If we have allowed that accusing to continue in our lives, we will begin to accuse other without our knowledge. But, there is a way to know for certain. If the person you are communicating with gets offensive, more than likely there is an accusing spirit involved. It's not that we can't talk to people and say what we need to say, but it's how we say it, and that comes from an "accusing" spirit. You have probably experienced this yourself. You try to share something but then you immediately feel their walls go up. They aren't receiving what you are trying to say. You are even being nice about it. But they believe you are "attacking" them. Because my dear friend, it's not a fight in flesh and blood, it's spirit to spirit. So if we get cleaned up inside BEFORE talking to someone, I would predict that the outcome would be a lot different.

Exercise:

Write a list of accusations toward God (to include wishes unfulfilled, dreams that have not come true, disappointments, any bitterness, or anger, etc.) We need to come into truth about our own heart condition.

Then pray this prayer:

"Dear Heavenly Father. I recognize that I may have been accusing you and listening more to the enemy than to you. Forgive me and restore me to your heart. I forgive you Father, even though you don't need to be forgiven, but you do say to forgive everyone, and so I also include you. I release you to be God in my life and do what you will. I take responsibility for my life, as most of what is going on is from my own choices. You gave me free will, if you make things happen in my life, that is not free will. So I am sorry for accusing you and blaming you. Today is a new day, a new start. I release all those past disappointments, regrets, dreams, blame, and unanswered prayers to you. Restore me to your heart Lord. I know that all things work together for good to those who love you, and I will believe that. I will praise you when things are going good and I will praise you when things aren't going so good. There is a reason, and I will trust you with that reason. My life is in your hands, and thank you for loving me. And forgive me for listening to the lies of accusations toward myself. You have not accused me of anything, you love me, help me have this mind. Also, forgive me for accusing and blaming others. Help me to love and forgive each and every person, past, present or future, in Jesus name. Amen."

If a person prays a prayer like this, God responds. He begins healing that broken heart. He begins restoring; He completes the things we cannot. We cannot change our heart. As God cleanses it from the things we've confessed,

He heals and restores our heart. He begins penetrating more of His love into our lives.

A Prayer for you for deliverance:

"Accusing Spirit Go now in Jesus Name. You have been telling this person lies and half-truths long enough. Let this person GO now. Father, replace those wrong thoughts and old programmed thoughts, with good things, good thoughts, truth, love and hope. In Jesus name, Amen."

Staying free. How do you do this? If you begin to "think" accusing thoughts again toward God, immediately confess them and receive forgiveness. Remember, it is not sin to "think" a thought, but if we dwell on it long enough, it could become sin. This also includes accusing thoughts against others and against you. These thoughts come from the kingdom of darkness. When Adam and Eve sinned, they began thinking they were naked. No one told them they were naked. Even God asked, "Who told you, you were naked?" They couldn't answer. God knew the answer, it was that other kingdom speaking to them in their mind. That's where that kingdom can rule and rein, but no longer. In this next section, we will expose that kingdom and help you regain back what was stolen.

Kingdom of Darkness:

This is a good time to talk about the "kingdom of darkness." The reason being is that whenever we keep dwelling in past mistakes, sins, broken relationships, etc., we are fellow shipping with devils, and that is in that kingdom. Anything that we dwell on that is from our past causing your pain and torment you are "in" the kingdom of darkness. The Lord was very clear when He said to me, "Any time you re-live something in the past that causes you pain, you are dwelling in the kingdom of darkness." So as the day went on I realized that I had dwelt in that kingdom more than I thought I had and from that time on began paying more attention to my thoughts.

We need to know that EVERYTHING in our past is dead works. You cannot do anything about it. God cannot even do anything about it! Think about that! So why do you think you can? When you do this, you are living in that other kingdom. Self-pity binds us to the past. Did you know that there is no provision of God's love for the past? The Bible says that God's love is huge and great but only for things <u>present</u> and things <u>to come</u> (Romans 8:38). It doesn't say anything about the "things in the past." When the past was the present, then we had God's love there to make choices, but now that it is the past, it is dead and gone. Everything from this second and before is dead.

Hebrews 9:14 *"How much more shall the blood of Christ, who through the eternal Spirit offered Himself without spot to God, purge your conscience from dead works to serve the living God?"*

One day I was thinking about all the wrong choices I made. I began pondering on them and letting my mind wonder. I began feeling sad. After a few minutes I recognized what was happening and said out loud, "Yes, I made some poor decisions in my life, but that is the past. I repent for those decisions Lord and receive full pardon and forgiveness. I choose to live in the present, looking forward no back." When I did this, those thoughts left and my peace was restored. Now as I try to remember what I was "dwelling" on, it wouldn't come because they were gone.

I'm not saying you aren't to look to your past, because in ministry we have to look back into our lives to see where we are "stuck." What I'm saying is that we aren't to dwell there.

Ministry:

"Dear Heavenly Father. I recognize that I may have been accusing you and listening more to the enemy than to you. Forgive me and restore me to your heart. I forgive you Father, even though you don't need to be forgiven, but you do say to forgive everyone, and so I also include you. I release you to be God in my life and do what You will. I take responsibility for my life, as most of what is going on is from my own choices. You gave me free will, if you make things happen in my life, that is not free will. So I am sorry for accusing you and blaming you. Today is a new day, a new start. I release all those past disappointments, regrets, dreams, and unanswered prayers to you. Restore me to your heart Lord. I know that all things work together for good to those who love you, so I will believe that. And will praise you when things are going good and praise you when things aren't going so good. There is a reason, and I will trust you with that reason. My life is in your hands, and thank you for loving me. And forgive me for listening to the lies of accusations toward myself. You have not accused me of anything, you love me, help me have this mind. Also, forgive me for accusing and blaming others. Help me to love and forgive each and every person, past, present or future, in Jesus name. Amen."

A Prayer for your deliverance:

"Accusing Spirit Go now in Jesus Name. You have been telling this person lies and half-truths long enough. Let this person GO now. Father, replace those wrong thoughts and old programmed thoughts, with good things, good thoughts, truth, love and hope. In Jesus name, Amen."

You can also pick up the book called "Stopping the Accuser" that goes into greater detail on this topic.

CHAPTER EIGHT

Fear

Perfect love casts out all fear and torment (1 John 4:16)

As you begin seeking more of the love of God, and applying forgiveness to your life and to the lives of others, there are still other things that can help with your sanctification process.

We need to understand fear (our enemy) as we get to know the Love of God. The Bible is very clear that a mature believer discerns both good and evil (Hebrews 5:14). I found that when people are in fear, it's because they have not been loved or unable to receive love. And it's usually because they don't think anyone could love them because of all the things they've done in their life. We need to understand as believers, that when we are saved, ALL our sins are forgiven, yesterday's, today's and tomorrow's. This is why Christians have guilt and condemnation they don't believe they've been forgiven. It's evidenced if they cannot forgive themselves. Refer back to the session on forgiveness if needed before going on. You ask what unforgiveness has to do with fear? It is the direct opposite of faith (love). Forgiveness is God's love. Jesus came so that we can receive forgiveness and have it to give! He came so we could receive God's love and walk in fellowship with Him and with others. Fear will prevent good things from taking place in your life! Fear blinds us, but love and faith opens our eyes and ears.

Isaiah 35:4-6 *Then the eyes of the blind shall be opened, and the ears of the deaf shall be unstopped. Then shall the lame man leap as an hart, and the tongue of the dumb sing: for in the wilderness shall waters break out, and streams in the desert.*

Whenever love is absent fear is always present. They cannot dwell at the exact same time, you will have one or the other at ALL times. We cannot have light and darkness at the same time. We cannot be up and down at the same time. Neither can we have fear and love at the same time. If you find yourself living in doubt and unbelief, and the next minute believe, then the next minute you have doubt again, it's because when you doubt you are in fear, and when you believe (have faith), you are in love.

Why do I say that fear is the opposite of Love when many say Hate is the opposite of Love? Well, both are true, but here is a scripture: 1 John 4:18 *There is no fear in love; but perfect love casteth out fear: because fear hath torment. He that feareth is not made perfect in love.*

To me, it appears that fear is the opposite of love. And why we say "hate" is the opposite of love, is because it's fear at it's best! We hate things because of fear. We say things like, "I hate having to do that." But what we are really saying is, "I am afraid of doing that because I don't like it."

Faith vs Fear:

"Now Faith is substance of things hoped for the evidence of things not seen" (Hebrews 11:1).

Fear is False Evidence Appearing Real. It's the evidence of something not real. You need to understand that the enemy counterfeits everything that is of God. You need to understand that fear (the devil's faith) is the direct opposite of God's love (faith). Fear pushes, faith leads and we will live under one or the other at ALL times! Which will you choose?

I have found countless times that when a person has fear, they are not experiencing love. The Bible tells us that *"Perfect Love casts out all fear and torment"* (1 John 4:16). In my life, when I began to "feel" fear, I immediatcly recognized what was happening, that the spirit was trying to take me again which meant I was not, at that moment, receiving God's love. So I would pray, "God I'm sorry for fearing, and I receive your love right now. Thank you for loving me right now. I take responsibility, confess my sin of fear, and begin to receive God's love." And within minutes the fear is completely gone! Every time, without failure! I may "feel" it while I'm saying this, but afterwards, the feeling leaves because God is the one who freed me... my job is to recognize and confess, His job is to line my feelings up with the truth.

Fear comes in all forms, not just fear of heights or closed in areas. It can be dreading something, worrying, frustrations, confusion, anger, depression, lying, discontentment, and so on. Fear is the devil's faith and it is apparent we operate in this faith more than God's. Anything that is not of faith (love and truth) is sin. (Romans 14:23)

I remember when I started flying after 9/11. Not only did I have the regular fear that comes from flying but now added fear of terrorists. But my ministry calls for me to travel from time to time and I had to face this fear. I knew that I was delivered from the "spirit of fear" but now I had to go and walk it out. I remember being a little anxious in my mind several days before flying. I heard the Holy Ghost say, "I am going to give you faith when you need it, not before." So I realized I wasn't trusting God and wanted that faith now for tomorrow. It doesn't work that way. God is the great "I am." That means now. So the time came for me to board the plane. With each step, it was a struggle, but I kept saying, Lord you love me, with each step. The minute I put my foot on the plane a peace fell over me like never before. I received the "faith" to "do" at that moment in time. The trip was effortless and even a joy. Now when I travel, I know God will give me the peace I need, because I know He Loves me and I trust that.

When we have fear, many physical ailments can come from it. If you have stress, that is the politically correct way of saying, "I have fear." Stress comes from fear. Anxiety comes from fear. Phobias come from fear. Feeling rejected and abandoned comes from fear. Fear is at the bottom of almost every dis-ease out there. So is fear the root? Not necessarily. Because I found that behind fear is pride. Think about this for a minute. The reason we fear people is because we don't want to be rejected, feelings of rejection come from pride. You may not say this but pride says this, "How can they reject me, they don't know who I am." I heard a statement that I believe is true: A humble man doesn't get offended. If we don't have pride, what is left? Love.

What are the ailments I'm talking about? Auto-immune diseases, high blood pressure, nervous system problems, Irritable Bowel Syndrome, parasites, Depression, Insomnia, Ulcers, Acne, Diabetes Type A, Hay Fever, irregular heart, muscle function, back aches, muscle contraction and Candita - to name a few. Look it up for yourself, it's in the medical journals. What is the stressor behind these things? Fear.

Long-term fear produces a cortisol drip that keeps your body in a state of high anxiety—a feeling of running all the time. I remember when I found out that this was what I had, I understood my drive to stay busy. I could never sit still but juggled several tasks at the same time. And of course, there was no peace and my mind raced all the time.

When your mind is constantly thinking of the future it affects your heart. Many don't think of the future in a good way but in fear. For example, "What will I live on?" "What if I get sick who is going to take care of me?" "What if I get hit by a car?" Luke 21:26 says that men's hearts fail them because of fear. This isn't saying you are never going to fear, it's talking about someone who consistently stays in fear.

Let's begin taking the Word more serious and cooperate with God. When we do the Word, we will fulfill all the promises written. Again, if we keep this ONE commandment, we fulfill all, and blessings follow. To love the Lord your God with all your heart, soul and mind, and strength, and love others as you love yourself, upon these hang all the law and the prophets. Fear comes when we aren't loving or experiencing love. People will fail you, but God never fails you. Stop trying to get from others what you can only get from God. His love is perfect and unconditional. Our love is not always so. When we receive God's love, all fear has to go, and then we can freely love others without fear.

Spirit of Fear

Now that we know that fear is sin, we also need to know that fear is a spirit. "For God has not given us a spirit of fear, but power, love and a sound mind" (2 Timothy 1:7).Here is something for you to apply right now if you live in a state of fear: 2 Timothy 1:6 says this, *Wherefore I put thee in remembrance that thou stir up the gift of God, which is in thee by the putting on of my hands.*

This scripture comes right before, "God has not given you a spirit of fear..." So the antidote is to stir up Power, Love and a Sound Mind that is within you! Lay hands on yourself if you have to... and say this, "Stir up power, stir up love, stir up sound mind. For God has not given me a spirit of fear but power, love and a sound mind."

So let me ask you. Which do you possess? Fear or love; Stress or a sound mind; Cowardice or power? I found that when we don't have power, love and a sound mind, we dwell in fear.

Notice how I said, "Which one do YOU possess?" But in reality, which one possesses you? I'm not saying you are "possessed" I'm saying which one has control in your life? Then we need to be delivered because it is "within" us.

I had to reconcile all this within my own heart because I was taught that when you receive Christ as your personal Savior, only the Holy Ghost is in there. Many stay in this mind set because they fear the devil. I discuss more in my book, A Matter of the Mind, so be sure to check it out. You may have heard the scripture that says if you are free from one spirit and don't fill up the place where that spirit left, then it can come back with seven worse than himself and take up residence in you again (Matthew 12:45). (Remember, these are "in" you, not "on" you. I used to say I was oppressed by the devil, but this is not completely accurate because I don't "feel" fear outside of my body but within. So when you experience fear, is it on your shoulder or in your body? You decide.) So, for those of you who fear being delivered, take heart. This is talking to people who don't have the Lord. When Jesus was healing people, remember, the Holy Ghost and salvation hadn't happened yet. Only when Jesus rose from the grave was this possible. So when they were delivered from a spirit, they were empty, they had to purposely seek out God to fill them. But when we get rid of an evil spirit, the Holy Ghost living inside us fills up that space in our lives because He's already there. If you were anything like me, I had a lot of knowledge, but it was only head knowledge. So when a spirit leaves, we are making room for that head knowledge to become heart knowledge! Yes, we need to still seek God to be filled in those areas, but don't fall into fear because you have what you need to keep evil from returning. This is what it means to exercise your faith, believing you are loved, believing the Word you have read, this is how we fill ourselves up. Many fear deliverance because they fear those seven devils! Be free now from that fear, in Jesus name, and be healed.

The Bible says that "we" are to keep ourselves unspotted from the world (James 1:27). That "we" are to cleanse ourselves from all filthiness of the flesh and spirit (2 Corinthians 7:1). That "we" are to keep ourselves out of the snare of the devil (2 Timothy 2:26). How? By being filled with the truth, His love, and His forgiveness. Fear keeps you unclean, and that's the enemy's M.O. (Method of Operation). The enemy can only produce fear, why? Because when he was cast out of heaven, not only was he stripped from being a favored angel with lots of responsibilities in Heaven, he was stripped from ever receiving God's love again! When we are separated from love, we are in fear. Since Satan is separated from God's love, he wants to separate you too! Don't let him any longer. Deal with this area of fear by accepting and receiving God's perfect love for you.

Ministry

I would like to lead you in a prayer of repentance. (If you want to be freed from the spirit of fear.) Because before anything can be cast out, you have to want it out.

"Dear Heavenly Father, I come before you recognizing that fear is sin, and also a spirit. For you have not given me the spirit of fear but power, love and a sound mind. I want that power, love and a sound mind Lord. I ask you to work this into my life. I give you permission Lord to do your will in my life. I fall out of agreement with fear and all it represents, and take responsibility now for entertaining it. I ask for your forgiveness and help me take my life back. I'm no longer going to be a puppet to be used by fear any longer. I also stand in the gap for my generations and ask you to forgive my fathers of the fear they had that may have been passed down to me. Thank you for forgiving them and breaking the bloodline curse off my life. Thank you for teaching me this truth so you can make me free. In Jesus name, Amen."

Ministry Prayer casting out the Devil:

"Father, you have given me power through the Holy Ghost to cast out evil spirits. This dear saint recognizes that they have a spirit of fear. So by the power of the Holy Ghost - Fear GO now, release this dear saint in the name of Jesus. You are no longer permitted to reside within this person's heart and mind. Let them GO in Jesus name. Father, I ask that the Holy Ghost within them stretch out and fill the area where the spirit of fear left so they are not empty. Help them to focus on your love, as it's your love that will cast out fear and keep it away. Help them to receive your love every day more and more. Flood them with your peace, joy, compassion, love, forgiveness, patience, and truth that comes by trusting you. Help them to trust you and know you even more. In Jesus Name."

Overview

This segment is a quick study how to stay free from fear once you have been delivered from the "spirit" of fear. Even though you have been set free from the spirit, there may be residue left behind and it manifests through situations, memories and feelings. Each and every one of these issues will need to be dealt with as they come up. But once they are out, they are out. The Bible says that the enemy won't get a foothold in our lives when we love and forgive. (2 Corinthians 2:10-11; Matthew 22:38-40; Mark 12:28-34.)

❑ Become acquainted with God:

1a) I will never break my promises:

Become acquainted with God's love. Mark 1:10 "You are my beloved son in whom I am well pleased." We need to hear this from our Heavenly Father - by faith. We need to know that we are accepted, that God is pleased with us, and that we are His beloved son/daughter. We need to know this.

1b) I will never leave you:

We need to know Him deeply and intimately so that we will know He will never leave us. Many think God has abandoned them, yet He has not. It's only because we don't "know" Him. We need to take the time to know Him. How do you get to know others? By spending time with them. Also, remember by studying about Jesus, you are getting to know God. Because even Jesus said He couldn't do anything He didn't see His Father do, nor say anything He didn't hear His Father say. You need to have a healthy interpretation of God and His relationship with mankind - it's not hard, pressing or wrathful for those who are His. It's kind, loving, and joyful. You may need to do a check on your perception of God. If you think Jesus is playing interference for you and God, then again, you need to have your mind renewed in truth. I encourage you to read the life of Jesus from the Bible for in doing so, you are reading God's life. Jesus came to show us the Father, not show us Himself.

1c) I will not remember your sins:

❑ This is one of the hardest things for us to comprehend. That ALL our sins are forgiven. When they are forgiven, God doesn't use them against us - ever! No matter what you "think." He will not remember our sins! Our job is to confess them, and He purges them - and they are gone! We have to do it over and over, but He forgives over and over! If He tells the disciples to forgive 7 x 70 just think how much He forgives us? More than that I'm certain. 2 Peter 1:9 say that we have forgotten that we were purged from our old sins. If you are heavy laden with care right now, it may be that you have not confessed them lately. Stop and take some time to do that so you remain clean before the Lord. It's not that you will become perfect, but your heart will become perfect before Him because you trust Him enough to take these things to Him. Fear will cause you not to want to... but push past that. Don't run and blame others like Adam did in the garden, run TO God. Fear causes us to run away and prevents good things from happening to us. Stop that right now by receiving God's love and forgiveness right now.

❑ Knowing the future. How many want to know the future? Well, there is only one who knows, and that is God. Anxiety is a result of thinking ahead into the future. However, if we commune with the Holy Ghost, since He knows the future, we can know it too. (John 16) One area of "knowing" is that we are going to Heaven. Another area is that the enemy is defeated, and going to lose the war. We can even see what it will be like in Heaven. We can know the future if we search the scriptures. But if we think ahead in our own imaginations into the future, this will cause fear. We are to cast down every imagination that exalts itself over the truth (2 Corinthians 10:5). We are not to think ahead, the Bible is clear that we are not to take thought of tomorrow. Matthew 6:34 "Take therefore no thought for the morrow: for the morrow shall take thought for the things of itself. Sufficient unto the day is the evil thereof." God knew that we can only handle today.. So stay in this moment and trust God with the rest.

⊓ Planting good seed - you will begin to reap a good future by planting today. Renew your mind daily and you are sewing seeds into your future. Then, even here you can know your future by the fruit you are planting. We are to put our mind on things above (Philippians 4:8). We have been given the mind of Christ (1 Corinthians 2:16). We are to think like God thinks. By doing this, we are planting truth into our heart that will reap a good harvest, not only in our lives, but in generations to come.

Ministry:

"Father, I ask for your perfect love to flood this person's heart and life. I ask you to help them find their identity in you. I ask you to help them get wisdom and understanding about who you are in their life. You said that if we ask for wisdom you will give it to us, and so I pray this for them right now. I also ask you accompany it with understanding so that your Word isn't just laws and regulations but truth that will make them and keep them free from all fear and torment. Let your mind be in them. Let them run to you not from you when they make a mistake. Help them get a revelation that fear prevents, but love receives. Help their minds be renewed daily in all truth. Write your Words upon their hearts Lord and hide them under the shadow of your wing. Make your love known to them Lord and help them receive it. Perfect love, your perfect love, casts out all fear and torment and we have confidence in this scripture that our job is to receive your love, your job is to keep fear away. Thank you for loving us and keeping us. In Jesus' name, Amen."

Further Study Resources:

We also offer a workbook called "Fearless Living." You can pick it up on our website at www.truthfrees.org or on Amazon.com. It has been used to teach in churches, anxiety groups, and personal study.

Another book is called, "A Matter of the Mind." It is my autobiography how the Lord delivered me from 30 years of anxiety, and now teach others so they too can find freedom. Many have been healed and on to helping others, how about you? Pick up this book on my website or on Amazon.com.

Dread

We have placed this in the chapter with fear, because dread is a manifestation of fear. Dread comes from fearing something or not wanting to do something.

Have you ever felt dread? Perhaps you never gave it much thought? But I found this is the most sneaky and cunning spirit yet. Many don't even know what dread is. Many don't realize it is fear! Regardless what your situation is, this teaching is one of the most important to helping you get your life back! To help restore you to peace without guilt or shame, without frustration, anxiety, or worry, without fear and irritation, and most of all "feeling" overwhelmed.

I believe we can all agree that we know what it feels like to be "overwhelmed." When we have twenty thousand things to get done in a day, or you just got a job that just seems way over your head, or you are doing things that just keep piling up. Well, you get the picture. You started out good, but before long, there is a pile of things to do and now you "dread" 'doing them.

Many churchgoers find themselves overwhelmed and it leads to burn out. They simply quit, sometimes even leave the church and take several years to recuperate. I know; I was one of them. It seems I start out okay but things just get too hard to handle, so I quit and move on. Sometimes I go to another job or church with determination to not get involved. But, if you are anything like me, "involved" is my middle name. So we try to not get "too" involved, but you know what happens then, you either are or you aren't and you are right back where you started. I didn't know what my problem was; well, not until I learned that it was a "Spirit of dread." If you have felt overwhelmed, confused, just plain heavy and tired, no energy or interest to do something, then it's pretty certain you have this spirit. The Bible says that I can do all things through Christ who strengthens me. Dread says, "It's too hard, and I can't do it." Here are some other statements that dread says:

- ❑ "I don't want to."
- ❑ "I don't feel like it."
- ❑ "I am too tired to even think about it."
- ❑ "I wish I didn't have to go."
- ❑ "How long is this going to take?"
- ❑ "What about............"
- ❑ "I'm just doing too much, I can't do another thing."
- ❑ "I want to run away from home."
- ❑ "I need to get away from here."
- ❑ "I'm so confused."
- ❑ "I'm so overwhelmed."
- ❑ "I'm so frustrated."
- ❑ "I'll do that later."
- ❑ "I dread the kids coming home from school."
- ❑ "I'm afraid I can't do that."
- ❑ "I don't want to do the dishes.

Does any sound familiar? Then you are subject to the "Spirit of dread" playing you like a fiddle. When (not "if") you experience these thoughts again, you have the power to cast out that spirit of dread each and every time. It doesn't matter how many times you have to do it, keep doing it because one day you'll not have to do it so much. Again, you are renewing your mind with the Word.

As I was preparing for this teaching, dread tried to stop me from writing it. I just didn't "feel" like doing it. I had other things I wanted to do, so I was thinking of putting this off even longer. But as you know, when you put something off that you can do today, that is sin because procrastination is sin. So not only is dread there, now sin is piled up on top of it. Then I would realize what was happening and immediately I confessed I entertained dread and told it to leave. Within minutes the overwhelming feeling went. My body was restored to feeling at peace and I was focused. I felt a new day began (even though it was mid afternoon) and was filled with excitement of what I'm doing in this ministry. It was no longer "dread" to me, it was a joy.

This is a lesson for you too. No matter how real the feelings are, it's not you! It's that spirit of dread using you as a puppet to act out its nature. Believe me, I know what I'm talking about. What will you lose by stepping out in faith and addressing that spirit? It's not what you will lose it's what you will gain. Peace, stability and joy!

Take a moment now and identify any area in your life that you dread doing. Once you make your list, <u>pray something like this:</u>

> "Father, I recognize that I have been in dread in these areas _____
> (name them). I ask you to forgive me for not recognizing it was the spirit of dread and for entertaining it and allowing it to control my thoughts. So I cast out the spirit of dread now in Jesus name. Restore me Lord God with your peace, love and joy. In Jesus name. Amen."

Each and every time you face "dread" you toss Him out! You do that through identifying it and telling it to Go. As you do that, be sure to seek more of God's love; because dread is really "fear." And the Bible says that perfect love casts out fear! Sometimes I find myself dreading when I'm trying to do things myself, in my own abilities and power. Such as wanting to figure things out, scheduling my time, and all along forgetting to bring God into the picture, acknowledging Him in every decision I make. Dread wouldn't be an issue if I kept my mind on the Lord. An indicator to me that I have a ways to go! But Praise God, I'm growing.

Ministry Prayer for You:

> "By the power of the Holy Ghost, I command the spirit of dread to leave you. Release them now in Jesus' name. Father in Heaven, I ask for your peace to fill their hearts and minds, I ask for your love to envelope them right now. Thank you Father, in Jesus' name Amen."

CHAPTER NINE

Guilt and Condemnation

What is Guilt?

The Webster's dictionary says, "to pay, to requite, payment, retribution, to pay, to yield, that state of a moral agent which results from his willful or intentional commission of a crime or offense; knowing it to be a crime or violation of law."

To put it in spiritual context, guilt is the initial onset that comes when we think we missed the mark, we didn't keep the law or we didn't do everything right. And with this guilt, we somehow feel the need to pay for it - which is condemnation. Frustration also comes by trying to keep the law (Galatians 2:21) and you can read more about that in the "Frustration" session.

Guilt comes when we have not received forgiveness for whatever it is we think we did. We think we have to pay for whatever we did, so we stay in that state of guilt. Many have been under guilt about their kids from decisions they made long ago, yet still carrying that guilt around today. It has become a part of their life. I know that a person who has not received forgiveness always walks around guilty about everything. In conversations, they would continually say things like, "I feel guilty about _____," I feel sad," "I feel so awful today and don't know why," "I just feel bad." These are indicators that guilt is present. But this is not to be so. Guilt was crucified with Christ. He bore our sins, yesterday's, today's and tomorrow's. The only way to abolish guilt in your life completely is to receive the sacrifice Jesus made.

How do you receive forgiveness? First you have to know Jesus Christ as your Savior. If you don't, then you'll have a very difficult time getting free from guilt and condemnation. Then once you have settled that, then you need to "apply" the sacrifice Jesus made on the cross to your own life. You need to "receive" the forgiveness IMMEDIATELY when you feel you have done something wrong. If you don't, then condemnation comes.

Guilt is from the enemy. It's his way of pounding you on the head for doing something wrong, that he may have even told you to do in the first place! Let's say you get tempted to eat a whole chocolate cake. You are drawn to that cake because it looks so good. (Remember, the enemy tempts.) Then after you eat it, you feel guilty for eating it. The very thing the enemy tempts you on, he then "accuses" you afterward and, if prolonged, guilt turns into condemnation. However, if you were tempted to eat that cake, then realized afterward you should not have, simply confess it as sin (if it is sin to you) and receive forgiveness. The longer you wait to confess and receive, the more condemnation will come.

Carried guilt, even after repentance and forgiveness causes us to accuse God. We become the "accuser" - we need to confess our sins of accusation toward God. Be specific too. Name off the things that you are feeling guilty for and then apply the sacrifice Jesus made on the cross at that moment of confession. What happens is that we don't do that. We do something we think is wrong, and then think about what we did over and over, and then guilt sets in. Remember what it says in 2 Corinthians 10:5, take every thought captive. Don't let the accusing thoughts take hold. They may come, but then you need to say, "Yes, I did that thing, I take responsibility for it. I confess my sin and receive forgiveness for it. I don't need to pay for anything at all, Jesus paid it all so I don't have to. So there devil, now leave.

When we feel guilt, we are putting ourselves on the cross in Jesus' place! Can you truly do that? No. But that's what we are doing. We are making Christ's sacrifice of none affect. We are slapping Him in the face, so-to-speak, and telling Him we need to do it ourselves. These are lies from the enemy and each one of these thoughts needs to be taken captive and cast out of our thinking. Only Jesus can "pay" the penalty. And remember, when we feel guilty, we are trying to "pay" for our sins or whatever we think we did was wrong.

What is Condemnation?

The Webster's dictionary says, "To pronounce to be utterly wrong, to sentence to punishment, to pronounce to be guilty, to judge or pronounce to be unfit for use or service". And condemnation in Webster's dictionary says it means, "The act of condemning, the cause or reason of a sentence of condemnation."

What an eye opener! When the guilt starts, condemnation is just around the corner. Because first we feel "guilty" (not applying the forgiveness through Jesus immediately to our situation), then because we dwell on that initial thought, the result sets in. The manifestation of that guilt is called "condemnation" and looks like this: We tell ourselves that we are so wrong, we are so horrible, we feel unworthy to receive any good and when we do receive good, we feel even worse because we don't think we deserve it. We even pronounce to others how unfit we are, how unworthy we are, how bad we are, how we just will never amount to anything." In other words, you have placed a sentence on yourself.

In the judicial system, guilt and condemnation is a daily routine. We can apply this to what we do to ourselves. When someone is found "guilty" then they are "condemned" (sentenced) to "pay" for their guilt. It could be jail sentence, retribution, or even death. So when you find yourself "guilty" what is your sentence? What are you trying to "pay?" What is the going payment these days? Loss of sleep? Self-worthlessness? Fear? Driven to please? See, in order to be completely guilt and condemnation free, the answer is simple.

Confess and receive forgiveness IMMEDIATELY for allowing guilt to rein in your body and ask God to reveal to you if there is any sin you are carrying that is producing the guilt.

If you are carrying around old guilt and condemning yourself for it daily, you need to confess those things you are feeling guilty for and receive forgiveness for them. ALL OF THEM! Not one thing you have done or ever will do is more powerful than the blood that was shed on the cross. If you think so, then you need to go back and re-learn what it means to be saved.

I find that when people are saved, they are saved through believing that Christ is the Son of God and that He died for their sins, rose the third day and now lives in Heaven. They receive this truth into their heart, and now they are saved. But the second part is missed. They now have to receive that sacrifice Jesus made into their own lives and nail every one of their sins to the cross. Receive complete forgiveness at the time the sin occurs, not wait until later, or don't receive at all, otherwise guilt and condemnation comes.

I have discovered there are two kinds of Christians. Those that believe they are forgiven and those that don't believe they are forgiven. Those that believe do enter into His rest, those that believe will struggle all their lives and fall into despair and hopelessness. Which one are you? You can choose today.

I'll give you an example of my experience:

I had felt guilty for not being a good mom for my son. If any of you have read my story in the book I wrote called, "A Matter of the Mind" you will see what I'm talking about. My son is now an adult, yet I carried that guilt still. And because of that guilt, all my life I tried, to "re-pay" him for how I was. I could never PAY for anything! All I was doing was staying in my guilt - which is sin. Because I didn't know how to apply forgiveness to my guilt! So one day while visiting my son, the Lord showed me that I needed to let that guilt go. I had to confess why I was feeling guilty. So I did. I began with saying, "I wasn't there for my son. I gave him to his father to raise him from childhood. I abandoned him." As a result of that thinking, I felt responsible for his happiness by trying to pay back what I didn't give him growing up. I realized then that I was taking on false sense of responsibility for my son's happiness. The Lord showed me that it's not my job. It was when he was a child, but those years are gone and he's a grown man now. He's over 30 years old, it's not my job any longer to provide for him or help him in his happiness. As I recognized the truth about why I was feeling guilty, and confessed them to the Lord, everything changed within me. The need to "fix" my son was no longer there.

My son and my relationship have improved greatly since then. I don't feel bad or hurt anymore (which is the same as guilt) if he doesn't call me on my birthday. I've set him free, and in setting him free I was set free too. My son is free to do and be all he wants, the way he wants, and I'm now there to enjoy him in his life just how he is. It is truly freeing my friends! And the truth is, he's God's son anyway, and it's His job to provide help in his happiness, and help him in life, not mine. I'm there for him, I can pray for Him, I can share in his life, but I'm not to "do" for him. That's God's job.

So with all that said, it's time to look upon your own life. Do you know of anything in your life that you still carry guilt about? I'm sure you can think of a thing or two. It's time to be set free.

Join me in this prayer:

"Father in Heaven, you are more than able to handle each and every sin and mistake I've made in my life. As a matter of fact, you even knew I was going to do them before I was even born! Help me get a revelation on your unconditional love. That nothing I can ever say or do is unforgivable. Help me to apply the sacrifice Jesus made on the cross for my sins. Help me to receive forgiveness. I confess that I have carried guilt with me too long. I confess my guilt of _____ (Then name off your guilt). I know that I have condemned myself - placed sentence on myself to pay for that guilt - but Jesus already paid for it. I will not put myself in the place of Jesus any longer because that is sin and idolatry. I receive the forgiveness of my sins that resulted in that guilt, and apply the forgiveness that Jesus wants me to have, now. And if anything from this day on happens that causes me to feel guilty, I will immediately stop and identify what is behind that guilt and take it to you in confession. I will receive forgiveness so that the condemnation will not take root in my life. Help me to stay guilt free Lord. I know that I can by applying forgiveness every day to my life. Help me Lord to get a revelation on forgiveness and receiving that forgiveness. After all, that's why you came, to free me from all sin which produces guilt. I receive your complete forgiveness, your perfect love, joy, peace, understanding, wisdom, direction and discernment, all in the name of Jesus Christ, Amen."

- Psalm 44:21 "God knows the secrets of your heart." You might as well face them too."

- Psalm 51:6 "God knows the hidden parts." Don't fear what you see, rejoice that you see them so you can be made free.

Conviction:

We cannot discuss guilt and condemnation without talking about conviction. Conviction is from God. He will show you the errors of your way, then forget it. He never pounces on your head when you make a mistake. He tries to nudge you and prompt you BEFORE you make a decision, and convicts you when you make a wrong decision, but NEVER gives you guilt. Why? Because He's forgiven you. A Christian is forgiven, whether they accept the forgiveness or not, that is why God doesn't condemn. We condemn ourselves by not facing the sinful things that put us in that condition. Jesus was condemned for us and so God NEVER condemns us! That's what the Devil does. So whom are you going to trust? The truth that God forgives immediately? Or a lie that we have to pay for your mistakes?

Conviction is to show us the error so we can make a decision of what to do about it. It's not to show you what is wrong with you to make you feel bad, guilty and condemned. But if you don't know what is happening, that's exactly where you'll end up.

John 8:9 *"And they which heard it, being convicted by their own conscience, went out one by one, beginning at the eldest, even unto the last: and Jesus was left alone, and the woman was standing in the midst."* Our hearts are convicted to stimulate action. When we don't apply "action" by repenting or doing what we know to do, it can turn into condemnation.

Acts 24:16 *"And herein do I exercise myself, to have always a conscience void to offence toward God, and toward men."*

Have you heard people say, "You have a guilty conscience." They are probably correct. It's not time to get defensive, it's time to "agree with your adversary quickly" and ask God if it is true. What if you do have a guilty conscience, what are you going to do about it? Wouldn't you want to be free? Our conscience also convicts us of sin. It's a good thing to get a check in your spirit; that is how the Holy Ghost guides us.

Remember when you rode in bumper cars, they had bumpers and you bounced off other cars? There were also padded walls so you couldn't go beyond the area where the cars ran. That's how our conscience works as bumper pads (buffers). And once you bump up against another car or the way, your car bounces off and goes into another direction. We are to be like these bumper cars and how you do that is when you "bump" into a sin, you confess it and receive forgiveness and go on your way.

Guilt and condemnation come if you stay in the same place and keep hitting that same issue. Once you hit the wall that is okay. The wall is there for your protection. So now take that think you bumped into before the Lord, confess it, and receive forgiveness asking Him to restore you and remove all guilt and condemnation concerning it.

Now what about the guilt that comes from something we do right? Where is the sin in that? Well, lets take a look. Why would we feel guilt for something we did right? Because we feel we don't deserve it. We don't want others to feel bad because of our blessing. These are all self-idolatry, self-loathing, false burden bearing, comparing yourself with others, victimized manifestations, self-pity, pride, etc. So you see, there is sin even behind a person who feels guilty for something good. What do we do about it? The same thing as shared before, identify the reason for the guilt and confess it to the Lord.

Ministry:

"Father, I ask for your perfect love to fill this person's heart. I ask for all guilt and condemnation to be exposed so they can be free. Help them to recognize and confess any sin behind the guilt, no matter how bit or small and release them once and for all. In Jesus' name, Amen."

We are never to live under any guilt or condemnation. Make that a reality today and take everything to the Lord that produces the guilt and allow God to wash it all away for good! When something new comes along that causes you to "feel" guilt again, identify what the sin is, take it to the Lord immediately, and stay free.

You can also pick up the books called: Overcoming Guilt and Condemnation, as it goes into more detail.

CHAPTER TEN

Take Every Thought Captive

We are responsible for our lives. Not only our physical lives but was is going on, but also on what is going on in the inside of us. So ask yourself, what is going on inside? Take a look below at the differences between God's thoughts (fruit of the spirit) and the devil's thoughts (fruit of death) and you decide what is dwelling within your heart and mind.

God's Thoughts	Devil's Thoughts
Truth	Lies, negative, dishonest, deception
Honesty	Dishonest, secretive, controller, manipulative
Pure	Suspicious, unclean, sinful, filthy, perverted
Just	Victimized, self-pity, distrusting, comparison, self-righteous, debating with God, demands justice and rights for self
Lovely	Ugly, impatient, self-hatred, hardness, unloving
Good Report	Gossip, accuser, slander, judgment, criticism, filthy communication, bad reports, blasphemy, wrath, malice, anger, profanity
Virtuous	Cowardly, prideful, arrogant, disloyal, unclean
Praise	Unthankful, doubt and unbelief, fear, isolation, self-preservation, self-exaltation, pride, self pity

Note: This is not to bring you under guilt or condemnation, but to bring things out into the light. The sin loses its power when it is brought out into the light. This is a good thing when you see yucky stuff. The Holy Ghost living inside you sees the junk and uses conviction to cause you to deal with it. However, if you don't know what is happening, you could run from God and not to Him. fear. But the truth is, you have to see what is inside you so you can be purged. However, there is a caution. If you are only dwelling on every thought, you could lose your peace. There has to be a balance because as you take every thought captive, don't just cast it out alone, but replace it with God's thoughts. Begin to praise Him for what just took place. Spend some time with Him at that moment. That way you will be equipping yourself for life! I talked in an earlier session about God's love that casts out all fear and torment. Don't you think these thoughts are tormenting? So not only do you recognize it as an evil thought, confess it to God, but also begin receiving more of His love at that very moment! That is how we are supposed to live each day. I encourage you to begin doing what I'm teaching in this session. So what forms our thoughts? I heard it said that we don't even come up with an original thought. We actually say, "A thought occurred to me." So the thought comes from someplace else. Our thoughts come from three sources - God, our selves or the devil. I have found in most cases that our thoughts and the devil's thoughts are almost one, because when anyone seeks ministry, it's because their thoughts have been agreeing with the enemy. But don't let that condemn you, be glad that you finally see the difference, now God can really begin working in your life.

When God came to Adam and Eve, they ran from Him and hid because they were naked. God asked them, "Who told you, you were naked?" They had a thought that came to them. Something told them they were naked and caused them to feel shame. These were thoughts that came to them because Adam disobeyed God and opened the door for the enemy to have free reign in their thoughts. We do the same today. Whatever thoughts we have that are not God's thoughts, the enemy has every right to your life because he uses those thoughts to gain access to your life.

So how do we recognize when we are thinking God's thoughts or the devil's thoughts? You probably already know that answer, one brings torment the other brings peace. But I found that many ignore what God is saying and cleaves to what the devil says because it's easier. No, it's not easier. It's easier to be free! The enemy is lying to you in your "thinking" when you think this. Remember, pay attention to your thoughts.

Let me ask you a question. If you had small children who were watching TV, would you censor the shows? Of course you would. If we showed our thoughts on TV, would our kids be able to watch? We need to take responsibility for our thoughts today, and stop being used as a puppet by the enemy. If you resist him long enough, he will go away. Be not weary in well doing, for in due season you will reap if you don't faint. If you feel like fainting, go to God for His strength! We can't do this alone - we need His power to do this.

Matthew 18:12 Jesus asked, "What think ye?"

So, what are you thinking? Philippians 4:8 *"Finally, brethren, whatsoever things are true, whatsoever things are honest, whatsoever things are just, whatsoever things are pure, whatsoever things are lovely, whatsoever things are of good report; if there be any virtue, and if there be any praise, think on these things."*

This scripture breaks the thought process down for us. So anything that we "think" that does not line up with this passage are the devil's thoughts (or our own stinkin' thinkin'). Anything, even thoughts, that are not full of faith, is sin (Romans 14:23).

1 Corinthians 13:5 says not to think any evil. This chapter, the love chapter, really goes into detail what we are to think on.

Why is thinking so important? Because what we "think" comes out of our mouth. And when it comes out of our mouth, that's when sin is conceived. The Bible says that what we think in our heart, so are we. (Proverbs 23:7) James 1:13 -15 says that temptation comes first, and it's when we act upon it that it becomes sin. Just because you think a weird or bad thought doesn't mean you've sinned. You are heading for sin IF you dwell on that thought long enough. Remember to take every thought captive that does not reflect the nature and character of God and tell it to go.

Our thinking has been the culprit!

Simply put: Positive thoughts are of God, Negative thoughts are of the devil. Even if the thought you are thinking may be true in nature, perhaps someone did do you wrong, but we are to still "think" good thoughts all the time. Like the saying goes, "If you can't say anything good, don't say anything at all." But some of us don't even realize they are negative thoughts. Many just say, "That's just the way I am" believing that those thoughts are right. It's been such a pattern in their lives that it "is" truth to them. But we need to understand that these thoughts aren't "us" they are from that other kingdom. That is why our minds are to be renewed every day because it only takes one wrong thought to send us spiraling down again. Like the Lords' prayer says, "...lead us not into temptation but deliver us from evil."

It has been apparent that everyone has thought problems. That's what I realized for myself and that's why I wrote the book "A Matter of the Mind." I knew it started with my thoughts.

If we had the "mind of Christ" we wouldn't be thinking any of the negative thoughts (1 Corinthians 2:16). This passage says we "have" the mind of Christ. So we as believers, have what we need to think positively.

Let's look at the scripture in the same passage, Philippians 4:4-7: *"Rejoice in the Lord always, and again I say rejoice, Let your moderation be known unto all men, The Lord is at hand. Be careful for nothing; but in everything by prayer and supplication with thanksgiving let your requests be made known unto God. And the peace of God, which passes all understanding shall keep your hearts and minds through Christ Jesus."*

The whole process of our sanctification is to have the mind of Christ. Having this one-mind (Philippians 4:2) results in peace. If there were no turmoil, worry, confusion, jealousy going on in our thinking, wouldn't we be at peace? Of course we would. 2 Corinthians 7:1 says we can cleanse our minds of all filth:

"Having therefore these promises, dearly beloved, let us cleanse ourselves from all filthiness of the flesh and spirit, perfecting holiness in the fear of God."

So how do we do that?

1. We need to have the mind of Christ activated in our lives, it's already there when you received Jesus as Savior and needs to become forefront

in our mind. As we get to know God through prayer, scriptures, and relationship those thoughts become more active and pretty soon those negative thoughts diminish. A matured Christian knows how to discern both evil and good so that they can choose wisely. You need this in order to "weigh the spirits" as the Bible tells us to do; to know if they are of God or not. Do a Bible study on the words "think," "thoughts" and "mind" to see what God says about all of this. When you understand what He is saying, you will then be able to recognize the thoughts in your own mind, whether they are good or evil. This is called discernment. Knowing the difference between good and evil (Hebrews 5:14).

2. Cast the thoughts out that are not of God, and keep those thoughts that are. 2 Corinthians 10:5 says to cast down imaginations, and every high thing that exalts itself against the knowledge of God, and bringing into captivity every thought to the obedience of Christ. We are to take EVERY THOUGHT CAPTIVE! At this point, decide if the thought is a God thought or not. Yes! Every thought. Did you know that if someone did something wrong to you and you began thinking bad thoughts about them you have just taken the bait from the enemy? No matter what happens in our lives, to us or around us, we are to "think good" at all times. Think positive. Make lemonade when life gives you lemons. Think good of all men - as the Bible teaches. This whole thought issue has to do with relationship with people. If there were no people, half of our evil thoughts would be gone because the people are gone. However, there is still ourselves, so we can think evil of ourselves the rest of the time. We are not to even think evil of ourselves!! Why? Because when we think negatively about ourselves long enough it can produce self-hatred, self-bitterness, self-rejection, thoughts of self hurt, etc., and when these thoughts go on long enough could result in physical ailments. For example, someone who hates themselves and says things all their life to themselves like, "You are so stupid," "No one will ever love you," "I wish I were dead" you are attacking yourself. If this persists for a long period of time, your body will finally agree with you and begin attacking itself, called "white corpuscle deviate behavior." The corpuscles gather in an area and have a pity-party on your behalf and begin eating you, resulting in all kinds of auto-immune diseases.

3. Understand that these thoughts don't just pop in our heads, these thoughts come from what is in our heart! Mark 7:20-23, "And Jesus said, "that which cometh out of the man, that defileth the man, for from within out of the heart of men proceed evil thoughts, adulteries, fornications, murders, thefts, coveteousness, wickedness, deceit, lasciviousness, an evil eye, blasphemy, pride, foolishness. We need to come face to face with what is truly in our hearts. And if these thoughts start to surface and we begin responding to them, it's time to begin casting out those thoughts, as 2 Corinthians 10:5 says to do. But I find we don't do that. We think about it, and think about it, then we feel "bad" because of what we are thinking, we even begin to doubt if we are even saved. Many people think that if they think a thought, it's sin when we act upon that wrong thought. Remember when I said earlier that conviction causes us to "act"

accordingly, so does guilt and condemnation. Thoughts will cause us to do one thing or another. It becomes "sin" when we act upon the wrong thought, it becomes "life" when we act upon the good thought (James 1:13-15).

4. Know the enemy's thoughts. In order to be set free completely, we need to know BOTH good and evil. God's thoughts and the devil's thoughts, just in case our thoughts are in there someplace too, we need to discern ourselves. What I believe is this: When we think a thought, it's because it's something in us. Because the enemy can only cause us to think wrong if we have something in us he can draw on. For example, I cannot be tempted to rob a bank. It's not in me. I can't even be tempted to drink alcohol, because I no longer have that addiction. But I can be tempted to each chocolate. I am tempted to judge. I am tempted to fear man because these things are still "in" me. The process of everyone's life is to be sanctified in body, soul and spirit. This is a process! A process means there is time involved. So even though God has already purged me and cleansed me from a lot of things that were "IN" my heart already, there are still many more things to be cleansed from, and evidenced by what I still "think." If I have a dream that startled me, and I wake up and wonder why I dreamt that, first of all, I cast that "evil" thought out. But then I begin asking God what is in me that the enemy used to cause me to "think" (dream) that dream? And sure enough, there was something God wanted to get at. Sometimes He has to use the enemy in a dream to show us what is in us! Remember, God uses anything to get to us - even the jawbone of a donkey!

5. Separate the thoughts now. Remember, our thoughts come from one of three places: God, ourselves or the devil. Once I categorized them in my mind, I was able to capture the Devil's thoughts, bind them up and cast them out! But I could only do this when I knew truth. At first I had to do this a hundred times a day. Then it got less and less as time went on Because I believe by taking responsibility for our thoughts, taking charge of what is in there, recognizing if it's a wrong thought, and telling it to leave, is cleansing my heart at the same time. When we do this we are actually being a "doer" of the word because it says, "Cleanse yourself from all filthiness of the flesh and spirit" (2 Corinthians 7:1). I found that many people stay in bondage because they aren't willing to see what is in their own heart or they are afraid to see what is there or they don't believe that anything bad is in there. I came from a background that said once we are saved, all that junk is gone. Then why do we still have so many problems in our soul? We can't be afraid to see it but we need to so that it can be purged. Once we "see" it, half the battle is won! We take it captive, cast it out, and God does the restoring, purging, and healing in line with our own words!

6. Recognize that those things within you that the enemy uses are NOT you! They are the sin in you that God is wanting out. Romans 7:20 *"Now if I do that I would not, it is no more I that do it, but sin that dwelleth in me."* In other words, there are things I don't want to do because I "know" not

to, but then I do them anyway. We need to understand that it's the SIN in us using our bodies to live out its characteristic. We have simply allowed them to because we didn't know any better or we got lazy. In order to get them out they may have to manifest so you can see what is in you! God can only purge something when you know what it is. You can start by saying "Father, purge me from everything that is not of you." But then we need to get specific. Father, if there is any evil in me, tell me what it is - as David prayed. We have to see what is there before He can begin the cleansing process. This is the same with forgiveness, we just can' t pray a blanket prayer of forgiveness, we have to identify each person we need to forgive.

This is an every day practice a believer is to do. Our minds are to be renewed every day - His mercies are new every morning. Our minds are to be conformed, and continue being conformed, to the mind of Christ, it's a process (Romans 8:29). Some say that "Old things are passed away, behold all things become new" which is biblical. But then it becomes bondage to them because if they do have issues in their heart they don't want anyone to know it because they are supposed to be new, so they stay in their bondage. This scripture is a confirmation to our lives, it's a promise to aspire to. And any ways, it says "become" new -- that means we are being made new! So don't let that trip you up any longer.

When we know that it is the sin in us, and not us, we can stop being so angry and unhappy with ourselves. Now I can love myself better because I've separated myself from the sin in me. I still hate the sin, but I don't hate me! So many have made themselves ONE with the sin! You bought the lie if you think you are an angry person! The anger is the sin in you, because truthfully, you don't want to be an angry person, you may have even tried not being an angry person, yet it just comes out! It's time to go to work and ask God to help purge your heart of the anger that is within, and identify the root behind it.

I was a very angry person; I would fly off the handle at the drop of a hat. I even drove with anger and tailgated if someone cut ahead of me. And believe me, that was all the time. I drove over an hour one-way to work for 17 years! By the time I left that job, I was no longer angry. During those 17 years the Lord used that commute to deal with my heart. Then to top it off, I was delivered from the anger of my earthly father. He demonstrated anger and so I confessed his sin of anger to God and He purged me from it! I would forgive those who pulled out in front of me in traffic and I didn't feel that "rage" come up from within me any longer because it was gone! If someone pulled out in front of me, or cut close to me in traffic, I felt nothing. I was in complete peace, how awesome is that? But again, it was a process because I had such deep-rooted anger. And by the way, anger is a root of fear. And if you know anything about my story, that was my main problem. So as I was being set free from fear, anger was leaving too.

Simply put. Pay attention to your thoughts and cast down (out) any that are not God's thoughts. Even if the thought is true - if it's not a good thought, you are not to dwell on it at all. If you get a thought, take it to the Lord, deal with it at that moment of inception and you will stay in peace. And since those thoughts came from someplace within us, we need to go to God and ask Him what is in us. There was a reason that thought came up in the first place, perhaps God is wanting to bring your attention to something within that He wants out! It's not time to go into condemnation and fear or run from it or ignore it. It's time to get excited because God is doing a work. Remember, things have to manifest in you before they can be removed from you. Reminds me of a story I use in ministry called "The shrapnel." My husband was in Vietnam and bombs blew up all around him sending pieces of metal his way. Many of those pieces penetrated his body, so when he returned back to the U.S. he still had that shrapnel in him. One by one they all began protruding out of his skin. They would begin festering, hurting, reminding him of how it got there in the first place. It wasn't a pretty sight and for years suffered PTSD. However, when the metal finally worked it's way out, and sometimes had to be surgically removed, the sore was healed. That's how God purges our sins - the way it went in is the same way it will come out! But once it's out, it's OUT!. If you suffer PTSD, be sure to go through the teachings on "Trauma."

I want to add that once we commune with God, fellowship with Him, and learn of Him, we begin to think like Him. The more we do this, the less we have to "fight" with our thoughts! Our heart changes, and when our heart changes and is filled with love, compassion, peace and joy, that is what we begin to think about. It's from the heart where evil thoughts come - the heart feeds the mind. Sometimes the enemy does put a thought in our mind that is wild and weird, and we really don't know where it could have come from. But even in those times, I would go to God and ask if there was anything in you that caused that thought to stick. I personally found that I either watched something on TV, or heard something negative, or it was actually something God was dealing with in my heart that causes these thoughts to come. I encourage you to be thankful when things come into your mind because it gives you opportunity to exercise your faith to deal with it. Go to God and confess any wrong thoughts to Him, ask Him to cleanse your heart and mind from that thought and anything that is rooted in it that could be in your heart. God looks at the heart of man, He doesn't look at our minds. Why? Because from our hearts flow the issues of life (Proverbs 4:23). So whatever is in our heart, that is how we will act. After you settle things with God, then bask in His love and forgiveness. Get back into the center of His love, and all fear (and ugly thoughts) vanishes. That truly says it all. "Perfect love casts out all fear and torment." Where do these get cast out of? Our hearts and minds.

Some people believe that they can't have anything evil in them. Boy, this is a whole other teaching, because if God's love casts out fear, then it is obviously it's inside us?? There are so many passages that back this up. Romans 7, Mark 7 - both accounts talking about evil coming from the heart of man. In Romans, Paul is talking and in Mark, Jesus is talking. Run a reference yourself on "heart" and "evil." There is a passage that comes to me that talks about an unbelieving heart is an evil heart. Hmm...

I want to share a couple more personal accounts that came up during the re-editing of this segment.

I found myself in a state of rage toward my husband. I was very surprised at myself because I knew I was delivered from anger as shared previously. But this was "rage." There is a difference. Rage is man's wrath. Rage causes us to act out. As my husband was saying something, I jut wanted to haul off and punch him. This was not natural to me and so I knew it was a spirit, but it felt real all the same, and it did offend my husband. So I had to go to God. As I was talking to the Lord I also included my husband and we began our search. The Lord almost immediately showed me why I was full of rage. I was in fear of a generational disease, Huntington's Chorea. I had been hiding from that in my mind and was in fear of looking at it straight on. It had been boiling in me for over 25 years when my father was diagnosed with it. I didn't even know I was in fear of it until it came up. I was always afraid to talk about it, I tried ignoring it, I even prayed off generational curses, but yet the fear was still there. Once I exposed that fear, the anger left!

The next time rage rose in me wasn't too many days later. I said, Lord what is going on? He reminded me that a few weeks earlier I had prayed he remove more stuff from my heart and He was doing just that. So I cooperated with Him and began looking into this level of rage. My husband and I had a "tiff" it wasn't that big of a deal, but the rage rose in me. My feelings that came out surrounding this were feelings of being betrayed, lied to, stolen from, ripped off, abandoned and rejected. They weren't coming from my husband, they were coming from another person years ago that was just surfacing. My husband and I began talking and he asked me, "Who stole from you?" He recognized the attitude I was having was manifestations of this kind of thing. As I thought about that question, I saw one person come to mind. I had thought I forgave him, but it looked like another level came to the surface. And when I began sharing with him the story of a guy who stole all my stuff, that's when that anger broke off. The rage within me was gone. See this guy first caused me to leave my son's father. I packed up all my stuff in a U-haul and drove to Florida to start a new life with him. My son was 2 at the time and we were going to have a wonderful life. Well, that was short lived because not many days later I found myself on a plane ride home. He promised to send me back my stuff, he did all right, but only the stuff he didn't want. As I began sharing that story with my husband, I became lighter and lighter. It was a level of intense fear that was deeply rooted in me because of the abandonment, lying, stealing that actually took place in my life. So I was responding to Tom in that attitude and action even though it wasn't about him. Since Tom is a mature believer and knew what was going on, we didn't fall apart. It was hard, because the feelings were real, but we also knew it was a spirit that had been tormenting us. So we both confessed to the Lord and cast out the spirit of rejection, accusation, lying, fear and abandonment. We knew that if we submitted to those thoughts, we could lose everything. I can see how easily a marriage can fall apart when we don't understand what is going on and where that attack is really coming from. We don't wrestle with flesh and blood but with evil spirits!

Ministry:

"Father, I come before you with my brother/sister in the Lord. I know from experience that our thoughts need to be renewed and conformed to your thoughts. Help my brother/sister to identify every thought to decide if they are your thoughts or not. Help them to get more of your thoughts in them through Bible reading and fellowship with You. Help them to recognize when the enemy is thinking a thought through them so they can tell it to "GO." Help them to know that they have this authority to cast things out! I pray courage and fearlessness over their lives. I pray they take back their thoughts, and get rid of anything that is not of you. It may be a bit overwhelming for some at this point because of all the negative thoughts they have. But let them know that by exercising their senses (Hebrews 5:14) it won't take long for the thoughts to become less and less destructive leaving only your thoughts. Let them find comfort knowing that every person reading this is in the same boat, otherwise they wouldn't be reading this.

They are not alone, and even the most polished preacher has to take every thought captive, if they know to do so. And as thoughts come up that are not of You, help them to investigate further by asking You to help let them see what is in them that allowed that thought to come in the first place. Sometimes it could be things such as jealousy, fear of evil, doubt, confusion, bitterness and unforgiveness, comparison, feelings of incompetence, etc. And help them not to think badly of themselves for having these things. Help them remember its sin in them that has to manifest in order to be purged. Don't let them fear what they will see, but be happy they see it. Help them to cast out every imagination and high and lofty thing out of their thinking, and only dwell on whatsoever things are good! Let their heart and mind be stayed on You so that whatever comes from within, out of their mouth, will be what would come out of Yours. Just like Jesus, He only spoke or acted upon things He saw you do and say, and I want to be like Him. I know this is a process, but help them to remember when they mess up, to confess their sin immediately and receive forgiveness immediately and go on with their lives. We only stay in sin because we haven't received forgiveness. Bless my friends now Lord, and let them all experience peace within their heart and mind. In Jesus name, Amen."

More Teaching Resources

Caspar McCloud and myself wrote a book called "What Was I Thinking?" It goes into greater detail on getting your thought to work for you and not against you. You can pick up your copy at www.truthfrees.org or Amazon.com. You can also pick up the workbook. If you are a teacher, you can pick up the teacher's guide. These will help you and others discover the truth that makes us free.

CHAPTER ELEVEN

Connection in Mind and Body

Understanding the connection between the mind and body will help you when dealing with specific issues.

This topic seems to be controversial yet it is the foundation for understanding why we have dis-ease. From a personal standpoint, I couldn't understand why I wasn't well. Why, even though I had been a Christian for so many years, I wasn't getting better, only worse in my health.

So I ventured out into a teaching by Pastor Henry Wright from Pleasant Valley Church in Thomaston Georgia, and found what I was looking for. I saw the connection between sin and sickness, life and death, truth and lies, and more.

At this time, I began writing a journal, which later turned into a book of my journey from fear to faith called "A Matter of the Mind." I had to come to grips with the realization that most of my problems started with my thoughts rooted from a spirit of fear. Later I realized how my body responded to thoughts and saw the parallel in my own life.

I pray this information proves to be helpful for you to understand the truth behind the mind-body connection that may cause some of your dis-eases today.

I want to start by sharing an article I read called, Heart and Mind connection. I found this while browsing through some magazines. The title of the page says, "It's up to you." And I believe that is very true, but let me share some excerpts written by Roon Frost, an author for this magazine.

"Although diet, blood pressure, and other risk factors play an important role in developing heart disease and angina, these forces can be significantly moderated by a loving relationship," says Dr. Ornish. If almost anyone else made that statement, mainstream medicine would scoff. But Dean Ornish has probably done more than any researcher in the last two decades to change the way we look at heart disease.

"When people open their hearts to each other" Dr. Ornish says, "healing often happens. More precisely, a support group helps heal isolation, alienation and loneliness," allowing physical healing to begin from the inside out."

"Everyone talks about heart disease being linked to negative emotions, such as anger, depression and so on." Says James J. Lynch, Ph.D., professor of psychiatry at the University of Maryland Medical School, "But I view all these internal vascular changes as really hidden forms of communication, like blushing. Blushing is really a hidden form of caring. I blush because I'm afraid I'm going to be rejected, but I care about the other person, and I

don't want them to reject me. So, the vascular changes are the language of the heart only hidden." Lynch's own work with heart patients shows that their blood pressure goes up when they talk, and that it drops when they listen, "really listen."

I found this article quite interesting as it actually backs up what I'm sharing in this session. I think you can agree that high-blood pressure comes from stress. That's easy to understand because so many studies have been made. But there was a time when it was not at all considered as the reason for high-blood pressure. We need to be open to all possibilities and not close our minds to this. So as you continue in this session, I pray your mind be opened because that's where your battle is.

Why are people sick?

Where there is no peace, the body is sick. Peace is the "stuff" we need for healing and to continue in to stay healed. When we have peace our body's chemicals balance out. When we have peace, we don't worry, fret, stress out, fall into depression, get angry, jealous, and the like. And as you know each of these things listed does not produce peace!

The Bible says to follow after peace. And at the end of most of the letters written, it says, "peace be with you." Even Jesus' parting words were, "My peace I leave with you, not as the world gives, give I unto you" (John 14:27).

Peace is what causes homeostasis - balancing of our chemicals. Disease is a direct result of imbalanced chemicals, which is why we are given drugs, to balance out chemicals. Folks, we have everything we need for our bodies to produce the exact amount of chemicals every day, but many don't see this as a spiritual issue so they are happy to get that little blue pill to make it all go away. This is only covering up the real problem. There is a better way! God's way.

We need to take our peace - *"The God of peace sanctify you wholly, and I pray God your whole spirit and soul and body be preserved blameless unto the coming of our Lord Jesus Christ"* (1 Thessalonians 5:23).

We need God's peace to sanctify us, to run through our blood and our thinking, so that our body's are not condemned with disease.

3 John 2: *"Beloved, I wish above all things that you may prosper and be in health, even as thy soul prospereth."*

When our soul prospers (which is our mind, will and emotions) our body will respond with good health. If our mind is filled with wrong thinking, our body will respond with poor health. When our heart is at peace, without guilt or condemnation, our body is at peace resulting in good health.

John 5:14 - *Afterward Jesus findeth him (the one he healed) in the temple, and said unto him, Behold, thou art made whole: sin no more, lest a worse thing come unto thee.*

John 8:11 - The lady who was about to be stoned for adultery. Jesus said unto her; go, and sin no more.

To me this is New Testament thinking. Go and sin no more, doesn't mean we'll be perfect, it means to make better choices, but when we mess up, Jesus is our redeemer from the curse of that choice!

Is Disease from a curse?

The blessings and curses are revealed in Deuteronomy 28 and Leviticus 26. The scriptures say that if we obey Him, we shall be blessed, if we don't, we shall be cursed. And as we see the listing of curses, they are diseases AND bad situations.

God says that if we listen to Him and line up with Him, He will bless us by taking away the diseases that our disobedience caused (Deuteronomy 7:12-15).

You should have this scripture memorized by now, but it's the main theme behind what is being taught here. "We are to love the Lord our God with all our heart, soul and mind, and love our neighbor as ourselves, upon these two commands hang all the law and the prophets" (Matthew 23:38-40 and Mark 12:29-31).

When we "love" God, ourselves and our neighbors, we "DO" all the laws and commandments of God. This is where the breakdown is. We don't! We can't seem to get past the crabby neighbor, or the mean boss, or forget and forgive those who hurt and abused us as children, or even question if God really loves us. All these things play in to our lives and affect our health.

How is this remedied?

Christ redeemed us! Galatians 3:13-14, *"Christ hath redeemed us from the curse of the law, being made a curse for us, for it is written, cursed is every one that hangeth on a tree. That the blessing of Abraham might come on the Gentiles through Jesus Christ, that we might receive the promise of the Spirit through faith."*

Isaiah 53:5 and 1 Peter 2:24 tells us that by Jesus' stripes (his scourging and beating) we are healed.

Then Why are Christian's sick?

The provision of healing must be appropriated through confession and repentance of sin, sanctification, prayer and ministry. Just as each individual must appropriate salvation through faith in Jesus Christ, so each individual must appropriate their healing provided by Jesus' stripes through faith in Jesus Christ. But more than faith is required for healing of disease.

Disease is a curse. Proverbs 26:2 says that to every curse there is a cause. The cause is sin and evil spirits. The cause (sin and evil spirits) of the curse (disease) must be dealt with before the blessing (healing and health) comes from God.

"As you have believed, let it be done unto you..." (Matthew 8:13) comes to mind. In my own healing, I first had to believe I could be healed. I had to believe God's desire for me was to be healed. I had to believe that God did not give me a disease. Because if God gave me a disease why would I be going to a doctor to get well? When I pinpointed where my belief system was at, I realized I didn't believe that God existed or that He loved me, or that He was in charge of every thing. I was taught that our disease is from God. I was taught that we are not healed because we don't have enough faith. I have heard countless individuals say that their disease has brought them closer to God. That is not what God intended. But God uses all things to draw us to Him; including being sick, but that was not His choice. He wants you to draw to Him because you want to, not because you have to. And when we say God gave us the disease we make him evil. Because anything that torments us is evil.

I had to believe it was possible for me to be healed. It was a process. Many can get a miracle, but I have found that if the sin issue wasn't dealt with in that individual after a miracle, in most cases they end up getting sick again! Cancer is an example. It seems that when people go into remission, it comes back - it's because the sin issue of bitterness, self-hatred, and unforgiveness was never dealt with.

We need to participate in this process and one area is confession of faults and sins in order to be healed. James 5:16 says to "Confess your faults one to another and pray one for another and you shall be healed." John 1:9 "If we confess our sins, He is faithful and just to forgive us our sins and cleanse us from all unrighteousness." And these are New Testament teachings! Why would they be there if we were free from the curse? Do you think allergies, hemorrhoids, heart disease, Psoriasis, brittle bones and the like are blessings? No. They are curses. As a matter of fact, each and every one of these are listed in Deuteronomy 28. Deuteronomy 28:1-14 lists blessings, from verses 15-66 lists curses, which by the way lists a wide range of disease we see today - and even in Christians. So obviously something is connected here. A scripture comes to mind, "The Lord rains on the just and on the unjust" (Matthew 5:45). Meaning, curses can come to anyone who has not dealt with the issue behind the curse. And that issue is not loving the Lord God and obeying His commandments. See, Jesus didn't come to take away the law, He came to fulfill it. What he took away was the "curse" IF, and only IF you love the Lord God with all your heart, soul and mind. That is why that scripture is the foundation for this ministry, by keeping that one commandment, you keep all, fulfilling the requirements God made on us for healing and blessing.

There are conditions to God's word. It doesn't mean we are back under the law. What we are, is free from the penalty of sin associated with that law.

It's not enough to only believe, the devils even believed! But as Christians, we believe by taking action to confess our sins and receive forgiveness for what we see.

God Heals Today

Our job as believers is to believe, believe the whole Word! All of it, not just the parts we like. We need to believe that obedience brings health. We need to believe that we are healed when we put into action the conditions for healing. This has nothing to do with salvation. Once you have received Christ into your hearts as your Lord and Savior, that puts into motion the ability to live out what God wants for you. The Holy Ghost takes residence in you, seals you until the day of redemption, and in the meantime begins to convict you of things in there so you can come clean before God and be delivered. This has nothing to do with salvation; it has to do with sanctification - a process of changing into the image of Jesus. Being saved is required before life can really begin, it is just the beginning or doorway to life.

The books of Matthew, Mark, Luke, John and Acts demonstrate the power and will of God to heal through the many recorded miracles, signs and wonders. God showed us that healing is available because Jesus bore our sicknesses in His body on the cross. (Matthew 4:23-24; Matthew 8:16-17; Matthew 12:15; Matthew 14:14; Matthew 14:36: Luke 4:40-41; Luke 6:17-19; Acts 10:38; Acts 5:12-16.)

Romans through Jude emphasize the sanctification of the believer. The putting off of the old sinful nature and putting on of more and more of the nature of Christ through the work of the Holy Ghost. Part of the reason for this emphasis on sanctification is to show that without sanctification there will not be the healing of disease, because it is the lack of sanctification (sin and spiritual problems) that is causing the disease. (1 Thessalonians 4:3; 1 Thessalonians 5:23; 2 Corinthians 3:18; Ephesians 4:21-23 and rest of chapter; Ephesians 5:26-28; Deuteronomy 7:11-15; 2 Corinthians 7:1.)

Healing is the Fruit of Repentance.

Deuteronomy 7:11 Disease prevention is keeping the Word. Here are other scriptures to look up and study. Let the WORD teach you!

Read each one and write down what you believe it says to you. Ask the Holy Ghost to guide and teach you.

- 1 Corinthians 15:34; Hosea 4:6; Isaiah 5:13; Deuteronomy 28:1-2 and 15; Proverbs 26:2; Job 3:25; Psalm 103:3; Isaiah 26:3; John 14:27;

- 2 Corinthians 10:5-6; 2 Timothy 2:23-26; 1 John 4:18; Ephesians 5:26;

- Proverbs 12:4; Romans 7:17 and 20; Jeremiah 5:25; Isaiah 59:1-2; 1 Peter 2:24

Evil Spirits:

Along with believing, then confessing our sins, we now need to identify if there any evil spirits at work in our lives. When Jesus came upon someone who had an evil spirit, they weren't happy or healthy, they were tormented and sick!

Jesus didn't give them a maintenance program or a schedule to a weekly group meeting, He cast them out! He didn't talk to each individual demon and convince them to leave. He cast them out!

Not every thing is an evil spirit, but if there is one there we need to address it. Many believe that when you are a Christian you cannot have anything but the Holy Ghost in you. I believed that for a long time too, until in my 18th year of Christianity the Spirit of Fear, Death, Witchcraft, Unloving, Perversion, and Seducing spirits were cast out. And I "felt" them go! So I had to change my theology on the matter. It's an issue of control.

What has you? Are you in a state of anxiety and panic all the time? Then that spirit "has" you. If you are having problems with love and forgiveness, then the spirit of unloving and bitterness has you, and so on. It's time to just face the truth and get on with things, not what we have "known" and "learned" through our lives. Many of us are stuck because of those things. Let's let go of the "traditions" of men and seek God.

There are several evil spirits, here are few: (We will discuss this in a later chapter). Deaf and dumb spirits (Mark 9:25). Spirit of fear (2 Timothy 1:7). Antichrist spirit (1 John 4:3).

A strong man is an evil spirit. Satan's palace is the person he inhabits. Luke 11:21-22 talks of the strong man, but a stronger can take him. And that stronger one is the Lord living within us so that we can take him by storm, he doesn't take us. So when we get out of bed, the enemy scatters, not us. When we understand this, we are well on our way to being free. Do you know anyone who is a scatter brain? Who is scattering whom?

In the case of bitterness, there are several things that happen. From that root of bitterness we will take on other spirits. The Bible says that when that root of bitterness comes up, it brings forth fruit. What are the fruit? Anger, fear, resentment, jealousy, envy, strife, hate, wrath, murder, retaliation, control, and more (Hebrews 12:15.

Is There a Remedy?

Each sin we allow into our lives is a direct result of unforgiveness to some degree. The door is opened to the enemy to come and go as he pleases. 2 Timothy 2:24 "The servant of the Lord must not strive; but be gentle unto all men, apt to teach, patient, in meekness instructing those that oppose themselves, if God peradventure will give them repentance to the acknowledging of the truth, that they may recover themselves out of the snare of the devil, who are taken captive by him at his will."

When you recognize what is happening, you can recover yourselves by taking responsibility, and repenting.

Satan Wants Our Blood

Leviticus 17:11 "The life of the man is in the blood." Satan knows that by drying up our blood, it will result in many illnesses. When the blood dries up in our bones, it results in autoimmune diseases such as allergies, bone disease, rheumatoid arthritis, crone's disease etc. All autoimmune disease is a result of the blood drying up in the bones. "A merry heart does good like a medicine, but a broken spirit dries up the bones" (Proverbs 17:22)

Our spirit is broken because of a hurt or an offense. It could have been from something that happened years ago or even today.

Forgiveness is the antidote for the bones drying up. Forgiveness causes us to get our hearts right with God. We are doing the Word when we forgive. James 1 says to "be a doer of the Word." Forgiveness is what God brought through the sacrifice that Jesus gave. God knew that by balancing out our hearts in truth with Him, the result is perfect homeostasis - balanced chemicals.

What will You Choose?

Will you choose to forgive each and every person that ever hurt or offended you or will you keep all those hurts because you think if you forgive them it gets them off the hook. That is true in part, but the main person off the hook is you! Once you forgive, you are released from that person's junk! And now they are free game for God to meddle in their lives. 2 Corinthians 2:5 says that if someone gives you grief, to forgive him and go as far as to comfort him lest that person be swallowed up with much sorrow. Well, some of you are saying, "But they deserve it." But let me finish what that passage says - if you don't forgive, you are opening your life up for Satan to get an advantage over you.

Prayer for You:

"Father, this teaching is by far one of the hardest to comprehend yet it is the most important to understanding sickness. Many instances in the Bible you indicate that sin and sickness are related. You told the lady who was about to be stoned, go and sin no more. You told the man whom you healed, "Go and sin no more lest a worse thing come upon you, and you also said to the lame man, "Thy sins be forgiven, rise and walk." So we need to come to a realization that this is true for us today. I pray that this dear saint believe who you are, believe you are God who loves them, believe you want to heal them, believe you exist! And I pray that they also recognize the sin within them and confess and receive forgiveness. If they have to forgive others, help them to do so Lord. Restore their bodies to perfect homeostasis Lord. Balance out the chemicals in their brain Lord. Restore the blood to their bones. Establish peace into their hearts and minds. And help them to identify any spirits that may "have them" Lord. Let them not fear any thing they see but know that you need them to see so they can be cleansed, purged, healed and delivered. I ask for an anointing of your Holy Ghost to manifest Himself in them, filling them with healing, truth, love and peace. I ask you to give them strength to walk out their sanctification, hand in hand with you. Let them understand that their job is to recognize, take responsibility, repent, and receive forgiveness. Your job is to heal, deliver and restore. Grant them peace in their minds now, in Jesus name, Amen."

CHAPTER TWELVE

How to Walk in the Spirit... of God

"How to walk in the Spirit of God" will help you learn to choose God's path because there is another path we can follow. It's that other kingdom that we battle with every day. In order to walk in the Spirit of God, we have to discern both good and evil because of Adam's disobedience he received sight to see both, so do we. As believers, we now have the life-long task to continue to choose to walk in the Spirit of God renouncing that other kingdom that joined us at birth (Psalm 51:5). Welcome to your life as a believer. Many who find this out think it's too hard of a task to bear and some fall by the wayside. We see that in scripture when Jesus would teach a hard saying that people would turn from following Him. Don't let it be you. See this as an adventure and exciting to be called a child of God who loves you and is here inside of you to walk with you.

The Bible is full of can do.... not do nots... even though it may seem that way to the naked eye. We have to read the scriptures properly through the eyes of the Spirit so we can see where God is coming from that is for our benefit. This is why I'm writing this book. Many are not seeing this life through the eyes of the Spirit of God but the spirit of man (flesh and soul) and will trip us up every time. When we understand that we are MORE spirit being that flesh and blood we may see that we have been given the POWER to become the children of God and live so (John 1:12).

I wanted to share what the Lord helped me to understand because this is one area that transformed my life. My husband even said that he saw a paradigm shift that was so profound. I hope the same happens for you because this is where the rubber meets the road and lives change for the better.

What I share in this book is only a glimpse, otherwise I would have to add the whole Bible because it is full of "how to walk in the Spirit." But wanted to share a few things that would stir up your thoughts and heart to seek out more for yourself.

The day the Lord showed me these truths that caused me to be more aware of my walk was the day I saw how far off the beaten trail I had wondered at times. Sometimes I would walk in the Spirit and sometimes I didn't. It was hit and miss. I would rejoice when I did and suffer when I didn't. The Lord had me look back on my life after getting this revelation, and showed me some of the choices I made were not in the Spirit. It was very clear. Then He said something quite fascinating. What if I could "know" before I took a step if I was "going to" walk in the spirit or not? That's when He gave me this amazing insight, because we can!

Until the writing of this book, I didn't know there was a real clear path to follow. I just hoped I would get it right but then only to find out later I didn't. I never really knew. I could look at the outcome and see if it was from the Spirit or not after the fact. But what if we can "know" the true "north" of God's heart before we decide? What if we can see clearly the direction for our steps?

I have often said that I don't talk on anything the Lord hasn't brought me victory or clarity in, and this is one of those times. Romans 15:18 says that Paul only taught on what the Lord brought Him through. So know that what I share will give you hope to know you can do it too.

I believe this teaching will be a strong tower to those wanting to learn how to walk in the Spirit of God not in the spirit of man. Isn't that what following Christ is all about?

"Lord open our eyes that we may see and learn and choose clearly to walk as Jesus walked, in the Spirit of our Heavenly Father. In Jesus name, Amen."

Romans is filled with how to Walk in the Spirit, let's take a look at a few more passages to get clarity.

Romans 8:4-5 *That the righteousness of the law might be fulfilled in us, who walk not after the flesh, but after the Spirit. For they that are after the flesh do mind the things of the flesh; but they that are after the Spirit the things of the Spirit.*

We have ourselves on our mind when we walk in the flesh, and those who walk in the Spirit are thinking of greater than themselves things!

Earlier I alluded to Galatians 6:22 which lists the fruit of the spirit. Now I want to dive into it a bit more and discuss what the fruit of the spirit is not! Remember, a matured believer knows what is good and evil (Hebrews 5:14).

Galatians 6:16-21 *¹⁶This I say then, Walk in the Spirit, and ye shall not fulfil the lust of the flesh. ¹⁷For the flesh lusteth against the Spirit, and the Spirit against the flesh: and these are contrary the one to the other: so that ye cannot do the things that ye would. ¹⁸But if ye be led of the Spirit, ye are not under the law. ¹⁹Now the works of the flesh are manifest, which are these; Adultery, fornication, uncleanness, lasciviousness, ²⁰Idolatry, witchcraft, hatred, variance, emulations, wrath, strife, seditions, heresies, ²¹Envyings, murders, drunkenness, revellings, and such like: of the which I tell you before, as I have also told you in time past, that they which do such things shall not inherit the kingdom of God.*

As you read though this, you will see that the spirit and flesh war with each other, so that is our battle. And it will depend on you to choose!

Many who live under laws, that either they believe God has given or they have given themselves, are not living in the Spirit! Because it says, *"If you are led by the Spirit, you are not under the law."* How do you know if you are living under a law? If you demonstrate any of the traits listed. These are things of the flesh and they that do them shall not inherit the kingdom of God. And I believe that to mean, cannot possibly be Walking in the Spirit.

This is not to get you feeling condemned or doubt your Christianity, but it's to get you to see your own heart. If you see any of these things working in your life, don't run from God, run to Him and repent, confessing what you have entertained and allowed the enemy to hinder you with.

We can go through life carnal (kicking and screaming) or walk with the Lord (as in the Spirit) as an overcomer. Both will get you into Heaven, but what road you take to get there is up to you. Allow God to work in these areas and help you trust Him. This isn't talking about salvation, because carnal individuals who have accepted Jesus as their Savior are also saved, they just don't live a very productive and prosperous life. It's when we give ourselves totally unto the Lord that we really get to enjoy the benefits and promises given to us in the Word (Matthew 22:38-40).

Can We Go By Feelings?

If we understand where we are right now we can choose. If by now you have discovered you have been walking more in the flesh than in the spirit, that is a good thing! Now you can choose better from this day on. Now you know what it "feels" like to walk in both. Yes, we can use our feelings too. Many say not to use your feelings, but we can if we are following the Spirit... what is joy? A good feeling! But we do know that if we follow after those feelings that come from wrong fleshy carnal thinking, then of course, those feelings lie, and don't entertain them. So there is a fine line when listening to our feelings.

Can We Have Clear Direction?

In my case, I didn't know WHAT the Spirit was and what it was not. I knew from the outcome but had to go through a lot of apologizing, repenting, pain, after the fact. I believe the Lord wants us to avoid these unnecessary feelings by choosing to simply follow Him. Since the Lord has shown me, now I'm showing you. We can know the ways of the spirit, because all ways of the spirit are in the right direction! Do you remember that children's game "Shoots and ladders?" Well, I'm giving you the key to climbing the ladders rather than sliding back on shoots all the time. That's the more excellent way, don't you think?

Have you ever said, "I thought it was God?" when you find out later it really wasn't. We believe we heard from God. We believed we thought this was the decision to make. Let me submit to you that we can really know it's God before we go... by continually *Walking in the Spirit*. Remember, keeping our own needs off our mind!!!!

Practical Application: Lets say you need to make a decision. You need to ask yourself what or who are you thinking about? Who will benefit from this decision? If it's to benefit you, it's probably a fleshly or carnal response. If it's about how to bless another without any benefit for you, more than likely it's in the Spirit of God. Because sometimes, we do bless others but with a motive that something is in it for us too. There were times I would do conferences in amazing beautiful places because though I did minister, I also saw the benefits for me... to enjoy the sites! Now, it's not wrong to enjoy where we are at, but if the motive and direction is to hurry through the ministry to go bless the flesh, that's another thing.

That's the easiest and clearest way I can put it. We are learning to separate the two and see them both clearly to clearly choose our steps.

Mind of the Spirit and Flesh

Romans goes on to talk about the "mind" of the spirit and the "mind" of the flesh. Romans 8:5 *"For they that are after the flesh do mind the things of the flesh; but they that are after the Spirit the things of the Spirit."*

This is very clear that the battle is in our minds. Again, what or who is on our mind when we make a decision? That's where it starts to see whether we will walk in the flesh or spirit. Did you know that we will walk in one or the other at ALL TIMES.

But you don't have to hope, guess, or once in awhile get it right any more, you can choose!!

Where is your mind when you make a decision? Is it about what you can get? Or is it about what you can do for the Kingdom of God?

Now before you say, "What about me?" Get this really clear. When you walk after the spirit the benefits for YOU are abundant life!!! This impacts your health, your provision, your relationships, your family, everything! The very things you may even be wanting in the first place will come upon you and overtake you!! (Deuteronomy 28:2).

Remember, seek FIRST the kingdom of God —which is walking in the spirit— and ALL THESE things shall be added. That means you don't even have to go after them. Remember, God knows what you have need for even before you ask (Matthew 6:8).

We Have a Part to Play

We just don't get up and walk aimlessly, we choose our steps daily. If we are applying what I'm sharing, the Lord will direct our steps because we are in step with Him. Have you ever started going in one direction and realized it was the wrong direction? I have noticed I do that when I haven't committed my ways unto the Lord, fully. I found some scriptures that backs this up:

Psalm 37:5 *Commit thy way unto the Lord; trust also in him; and he shall bring it to pass.*

Proverbs 16:3 *Commit thy works unto the Lord, and thy thoughts shall be established.*

Proverbs 3:6 *In all thy ways acknowledge him, and he shall direct thy paths.*

We are all growing, learning, and applying the truth to our lives. Know that God knows this, but don't give up even if you don't get it right every time. Remember, as a child of God, you will only fall into the arms of the Lord. You cannot fall anywhere else if you are in Him. Remember that. Jesus is our net! When we received Christ, He becomes our safety net and will catch us. Let's never forget that.

A friend of mine gave a great illustration of this. She loves horses so God would give her illustrations using horses. She shared with me that we are all in God's corral. There is a fence all around us when we become His, so no matter if we get lost, fall, or stuck, we are still in the corral. We can never fall out! I think that is a good illustration to hold on to.

Take the Challenge

I challenge you to choose today to think like God thinks. Pay attention to who is on your mind when you take a step forward. Is it what you can do for the Lord or what you can do to bless yourself?

I like what 2 Corinthians 4:5 and 7 says, *"⁴For we preach not ourselves, but Christ Jesus the Lord, and ourselves your servants for Jesus' sake... ⁶but we have this treasure in earthen vessels that the excellency of the power may be of God, and not of us."*

So to walk in the Spirit is not about us... but servants of God demonstrating His love and kindness to the World. We have to cooperate with God, but it is still Him! We have this treasure within us to walk this out, but it's still God doing it. Many times when we share our testimonies it truly is all about us, but we need to share our testimonial giving God all the glory... because we are simply vessels of His glorious power. And what comes out of you will determine what you are full of.

2 Corinthians 4 goes on to finish this thought... *¹⁶For which cause we faint not; but though our outward man perish, yet the inward man is renewed day by day. ¹⁷For our light affliction, which is but for a moment, worketh for us a far more exceeding and eternal weight of glory; ¹⁸While we look not at the things which are seen, but at the things which are not seen: for the things which are seen are temporal; but the things which are not seen are eternal.*

To sum it up... our flesh will perish but our spirit (inward man) will not... it is renewed daily. We may have some affliction in the flesh, but it is only for awhile and does not compare to the eternal glory waiting for us! By seeing things in the SPIRIT you are able to also walk in it. That is why we are to walk by faith and not by sight. Because things seen is temporary and will be burned up in the end. When we walk in the Spirit of God we are making our footprints known to the heavens and that is what remains!

For more on this topic, pick up the completed version at www.truthfrees.org or amazon.com. The book also comes with an on-line program that helps you learn to walk in the spirit in 21 days! Filled with insights and revelations and a video from me personally, will help guide you along. Here is a testimony of one who went through the program:

I did it! I completed the book and I actually feel God's presence more! I know how to walk in the spirit now, and it's up to me to choose daily. I loved the video portion, as it's a way to encouarge me to continue and not give up! It was a delight to see you every day. I'm not going through it again!!! I look forward to enjoying the Lord even more.

From Australia

CHAPTER THIRTEEN

Victimization

I find that this issue is hidden through self-deception. Many say they have been victimized because of actual wrong acts against them. So they stay in that victimized state. We need to shake that off. A person who is holding onto victimization is holding onto the past. This person is holding onto unforgiveness and waiting for absolution - that will never come - well, not in the way they expect it. We are to let go of every sin that so easily besets us and run the race (Hebrews 12:1). We can't run carrying a bunch of this junk! This session is to help you identify your own condition (not other people's condition) and to gain understanding in this area for freedom! There are some, unfortunately, that don't want to give up their victimization because they use it for their own gain. We aren't going to address those individuals, we are going to address those who want to be set free, healed and delivered. Victimization causes problems in relationships, at work, and with us. It can even produce health issues because fear and stress is apparent.

I've listed several manifestations of a person who has been victimized. If you display any, this is not to condemn you, it's to help you see what is in you so that God can cleanse and heal you. So, hold on and let's see what God will do.

Anyone who experiences any of the following has a victim mentality:

- ❑ Needs to justify self to others
- ❑ Needs to prove they are okay
- ❑ Needs to be understood at all costs
- ❑ Complains about everything
- ❑ Never really satisfied, finds something wrong in everything
- ❑ Looks for other people's mistakes and points them out
- ❑ Takes care of themselves but lets people know they are all alone in this
- ❑ Making sure everyone around them thinks well of them
- ❑ Whatever others do for them, it's never quite enough
- ❑ Expects out of people what they "think" they deserve (an "everyone owes me" mentality)
- ❑ Low self-esteem and self-image
- ❑ High self-image

- Self-pity (no one understands and their plight is the worst of all)

- Their situation is unique

- Compares their sufferings to others - thinking no one's is worse than theirs

- If someone never went through their exact situation, they won't listen to counsel from them

- Self-hatred, self-conflict, guilt and shame

- Feeling worthless and insecure

- Needy (People avoid them because after visiting with them they feel drained.)

- They will only receive council from the "Pastor" no one else will do

- Pushes away possible relationships - clinging and controlling which results from abandonment and rejection (as with the "needy")

- Wants to tell their whole story, looking for sympathy and pity

- Blaming others - not taking responsibility - because after all "I'm the victim"

- Self-righteousness, pride and arrogance- sometimes religiosity

- Idolatry (putting one's feelings above everyone else)

- Cannot receive love

- Gives love conditionally (with self in mind)

- Has self on their mind all the time, "What about me"

- Fear of letting others get ahead of them

- Talkative

- Looks for approving glances

- Everything that happens is about them (i.e. when they walk into a room, they think everyone was just talking about them) turns everything inward. "Takes things personally."

- Wants to be justified and validates their feelings

- Wants everyone to know how much they have been hurt - tells their story to anyone who will listen

- Defensive and abrupt

- Very suspicious - thinking people are out to get them

❑ Talks about their "good deeds"

This is only a brief list of the fruits of individuals who have been victimized. Victimization doesn't only mean being attacked physically, but also emotionally and spiritually.

I believe that most people have been victimized in one way or another. If you identified with any one of these, then it's time to get to work. And for those who can name off several people off the top of your head that demonstrates these things - judge not, remember, when we see something in others, its because its what we have ourselves, Selah.

Even if only one of the above rings true for you, remember, one lump can leaven the whole lump. A person who has been victimized cannot see their own condition – they're always thinking it's someone else causing them their problems. Victimization is something that many won't believe they have, and that's the problem. Until we realize we have these traits and are a victim, we will struggle all our lives with ourselves, others, and especially with God.

Why?

A victimized person is in a constant state of blaming someone. It's every one else's fault they are the way they are.

In ministry, I find that when I share some truth with them about their lives, they don't comprehend a word, but continue where they left off with their sad story. They don't "see" that they have a responsible part in all this. Some may admit that they blame people, situations, but don't think it's their job to get out of it. They think that someone needs to come along and fix everything. So because of this, they inwardly blame God and accuse Him of not being the God they "expected'" Him to be.

Self-pity is a large part of this. Self-pity causes us to get stuck in the past, and that is where the kingdom of darkness reside. Each time someone has self-pity, I would imagine their thoughts have been on what has happened to them. It then is the breeding ground for depression, anger, jealousy, strife, fear, discontentment, self-deception, blame, denial, judgment, critical, controlling, lying, justification, etc.

Every person ministered to along these lines are confused about "why" they are sick, or "why" bad things are happening to them, "why, why, why." A person who asks "why" all the time, is not looking for answers. They are looking for someone to "fix" everything like magic.

I bet by now you have this scripture memorized: Jeremiah 5:25 *"Your sins and iniquities are withholding good things from happening to you."*

Victimized or not, we withhold good things from happening to us.

So what are OUR sins and iniquities as victims? A person who does not forgive is a person who thinks, "If I forgive them this lets them off the hook and that isn't fair."

This person wants complete justification and gratification that this person gets what they deserve.

If not dealt with, this person falls into more victimization. It becomes stronger and stronger and now they cannot even "feel" any longer. They get "numb" to everything and everyone, thinking they are better. The truth is they are not better, they are worse because now the unforgiveness has dropped down into their spirit and become hardened iniquity. Only to fester and stew until they decide to repent.

Once a person sees what is in their heart, which is the first step to any healing, they need to take responsibility. Responsibility for what? We need to pick up our bootstraps, and stop blaming the past, present or future for our own situations. Sure, perhaps someone caused a lot of heartache – that is not to be discounted at all – but it's time to get on with life. By taking responsibility of your life today and what you will become, you are on your way to restoration. As Christians, we are no longer victims. Even though things happened to you, you are responsible for this day forward, and we are to follow after our Savior's example. To love and forgive those who despise you, who hurt you, and who use you (Matthew 5). So we don't have any excuses any longer, do we?

Need for Justification

Let's look at needing to be justified. The Bible says that God is just. If this person doesn't think they have been justified, they are actually blaming God. They demand justice for their pain! But no one can provide that justice, especially if a person's pain came from a long time ago (I'm not talking about illegal acts; I'm talking about relationships). If a person feels unjustified, they are calling God a liar. Let's just say it for what it is. The TRUTH sets us free. We need to see what we are thinking, we need to face what we are thinking, and we need to take responsibility for what we allow in that thinking from this day on.

Did you know that if this were a perfect world and this person's "abuse" was justified by a court of law, and gratification was completed, this person would find something else to feel unjustified about? It will never end, because this spirit DEMANDS to be justified. The problem is, it never will!! It's a spirit; it's his nature and will do nothing else. This has to GO! This mentality has to stop!

A victim's secret desire is to see those that have caused their pain suffer as they have. But that is completely contrary to how Jesus would have us respond.

Luke 9:54-56 *"And when his disciples James and John saw this, (talking about people who did not receive them) said, Lord, would you command fire to come down from heaven and consume them? But Jesus turned to them and rebuked them saying, Ye know now what manner of spirit ye are of, for the son of man is not come to destroy men's lives, but to save them."*

Jesus came to save men's lives not destroy them. The very people that have victimized you are the same people God loves! The very people, who don't agree with you, are those whom God has compassion for. AND when we desire to see bad things happen to those who we think deserve it, is coming from a "SPIRIT." Jesus' desire for all men is that we are saved, delivered, set free and healed. There is no respect of persons with God. All men are equal in His sight and have the same opportunities in Him.

Luke 6:27-35 *"Jesus said to love your enemies and do good to them, which hate you. Bless those who curse you and pray for them who use you. And if anyone hits you on the cheek, offer the other, and if any take away your cloak, give him your coat also. If anyone asks for anything, give it to him, and don't ask for it back! But love your enemies and do good, and lend, hoping for nothing again, and your reward shall be great, and ye shall be the children of the Highest, for He is kind unto the unthankful and to the evil."*

Jesus demonstrated in his own life how to respond to being victimized. I see that he was the most victimized of any person on this planet! Yet He didn't take on any sins!

Jesus looked at every life as valuable. We too need to look at every life as valuable. I know why He asked us to love our enemies, as Luke 6:27-35 says, because He loves everyone and wants us to love everyone.

At His last breath He said, "Father forgive them for they know not what they do" (Luke 23:34). He loved and forgave the very ones who committed Him to death! And here we are, not willing to put up with anyone who says an unkind word!

We need to come to terms that justice only comes from God, and whose to say what that justice is for them? So you need to lay all that aside, cast those thoughts of "revenge" out of your mind, and begin to live as Jesus taught. He wants you to love those who are hard to love. Forgiving those whom you think shouldn't be forgiven. He knew that by doing this, you save both yourself and those around you from much heartache and pain.

There is injustice in the world, even in our own situations. You may see others should be treating you better. This could be true, but it is not up to you to see fulfilled. As Christians, we can see when things are not right, but instead of showing mercy, grace, patience, longsuffering, etc., we end up getting angry, frustrated, resentful and bitter, unyielding, actually the exact opposite of what we are supposed to do... If you can't say amen, say ouchy!

So what do we do?

Once you recognize any of these traits in you, we need to apply forgiveness, which includes being forgiven. A person who has been victimized has sins to confess! They are "retained" sins.

John 20:23 *Whose soever sins ye remit, they are remitted unto them; and whose soever sins ye retain, they are retained.*

This passage clearly says that when we don't forgive another we GET their sins! But if we forgive immediately, they bounce off of us and back on them. It's like that children's nursery rhyme: I am rubber you are glue, whatever you say or do, bounces off of me and sticks to you."

For example, when a woman has been sexually assaulted, what are her sins? Her sins are those that she retained from the attacker such as : feelings of unworthiness and shame, hate, rage and anger, fear, rejection, embarrassment, unforgiveness, resentment, bitterness, self-pity, selfishness, feeling dirty, and guilt, to name a few. These are the "sins" that are retained from that abuse. When we don't forgive our abuser, we take on their sins!! So it's clear that any victimized individual will have sins and iniquities to deal with. These are they, which are preventing good things from happening to you. (Jeremiah 5:25 and Isaiah 59:1-2) Then as you see your part, and receive forgiveness, you can see clearly now to forgive the abuser.

This doesn't mean that we are saying what a person did was right, it means we as victims need to make a decision to release them to God. We do that by forgiving. As long as we hold onto any resentment or anger or unforgiveness and bitterness this person will remain a part of our past, connected to us, putting a block between God and us and them and God. After all, God loves them too and wants them healed. Once we forgive them, they are freed to God. But as long as we hold ties to them with unforgiveness, it doesn't leave much room for God to move in their lives. And, we won't be able to love as Jesus taught!

God is the avenger, He repays. NOT US! When we get that out of our heads that we will see "justice served" it will help us move into the life we so desire. The Bible says that all evildoers will be cut down, but it's not for us to "see" that take place! That is also sin. The Bible tells us not to be glad when we see someone who was evil get his or her "just desserts." That is pride and arrogance on the victim's part. (Proverbs 24:17 says not to rejoice when an enemy falls.)

Let's see how Jesus coped with being victimized. He said not a word to His accusers! He never tried to justify Himself to others. He knew He was the Son of God. He knew why He was there. He knew what the future held and what He was going to be doing. He had no fear what "men would do unto Him." He was victimized, yet without "retaining" any sin.

It's time to stop trying to get people to pay back something they can never pay! It's a black hole, never to be filled. You can stop this vicious cycle by:

- ❑ Acknowledge or recognize God loves you.
- ❑ Asking for God to help you get a revelation on His love for you.
- ❑ Recognizing that you have been victimized.
- ❑ Accepting the fact that you may never see that person's sins against you justified in your eyes.
- ❑ Realizing that you are not going to be repaid by the abuser.
- ❑ Understand that God is your portion, nothing else will satisfy.

Acknowledge things you believe God has allowed in your life that you feel were wrong and confess them to Him. Be honest. We need to recognize what we have been blaming God for.

Be accountable for your sins. Take Responsibility. Decide today to stop the cycle of wrong thinking and wrong "needs" to be happy. Decide today to stop blaming your past and God for your current life. But look toward the future, with new hope.

Confess your sins AND receive forgiveness for your sins. (This is the most misunderstood part of confession. Many confess, but they don't "receive" forgiveness. You replace those sins with God's love by receiving! If you aren't sure what your sins are, refer back to this session. Ask God to help.

Then decide today to work with God to stop allowing those old thoughts and sinful acts against you to dwell in your mind. 2 Corinthians 10:5 say to take every thought captive and cast down all imaginations that exalt itself over the knowledge of God. Anything that does not bring you peace or comfort is not of God! Replace old thoughts with truth. Every time an old thought tries to come back, tell it "You are a liar, God loves me, He is my avenger, He is my provider, so you have to leave."

Keep on keeping on. You may have to do this 50 times a day, and for some time. Depending on how deep your victimization was. But the end will come, and you will be free! In freeing yourself, you are freeing others. Your heart will change toward people and they will change toward you. You will not even attract people who are themselves victimized. Because as you know, many people attract the very thing they want to be free from. We find people with addictions are attracted to those with the same addictions. It's a spiritual battle. When you get free from some of those issues, they are no longer in you to attract. You will be at peace because now you are living in freedom.

Join me in this prayer if you desire healing in this area:

"Father God, what an awesome privilege to be able to come to you about everything. How joyful I am to know you care about every detail in my life. I realize that I have felt like a victim, but no longer. I recognize my heart condition and realized that I have been keeping you from really blessing me. I confess my sin of Unforgiveness, rage and anger, bitterness, self-pity, accusing, blame, jealousy, strife, fear, discontentment, selfishness, self-deception, denial, judgmental, critical, controlling, lying, justification, confusion, wantonness, self worthlessness, bitterness, retaliation, unbelief, resentment, (continue naming others that come to mind). I now RECEIVE forgiveness Father. I thank you for forgiving me and filling me with YOUR truth and love. Replacing those sinful ways with all you are. Replacing those thoughts with your thoughts. Cleanse me and purge me today, Lord, continue keeping me clean in this area. I am not a victim any longer and will no longer blame you either. I will accept what has happened in my life and trust you in all things. Let me keep my mind clean Father, by casting out every thought that is not of you. Help me Lord. Help me to believe I do not need to "see" someone pay for my problems. I release them to you. Help me to forgive them Father, completely and once and for all. In Jesus name, Amen."

From God's heart to you:

"My child, I love you. Receive my love. I have seen all that has happened to you. I am sorry that you felt I left you and abandoned you in your life. I have not. These things happened because there is evil in the world, but I have overcome that evil. Trust me now. Believe that I have every detail of your life before my eyes. Rest in me, take comfort knowing I "know" all things that have happened to you. I am just and good, it may not seem like it at times, but that is the truth. Believe in the truth only. Forgive those who have hurt you.

Forgive yourself. Let my love penetrate those areas that you have closed off from the world. Open your heart to trust me, I will NOT fail you. Remember Job? He said, "Though I slay him, yet will he trust Me." He knew that no matter what was going on around him, all things will WORK TOGETHER EVENTUALLY for good. And as you know, it did. He was restored of all that was taken, and more besides. This is in store for you, but you mustn't give up hope.

Continue hoping in me, for your redeemer draws nigh. Fear not to see what is in your heart, these things I see already and they don't surprise me. Open your heart to me, and let's get out what needs to be pulled out for you to obtain that perfect peace you so desire. Your peace can only come when these things are pulled out. Let me work in your life, don't struggle any longer. I will never leave you alone, remember that."

How Do I live with a person who has been victimized?

As you have read through this, you will now see that a person is not acting victimized of their own accord. Even Jesus said, "You know not what spirit you are of." (Luke 9:54-56) Paul Said, "It's not I but sin in me that does it." (Romans 7) We need to realize that this person has no clue (in most cases) why they are the way they are. These individuals are "high maintenance." This means that you know that when you are around them long enough you feel "drained." And it's true, they are so needy, that they will suck the life right out of you because of the emptiness they have that DEMANDS to be filled!

So what do you do? First thing we need to do is forgive them. Jesus put it wonderfully, "Forgive them for they know not what they do." Because it's a fact that those who have been victimized cannot see within themselves clearly. And by forgiving them, allows God to work IN them!!! You may be used in the process, but know that God selected YOU in their lives to do this. This person needs to be loved. 2 Corinthians 2:5-11 says that by forgiving and showing love to someone who causes us grief, we are helping them come out of their "much" sorrow, and not only that, we are saving ourselves from the attacks of the devil!

John 20:23 says that if we don't forgive others, we get their sins! To love means to overlook their offenses, and their "sins" won't become a part of us.

As we "do" what I just shared, the Lord gives you what you need to be in relationship with that person, especially if they are in your household and you cannot get away from them. You will actually have compassion toward them instead of contempt. God will cause you to have peace and what they say or do won't affect you any longer. Our main objective as believers is to love everyone —even the unlovable.

Just look how Jesus dealt with people. He was kind to the unthankful and evil:

Luke 6:35 *But love ye your enemies, and do good, and lend, hoping for nothing again; and your reward shall be great, and ye shall be the children of the Highest: for he is kind unto the unthankful and to the evil.*

CHAPTER FOURTEEN

Abandonment and Rejection

Abandonment and Rejection are wide spread in America today, and many don't even know they have fallen victim to these. While many others know exactly what this means and have lived with it, yet not really knowing how to get out of it. So for both instances, I believe this segment of teaching is going to help you, just as it did me when God set me free.

It has taken me personally a number of years to come to knowledge about Abandonment and Rejection All of the sessions that I provide in this book, and all of the teachings I do in ministry are done after I've seen these principles become real in my own life. That gives me a deeper understanding of the issue so that I can teach with conviction and give hope to the hearer.

Let me start with the reason I teach on these two together. I put Abandonment and Rejection together because I realized that they both work hand-in-hand. For many years I dealt with rejection. I knew I was feeling rejection almost every day. I tried not to feel rejected, I've been ministered to on the lines of rejection, and I even thought I was completely free, then only to realize I wasn't. You know what I mean, something would happen, and I would "feel" that pain of rejection again only to have to start over figuring out what my deal was.

This is where I am today, I don't need to "try" to figure it out anymore to be free, I am free. That is why I feel I can teach on this subject with some authority. I had to stop working so hard on rejection, because I was just going around in circles. I had to first deal with abandonment.

Let's first look up the words in the Webster's Dictionary:

Abandonment: From the word Abandon which means: To forsake entirely; as to abandon a hopeless enterprise. To renounce and forsake; to leave with a view never to return; to desert as lost or desperate. (Synonyms: desert, to forsake, leave, quit, forego, give up, take leave of. Evacuate) Abandonment then means: "A total desertion; the state of being forsaken."

Rejection: From the word Reject which means: To throw away as anything useless or vile; to cast off, to refuse to grant, to refuse to accept. Rejection then means: The act of throwing away, the act of casting off or forsaking, refusal to accept or grant.

From these definitions, can you identify which one you have? Which one seems to be stronger in your life?

Below describes someone who has been abandoned:

- ❑ Being ignored by someone you love

- ❑ Left alone, no one to help, especially by those who should love you

❑ Having to take care of yourself

❑ Not able to trust anyone, including God

❑ Thoughts of having been left alone by God

❑ Having been left by a parent or guardian

❑ Having been adopted

❑ Having been made fun of by peers, children, family members

❑ Having been left to fend for yourself by friends, co-workers, and those of authority

❑ Having been a scapegoat

Below describes someone who has been rejected (These feelings come from being abandoned):

❑ Feeling that you don't belong

❑ Feelings of unworthiness and having no value

❑ Feelings of uselessness

❑ Not feeling loved or accepted

❑ Feeling that you aren't important, nor your needs

❑ Feeling that no matter what you do, it's not good enough

❑ Fear of man

❑ Perfectionist

❑ Driven to perform to be loved

The differences are clear. The Abandonment is an "act," the rejection is the "feeling" or "response" to the act.

This is not a complete list, because I'm sure you can add to the list based on your own experiences, but these are the areas I had problems with in my life. And let me tell you that as long as these are inside a person, the very opposite of what we desire will happen.

You may wonder why no one likes you, or it's hard for you to make friends, it is more than likely that your own feelings of rejection are rejecting them! Your own feelings of abandonment, causes them not to want to come into a relationship with you. After all, if we don't come into a good relationship with ourselves, how can we expect others to?

I've heard so many people say, "But I'm a good person." Yet there is so much havoc in their lives. This person is self-deceived because we have to be a "good person" to ourselves first before we can be to others.

But let's take a quick peek at what God says about being a "good" person.

There is none-good, no not one. Even Jesus said, *"Why call me good. There is only one that is good and that is God"* (Matthew 19:17). So in reality, when someone says, "But I'm a good person" they are self-deceived and the truth is not in them. Once we realize that we are all in this together, that we all have frailties and weaknesses, that we still have a long way to go in our Christian life, then we have a good chance at getting where we want to be.

Jesus did hear the words so important to us too, *"This is my beloved son in whom I am well pleased."* God did not say, "This is my beloved son in whom I am well pleased "because" he is good.

We are loved first and foremost in spite of ourselves. We must get that truth in our heart so that we don't have the need or drivenness to perform for love and acceptance. It will never be "good" enough. Never. But the miracle of God's love is that He loves us anyway! That pushes through all the sacred cows and wrongful teachings of our youth to see a truth that sets us free! So we can simply "be" ourselves without fear of rejection.

Until we understand this truth, that God has not abandoned us, never did, never will, we'll stay in a state of fear and feelings of rejection.

And regardless of what you think about yourself, if you are saved, you are righteous right now.

I know, many of you are saying, "But you don't know what I've done, or where I've been, or what I've said." True, so let me ask you a question. Are you a believer? Do you believe that Jesus died for your sins? Have you received Him as your Savior? If you have, then you are righteous. I didn't say "good", I said righteous. Be sure you have those two words defined clearly because they are different, and mean different things. We get the "good" mixed up, thinking in order to be righteous we have to be good! Don't make that mistake again!

The only requirement for you to get God's approval and seal on your life is to believe. The Holy Ghost "seals" us until the day of redemption. So, then why are we still messed up? Because we never really "received" the full pardon for ALL of our sins. The reason we haven't is that we haven't been able to truly believe God forgives ALL sins. It can't be any clearer than that. We think the sin is too big or too small and we stay stuck. It's as simple as that.

So what has this to do with abandonment and rejection? A lot! We need only God's approval not man's, and we can only get it if we believe it. Then when others abandon us or reject us we won't fall to pieces but demonstrate forgiveness and compassion to the one doing the offense.

I'm going to teach you by sharing my story. For many years I have had the feelings as I listed previously. I knew I had rejection, but it wasn't until much later that I realized I had abandonment. I thought about it and thought about it, I asked God, "Where did this all start?" Because if you know anything about ministry, we need to identify the "door points" which means to identify when this started in our lives. So of course, it all went back to childhood. That's where I got my first experience with rejection. A Sunday school teacher made fun of me in class in front of all the other kids. From that point on, I lived under that "fear of rejection" for the rest of my life. But abandonment didn't get exposed until a few years ago. I don't even really recall how that came to pass, all I know is that as you begin facing things in your life, the Lord brings things up that need to be dealt with before going on to the next thing. I knew I had abandonment but I never really understood how to get rid of it. Well, it came. As I began thinking about this incident about the Sunday school teacher, what she really did was abandoned me. The feelings of rejection came after. But I never saw that until now! So of course, the "strong man" of abandonment was hidden behind the "feelings" of rejection. The 'spirit of abandonment' thought he had a home in my life for good. But he was wrong.

Then as I thought more on this, I had realized that I was abandoned by my earthly father. It wasn't that he wasn't there, it was that he wasn't there emotionally. As I realized my father couldn't love me or communicate with me the way I wanted, I was able to forgive him. I was able to forgive him for being "silent" to me because it caused me to fee abandoned and rejected. Whether he did it intentionally or not, isn't the issue, it's what I became because of that. And God wants me free, and in order to be free I had to forgive my father for abandoning me. I confessed this to the Lord and I forgave my father for being silent to me. Since then the memories of my father are quite different. He was actually a pretty good father, as fathers go. He was always taking us on outings, allowing us to bring neighborhood friends with us. He had put up a pool in the back yard, he taught us how to shoot with bow-and-arrows, and since he was in the Air Force as a flight technician, he would hide put candy in his flight suit for us kids to find. I couldn't see the "good" he was until the "hurt" was gone.

My father is not gone, but my Heavenly Father is still there. He isn't silent to me and he's always there. He even says to me, "Linda, you are my beloved daughter in whom I am well pleased."

The results of this have been tremendous. I cannot even write down each and every time I have the opportunity to "feel" rejection that it wouldn't come! I wouldn't "feel" any pain. See the feelings of rejection are linked to the fact that we felt we were abandoned, or even truly so. Rejection is a manifestation of the abandonment. Because many are abandoned today, it's not a feeling. It's a fact! Rejection is the manifestation that comes out of being abandoned. That is why I never really saw my freedom from the feelings of rejection; I didn't know I had to be free from abandonment first! (My people perish for lack of knowledge Hosea 4:6)

I'll share one story with you as a direct result of being freed from those spirits. And I want to tell you something. "Whom the Son has set free is free indeed." And I don't believe that only means in the hereafter, it also mean completely now! In some of my teachings, I talk about not "trying" to do this or that. Well when someone is completely free, they don't even have to mess with "trying" any longer because they just do it! I'm living proof that this is true.

Let me share a testimonial with you: I was working one afternoon later than usual, and as I left I thought I would stop by someone's office and bid him good night. I began a conversation with him, but much to my surprise he never even turned around to look at me. His back stayed to me the whole time I was standing there. I even asked a question a little louder, thinking he didn't hear me. But to no avail. That was a blatant act of abandonment. Being ignored, right? And guess what, I didn't "feel" any pains of rejection whatsoever. Now the fact that I was abandoned was real. But the spirit was no longer in me to make me "feel" it! That is freedom! And to take it one-step further. The next day when I saw him it was as though he never even rejected me and we just worked together as though it never happened. Now whether he realized it or not was not up to me, that was between him and his maker. My job was to forgive him of his act toward me and go on! Let me tell you that this was HUGE! You may have just experienced it today. Someone ignored you or rejected you and you got a deep pain in your inside. Wouldn't it be nice that no matter what anyone did to you, you wouldn't feel that pain????

Then because I knew what he did was not right, I forgave him. I didn't forgive him to get rid of my pain, I didn't have any, I forgave him because he needed to be forgiven, and that's what God has commanded us to do. Forgiving others is two fold, it not only keeps our relationship right between our Heavenly Father and us, it also keeps relationships restored between others and us as well.

Many instances of being ignored and rejected happened all day long for almost a week. One opportunity after another, and I do mean all day long! But I could only laugh because I was free. I wasn't "trying" to not feel rejection any longer, I just simply wasn't. And I believe now that I am free, I realize that I've been given rejection opportunities all along, it's just now that I'm free I won't have any part of it. And that spirit is going to go have to find someone else to bug.

Then because of that, I have been able to respond back to a person correctly, not through any pain of rejection (which of course can result in all kinds of wrong responses.) And better yet, WITHOUT FEAR OF MAN! Many of my rejection experiences happened at work. The need to be perfect was out of that fear of being abandoned and rejected. That need to be liked and accepted was out of that fear of being abandoned and rejected. See how it worked in my life? I wonder if it's not true for you, especially if you are still dealing with this.

And the opportunities of being abandoned and rejected don't only happen out there in the workforce, but in our own homes. The devil uses those closest to us, those we love the most to cause us to "feel" rejection because he knows that this will cause relationship problems.

This is another testimonial of what happened between my husband and I.

My husband came home from work late one night and I was so happy to see him. I hugged and kissed him and then ran back into the living room to finish watching a movie on TV. Then I ran back to him in a few minutes and did the same thing. This time he kind of backed off and looked at me with eyes that said, "What do you want?' I then said, "I'm glad to see you." And then I went to bed.

Now there was a huge opportunity to "feel" rejection. He did in fact abandon me to myself, and in times past I would get all hurt and pout and have to deal with that for hours. But this time it was so different. After he said that, I just went on my merry way, and went to bed. He came to bed and asked me if anything was wrong. I said, no, not at all, why? He said, "no reason." Then we went to sleep.

The next morning was when I realized what took place the night before. We talked about what happened because my husband said something strange happened to him. He actually "felt" rejection! He was surprised because he never feels that. He knew it was a spirit that jumped on him, but from where? I then understood. I couldn't be tempted to "feel" rejection any longer, so the enemy decided to jump on Tom. After Tom realized what happened, he did tell it to go and was set free, but that was a new one on him. He said to me, "So you didn't answer your phone this time?" I laughed because he was right. I didn't allow that feeling to even come through the door of my heart.

Another incident: My husband was planning a trip to be gone for a couple of days, I was alone, but guess what? I wasn't feeling rejected!!! Then something else came to me during the night while I was lying in bed alone. I wasn't in any fear of being alone! Why? Because God was there, he has not abandoned me to myself! God's perfect love casts out all fear. But then to go on to say, that because that spirit of abandonment is gone, I no longer feel fear of being alone either! What a bonus!!!!

Let me tell you a truth. I will continue to be abandoned (ignored) but I can now be abandoned without the pain of rejection. That is freedom! I can't stress it enough how free that is. I no longer carry "what they did" to me everywhere I go. As a matter of fact, I've become more bold and courageous. I am making decisions and doing things at work that I'm no longer fearing the outcome. Because even if the outcome wasn't right, I still couldn't feel rejection!!!! THAT MY FRIEND IS FREEDOM!!!!!!

Ministry Prayer for You:

"Dear Heavenly Father, you are so wonderful and so loving and kind to your children. Father I ask that each of your children reading this prayer now begin to get a deeper revelation on your love for them. Father, if they have recognized they have been living under the spirits of rejection and abandonment, I pray you give them hope of being free, even today. Help them to see that you have not abandoned them. You have not ignored them. You love them. And you think well of them. Help them to see where their abandonment issues began and who was involved and forgive them. If they have been abandoned by their father or mother, or abandoned by any one else, I pray that this area be filled with you. For you have not abandoned them, you have adopted them to be your own. Help them see that even though they may have been ignored or that their father was silent to them, that they see this and confess this to you, that they confess this pain to you now. And I pray that as they confess this that you heal their broken heart. Let them know that if their father on this earth could have said what they needed to hear, he would have. But since he didn't, that they hear these words from you right now, "I love you, I am proud of you, I am glad you were born, and you are a good son/daughter." Let them be filled with this truth, remove all pain and hurt from their lives and set them free NOW in Jesus name from the spirits of abandonment and rejection. I believe you are doing a mighty work specifically for each person reading this. You see each one right now who is seeking you, who wants to know you, who are determined to follow you. Free them Lord so they can go onto other things in their lives with a healthy attitude. In Jesus name I pray, Amen."

Something to think about: It took me years to get to this revelation in my life, but it only took seconds for Him to heal me and set me free. Don't blame God by your long journey to health; He is there to instantly heal. The long journey is us getting the truth in our hearts, seeing through things and understand what is going on. We need to continue looking inside of ourselves, because I can tell you that God is "quick" in the spirit, and will respond once we have the "truth" revealed to our hearts that helps unlock the door leading to health.

Another facet to look at is 1 Samuel 8:7 *"They have not rejected you, they have rejected me."* Sometimes we are abandoned and rejected because of whose we are! That's when we need to pray and forgive all those who reject us, not taking it personally (when you have dealt with the abandonment and rejection issues in your own heart) because the Bible is clear that we will be rejected at times. Jesus was rejected and abandoned, but the thing that kept Him going was the fact that God was there. Yes, in Jesus' case, God did abandon Him to the cross so that we never will be abandoned. Jesus took on that abandonment and rejection so we won't have to. So the next time you are abandoned and you begin to feel rejection, stop right there and forgive.

When Abandonment is Good

In ministry, I have received more requests about having been abandoned and rejected than any other issue in life. I had to ask "Why is that so?" Well, as I dealt with my own abandonment issues, and even wrote several books on it, there was something I failed to see. We are experiencing so much abandon because there is a time and place for it. But it's getting mis-placed and internalized not realizing God is trying to tell us something: that we are to abandon ourselves!

Let me explain. For so many years I have taken care of myself. Done things that are good for me. When I would conduct conferences or minister to others, I was still on my mind. I was living in a box I made for myself, and didn't even know it. After sharing this revelation with Tom, he called it my "pleasure box." But I heard the Lord say, "Go deeper." That doesn't mean to dig into more insights, but go deeper outside myself, into that area of real love, real humility, and selflessness. This is HUGE.

For years I would say that the Lord came to give life and life abundantly. But what we all do, and I have done it too, is say, "The Lord came to give me life and give me life abundantly." But that's not what it says. Today I wrote this in my journal: "Enjoy Life." I left out the "my" as I always would say. "Enjoy my life." And when I said, "Enjoy life" this includes everything and everyone. Not just me!

There is a scripture that also says, "All things work for good to those who love the Lord." And again, we would read it like this, "All things work out for MY good...." Again, we are being self-centered and self-deceived.

This was hard to see today, because as a minister, I've given a lot of my time, effort, to everyone I come in contact with who has contacted me for help, but there was always an element of "me" in there. What was in it for me? Would this be a connection with someone who may help me do something? When I would teach in LA, I would want to leave quickly after the meeting so I could go to Disneyland. When I conduct a conference in another city, I look forward to sight-seeing. These aren't bad things, but they have their place. I recall doing a conference once and the woman who held it wanted me to wait until her husband got home to pray for them as a couple. But I didn't. I said that I had to leave. But the reason I had to leave was because I wanted to go see the ocean! I left a great opportunity of helping a hurting family who just lost their daughter, to go "enjoy myself" by the beach! Now friends, that was hard to admit, but maybe my transparency will help someone?

But today, a NEW day (remember, His mercies are new every morning and we can start over every morning) I confessed to the Lord that I am willing to go deeper, OUTSIDE myself, into the things of Him. Because abandoning oneself isn't about being tossed aside, it means to abandon ourselves to the love and care of the Lord, which is then demonstrated by how we love and care for one another. Scriptures say that when you do something for another, you are actually doing it unto the Lord (Matthew 25:40).

I know of one such person in my life that actually lives this way. He gives selflessly to me, every day. He is a great example of living deeper, outside himself. It's been there all along, but I didn't see it, because I had myself on my mind all the time. And that is my husband Tom. I can recall countless times he gave to me when he could have kept for himself, so that I'll be comfortable, protected and cared for.

A scripture comes to mind that says we are to prefer others over ourselves. That means, to think of others more than we think of ourselves. You may already "know" that, but do we "do" it? The truth is, when we do that, our lives will be filled to overflowing, more than we can ever hope or dream. Let's take that plunge today! Let's go deeper outside of ourselves in the Lord's pool of clear clean water, truth, and love.

I had some repenting to do How about you?

Further Resrouces:

For more on this topic, pick up the book called "Abandonment and Rejection."

CHAPTER FIFTEEN

What is a Trauma? A trauma is something horrific that has happened to you that caused you grief, pain, and hurt, so deeply that it actually changed your heart toward life. The images and pictures play over and over, and this is what causes many problems today. It seems that when people have traumas, this is when the person's life shuts down and they are stuck emotionally at that time and place. The trauma has to be identified at the root so healing can occur. Post Traumatic Stress Disorder (PTSD) is often labeled on people who had such traumas such as loss of a child, witness of a horrible incident, car accident, unexpected death of a loved one.

How to find healing? If this incident stays alive because of a memory, how do we get that memory purged? Unfortunately, the memory may never be purged, we are chemical beings and our bodies have a photo-shop built in (photosynthesis) to take snap shots of things in our life. That is why you see different pictures along the way, but not every thing, just things that had an emotional attachment at the time.

But there is hope! Facing the picture again for one last time will help you be restored by following same steps used in forgiveness. You will find your peace because a trauma "sticks" in our mind and heart because of unforgiveness.

See it's not the trauma that is keeping you stuck, it's the "pain" associated with that memory that is keeping you stuck. By identifying who was involved, how it affected you, who needs to be forgiven, is the key to your recovery. Ask God to help you because some traumas are so awful, such as child abuse, death, etc., that we don't even remember or don't want to remember. But in order to get free at the "root" these things need to be exposed. God will be there, He will guide and help you. Ask for His wisdom and discernment and strength, and He will give it. So the first thing to do is recognize you had a trauma in your life.

Post-traumatic stress is the response to being emotionally overwhelmed. Depending on your emotional strength to start with will determine if you will suffer from PTSD. It's usually a delayed reaction to an emotional pain; it is not a mental illness. Ministry needs to take place in order to be free. A drug won't help. Drinking doesn't help, only the Love of God and forgiveness restores.

Post Traumatic Stress Disorder

The following are some symptoms of post-traumatic stress disorder. A person who is experiencing it does not necessarily have to have all of these symptoms:

Depression: Feeling rejected, worthless, and helpless; seeing no hope for the future.

Nightmares: Experiencing in dreams the traumatic events experienced in that trauma.

Flashbacks: Suddenly experiencing, with deep emotion, a vivid memory from the war. This is usually triggered by something that occurs in normal, daily life such as a certain sound or smell.

Anger: Outbursts of unreasonable and uncontrollable anger.

Emotional Numbing: Not permitting himself to be emotionally close to anyone. There is no desire to have personal relationships with others.

Survivor Guilt: With wartime veterans, they constantly wonder why others, considered to be better than himself, died and he did not.

Suicidal Thoughts: Thinking about ways to commit suicide because it seems that there is no way out.

Self-Punishment: Inflicting pain upon self to try to atone for the past.

Substance Abuse: Using alcohol and drugs to numb his memories, emotional pain, and feelings of guilt.

Blackouts: Periods of time in a person's life that there is no recollection.

Addressing Vietnam Veterans

The American veterans of the Vietnam War experienced many difficulties after they returned home. Most people did not begin to understand their problems. The opinion of most people was that the veteran should just forget about the war, find a job, and resume a normal life. They thought he could turn off the war in his mind the same way you switch off a television. Because of this mind-set, the veterans turned inward and carried wounds that had to be hidden because no one understood. Most Americans had no idea of the horrific things the Vietnam veteran had experienced. Worst of all, most did not want to know. They were too busy enjoying the materialistic pleasures of life the very things these veterans sacrificed themselves to provide.

There were no welcome home parades for the young soldiers returning from Vietnam. Instead, it was not uncommon for him to be spit upon and called a baby killer. It wasn't unusual for him to be ridiculed and rejected by the veterans who fought in other wars, because they had been victorious.

Recent years, things have changed toward that war, however, the damage was done and too late to rectify. Now we need to address each and every person who has been inflicted, one at a time.

Any veteran, whether he was in Vietnam or in the Middle East can recover from post-traumatic stress disorder. There is a way out. Help is readily available. The first step to recovery is recognizing and admitting that you are experiencing post-traumatic stress and that you need help. It is just as important to admit that you are experiencing post-traumatic stress disorder, as it is to admit that you slipped on the ice and broke your arm. No matter how strong your arm is, enough pressure put upon it will cause it to break. Denial of the truth prevents healing. "You shall know the truth and the truth shall make you free" (John 8:32).

Addressing 9/11 and Hurricane Katrina Survivors:

The same holds true with current traumas. People who were involved in these events first hand have these pictures playing over and over in their minds. In their dreams, in their daily thoughts, interrupting their minds, which causes problems both physically and emotionally. If we don't deal with these "pictures" and thoughts now, they will become a permanent fixture and only lead to more destruction. As with veterans of wars, we are seeing that long-term the thoughts of the things they witnessed in war has produced a society of homeless, unable to take care of themselves. We cannot let that happen again. We can't afford to allow our lives to be robbed from us because we didn't deal with the memory keeping it alive with pain. See, it's not that we'll ever "forget" what happened, what God wants to do is heal the pain associated with that memory/experience.

So how do we get free from this? (Forgiveness)

1. Identify the stressor/trauma.

2. Identify the surrounding circumstances.

3. Was there others involved and who were they? Make a list.

4. Write down what they did.

5. Then write down what you became from what they did. For example, if you were abused you may feel fear, anger, frustration, unworthiness, self-pity, confused, jealous, distrusting, hateful, ashamed, embarrassed, etc.

6. Once you have identified them all, you have just identified your sins. They are sins that you retained from this experience. They are not emotions as some would suspect, and that's why people are still in bondage. They are sins - your sins retained. And it's these sins that are keeping the trauma alive. Keeping nightmares, guilt, and the pain alive! Did you know even a victim has retained sins from that situation? Let's take a look. If a person was raped, what did they "become" because of that rape? They became angry, confused, hateful, distrusting, fearful, ashamed, worthless, rejected, etc. Looks like the same kind of things that were in someone who was abused, right? The Bible says that if we don't forgive others for their sins against us, we take on their sins! Yep! Every single one of them. (John 20:23). But if we forgive them, their sins don't come onto us but stay on the perpetrator.

7. Take the list of your sins that you retained and confess them before the Father in the name of Jesus and receive forgiveness. See it's these sins, these retained sins that prevent you from being free! 1 John 1:9 says that if we confess our sins He is faithful and just to forgive us our sins and cleanse us from all unrighteousness.

Once you have received forgiveness, now you can forgive the person who caused your grief. You are now FREE to forgive, truly forgive from your heart because your heart is clean toward them! (If it's a situation like a war, you do the same thing toward the person who was in charge, starting at the top! Yep, the president, commanding officers, the enemy, etc.)

Forgiving removes the pain of that offense done. You may still remember things, but the pain is gone, the hurt is gone. That is freedom! So then when you are free you can live as you have wanted to. I believe by trusting God in this, not only do you become free, but that which was lost or stolen is also restored., you are able to help others find their freedom. And because you are no longer experiencing the pain, you are now able to minister to others without falling to pieces. Because frankly, if someone was ministering to me but was still in pain about it for themselves, I question if they truly forgave.

Ministry Prayer for You To Pray for Yourself:

"Father, as I acknowledge the trauma(s) in my life and the truth that I may not have applied forgiveness to every area, I ask You to help me do that now. Freedom and healing comes from forgiving, and trusting You no matter what. Let me seek You in every situation Lord and apply the truth that I can be free. I don't have to suffer any longer. Forgiveness heals, help me to forgive everyone that ever caused trauma to my life. Thank you for this teaching. I ask for Your love and forgiveness, and believe that even though I went through something horrific, your love and truth is greater than that. Help me to see this Father and find freedom from any fear or painful memory. Release me from the pain of this memory and bring peace, in Jesus Name. Amen."

Ministry Prayer for You To Pray for Yourself:

Father, I stand before You with this dear Saint. I trust that this teaching rings true in their heart and life. Help them to undertstand that this is the key to help them find peace from their trauma. Let them remember the truth of Your love and forgiveness for them, so that they can do it towards others and find their peace and joy restored. I trust You to remove the pain from their memories and give them the desires of their heart. I left up Your name Jesus, because in Your name there is healing, joy, justice and peace. I thank you for meeting us here now. I ask You to balance out their lives, to bring calmness and peace. Let them receive Your love that casts out all fear and torment. Thank you for hearing our prayer, In Jesus name, Amen."

Further Resources

Pick up my book called "Traumas and PTSD" from our Website or Amazon. com. It has been a source of help for so many!

CHAPTER SIXTEEN

Righteousness, Peace and Joy

The scripture that is used in this teaching is: "The Kingdom of God is not meat and drink, but righteousness peace and joy in the Holy Ghost" (Romans 14:17).

After you have begun seeking more of the love of God, and applying forgiveness to your life and to the lives of others, there are still other things that can help with your sanctification process.

These are: righteousness, peace, and joy. I believe these areas have been lacking greatly in a Christian's life, otherwise people wouldn't be seeking so much ministry. There is a fine line between the "righteousness of God in Christ Jesus" and "self-righteousness" and a fine line between "peace that passes all understanding" and the peace that the world gives.

We will discover in this session these attributes that God has so graciously given us. He knew that these three things would help establish us and help us as we journey through this life. These three areas have to be real in our lives in order to live the life we so desire, they are righteousness, peace and joy.

Righteousness

Righteousness for the most part seems to be one of the hardest mysteries of God to understand and comprehend. Personally I know what the Word says, but somehow it has been difficult getting it into my heart so that it becomes "me."

Righteousness is vital to a Christian, if we don't know we are righteous right now, and what that really means; we'll struggle as a Christian.

The Kingdom of God is righteousness, peace and Joy in the Holy Ghost. For me, in times past, I would quote part of that scripture that says "the Kingdom of God is not meat and drink, but Righteousness, peace and joy" and I would stop there. But the rest of that scripture says, "in" the Holy Ghost. It's "in" the Holy Ghost that we are able to live in the Kingdom. These two small words "is" and "in" are powerful and need to be looked at closely. Where is the Kingdom of God? It is within us. How? Because the Holy Ghost came to live in us when we received Jesus as our Lord and Savior. So by deductive reasoning, we "are" righteous the minute we receive Christ, which is done by faith. The Kingdom of God "is" righteousness, which now dwells in you! We as Christians need to separate our actions from the truth. We may not do everything right, but we are still righteous! That has to be settled once and for all. We all wear the "robe of righteousness" right now! That's what is covering us and provides us access to the throne of Grace day and night. It's a cloak, a covering, signifying our sins are covered and we "are" holy right now and always. God demands holiness, and we couldn't freely come to Him until we had on that robe making us holy too. Jesus gave us that robe so we could have sweet fellowship with God.

Hebrews say, "There is now no condemnation for those who are in Christ" (Romans 8:1). The word we need to pay close attention to is "in." We have righteousness when we are in the Holy Ghost as stated in Romans 14. We have no guilt or condemnation when we are in Christ. We need to ask God to help us get a revelation on being "in" Christ.

When I receive by faith the complete work of Christ personally (forgiveness of my sins and iniquities - all of them) then I am in Him. I am living in Righteousness. When we are in Christ, His righteousness perfects us. God demands holiness to be in fellowship with us, so when He sees us, He really sees Christ's righteousness. Romans 5:8 says that those who believe (being righteous) are those whose iniquities are forgiven and whose sins are covered (which is the robe of righteousness). It doesn't say we are sinless, it says they are covered.

The Bible says that to "do" righteousness is to love our brother. Then I went on to think that to "be" righteous is to love ourselves. Because we can't love our brother until we love ourselves. (Matthew 22:40) When we love our brother we are "doing" righteousness and when we love ourselves it's because we have received the complete works of Christ within our own lives to forgive ourselves and "be" righteous. We cannot forgive ourselves or love ourselves if we haven't received Christ's sacrifice for our sins and received the forgiveness and love personally.

I believe many are still under guilt and condemnation, cannot forgive themselves, I believe it's because they have not applied forgiveness to their own sins through Jesus. In Christ means to believe that Christ's work on the cross is finished. Jesus even said, "It is finished." What is "it?" Love perfected in His sacrifice. We are completed when we receive what Jesus did for us. If someone is "free" it's because they have applied the forgiveness to their lives Jesus came to give. To be free means to be free from the bondage and control of sin. We are free from the law of sin and death (Romans 8:2).

Abraham believed and it was counted to him for righteousness. (Romans 4:3) What did he believe? He believed God justifies the ungodly. In other words, he believed that God forgives sins (Romans 4:5).

Nothing we "do" can "make" us righteous. Even loving our brother doesn't "make" us righteous. We need to believe we are righteous before we can "do" righteously. So the first thing to "do" is receive the completed works of Christ once and for all, which is forgiveness for our sins of yesterday, today and tomorrow. And then pray God give you a revelation on righteousness.

Romans 3:21-31 says that Righteousness means to believe that we have been redeemed by the sacrifice Jesus paid on the cross. BELIEVE and RECEIVE. Believe what He did, then apply it to our own lives by faith through the power of the Holy Ghost.

Note: I know I keep repeating myself, but this is one principle that needs repeating over and over. For me, I had a hard time understanding the Righteousness of God in Christ Jesus, and if you are anything like me, it takes going over many times.

Jesus said to the scribes, "You must eat of my flesh and drink of my blood to be part of me." That offended them. But this is true. We are "in" Christ when we understand what it means to eat His flesh and drink his blood. I'm not a scholar in this, but God has given me understanding through the Holy Ghost. This simply put means that when we partake in remembrance of Him during communion, our faith is being worked. Eating His flesh means that we are healed, drinking his blood means that we are forgiven. Healing and forgiveness go hand in hand. This helps me believe even more what I teach about health and sin. Even this scripture depicts it. We are healed and we are forgiven when we are "in" Him. But then why are we still sick?

Because not only do you need to "know" this truth, you need to believe and receive it. That's the hard part. But with God all things are possible. He will help you believe this and receive this. But He has to work through his Holy Ghost to teach you how.

Righteousness and doing things right are not the same. The Bible says to "do" what God has instructed in the Word. If you do it, are you righteous? Yes. If you don't do it are you righteous? Yes. Our action does not dictate our righteousness. However, when we live after the righteous one and believe all I have shared, then your actions naturally follows. "Doing" and "being" are not the same thing. That's why so many Christians are sad, they are mad at themselves because they just can't seem to do everything right. They feel guilty and bad all the time. It's because they don't realize that even in their sin and mistakes, they are still "righteous." Remember, the robe of righteousness covers them all, doesn't remove them! "While we were yet sinners, Christ died for us."

Trying to be good all the time will cause an individual stress. See, right acts follow those who believe they are righteous. If we "try" being good, we are in works of the flesh and destined for failure.

This is a prayer for you to speak to the Lord. It's only a sample, you can say your own prayer, but this helps you establish the righteousness in you once and for all.

"Father, I need a deeper revelation on righteousness. Open my eyes to the truth about it. Help me to see that righteousness is not outward things I do or don't do, but the inner heart of believing. I am righteous right now. Help me gain understanding Lord. Help me to remember that I am in you every day of my life. And when I slip up or forget, or act unseemly, let me remember that I have Jesus as my Advocate and Savior to forgive me and restore me to you. Father, help me to see that. I don't even have to try to be "in" you because receiving Christ places me in the "in" crowd automatically! Help me to simply receive the righteousness of Christ right now, not because of what I've done, but because of what you've done. In Jesus name, Amen."

In reading scriptures, Jesus could speak a word, and it was done. Why? Because he KNEW who He was! He knew He was the Son of God and was given all power and authority. Did you know you have the same ability as a believer? Someone who has truly accepted what Christ did on the cross has these same abilities? But why don't we? Because we don't have a revelation on the "Righteousness of God in Christ Jesus."

We need a revelation on the "power of Jesus' resurrection" (Philippians 3:10). What does it mean to Know Him and the POWER of His resurrection? It means knowing Him - all of Him. God the Father, God the Son, and the POWER of His resurrection is the Holy Ghost! We need to get a deep understanding of who is living in us, and what power He has - that it was the same Spirit that raised Jesus from the dead!

Do you feel dead, lifeless and/or depressed? Then you have no clue what that power is to you. And the Bible is very clear that only what you believe shall come unto you! And many are in this situation because they have lost hope. That hope needs to be restored. Hosea 4:6 says, "My people perish for lack of knowledge"

Once you get a deep down revelation on God's love in your life, it will also help you understand what being righteous is all about, then you will be able to see the "power of His resurrection" at work in your life! But as said before, the foundation HAS to be laid! First things first, then the other "knowing" comes.

See we all want to "know" everything. The need to know came from Eve. She wanted to "know" both good and evil, that is why she took of the tree of knowledge. She wanted to know. So now we have been cursed with that, but it can be broken. You can turn your desire of "knowing" to knowing the things I'm talking about. Not knowing why the neighbor has been gone three weeks, or why your kids haven't called, or why your husband does what he does... those aren't the kinds of things God talks about when He wants you "know." Because I find that when we try to know those things, that comes from our need to control. The need to "know" all things borders on witchcraft. Think about that.

So how do you gain the righteousness I'm talking about?

- Recognize you are not righteous in and of yourself. When we think we have it all together, that is "self-righteousness."

- By applying God's righteousness to your life by accepting the forgiveness of your own sins, you will begin to understand. You can also study the word "righteousness" by getting out a concordance and looking up the word "righteousness" in the Bible. There are 40 books listing this Word, it appears you have your homework assignment.

- As you find each word and read it in context (read all the scriptures before and after it), ask God to give you insight and understanding on what it means for you and your life. We need to understand what God says about it.

❏ Then begin praying and thanking God for His Righteousness living within you. Thank Him for all the attributes you see in Him, because they too are in you! Ask God to help you believe they are in you, because as you have believed, will be done unto you!

Peace

Take Your Peace! Peacemakers shall be called the children of God (Matthew 5:9)

How many of us don't have peace? I've heard people say, "I just want peace of mind." The same is true for those who want stability. I had a friend tell me once that she would pay a million dollars for stability. *"A double-minded man is unstable in all his ways"* (James 1).

Double-mindedness is our own thoughts against God's thoughts. Peace starts in what we are thinking. If we are in constant array of doubt, belief, doubt, belief, this is double-mindedness. The Bible tells us to be of a singleness of mind, having the mind of Christ.

Peace and righteousness go hand in hand. You cannot have peace without righteousness. *"The Kingdom of God is not meat and drink but righteousness, peace and joy in the Holy Ghost"* (Romans 14:17).

Peacemakers shall be called the children of God (Matthew 5:9) We are Sanctified by truth (John 17:17) We are Sanctified wholly (Psalm 103:3).

When Jesus left this planet, He left saying, *"My peace I leave with you, not as the world gives, give I unto you"* (John 14:27).

That seems pretty clear, but what do we do? We go around trying to fix everyone and everything around us so we can have some peace. That's not what Jesus came to bring. He said he didn't come to bring peace but a sword (Matthew 10:34). As you continue reading vs. 35, it explains what that sword is. It's having a right relationship with our family members, and with Him. So again, we go back to having a right relationship with others through forgiveness and love.

So how do you get the kind of peace Jesus is talking about? The Bible says that Jesus is our peace. Jesus represents a sound mind. Jesus represents the Word of Truth. The Bible tells us that we already have the mind of Christ. (Philippians 2:5) It doesn't say, we are to have it, it says we HAVE it! And when we have this mind, renewing it daily as the Bible teaches, we will find the peace that Jesus came to give. We have the mind of Christ when we "believe" we have the mind of Christ. We can also say the same about righteousness, we have righteousness when we believe we have it. It's very clear that we can only "have " what we believe. It can be there, it can sit right in front of us, but until we believe and receive it, it's nothing. (To have is to receive.)

Peace comes by getting the bad thinking out of our minds. I know that I have peace when my mind is at peace. Things can be falling apart around me, but if my mind is at peace, then it doesn't matter what is going on around me. But the only way my mind can have peace is to get the truth in there so that the lies are cast out. That is why we need to renew our minds every day. Junk tries to get in every single day, and if we go on too long, those thoughts can take over. That is why it is critical to keep our "minds on Him." When we do that, He keeps us in "perfect peace" (Isaiah 26:3).

And as we get the Word into our hearts, it begins to work into our lives resulting in "doing" rightly, "having" peace, and all the blessings that you desire.

The Bible tells us to put on the "shoes of peace." We put on peace by walking in truth. The truth is to heed what the Word says, and the scripture of all scriptures is Matthew 22:38-40. If we "obey" this scripture, we are putting on peace! And again, we cannot obey anything until we know the person we want to obey - as described in the session on "God's love."

I don't believe you can get in a prayer line and have peace placed on you. Peace comes when we pursue it. No one else can do it. And it's God's peace and His peace alone that has to dwell in you. We gain His peace by building our relationship with Him. Peace comes when we have righteousness. Peace comes when we trust and believe God loves us. Peace comes when we have patience, because we trust and believe God for everything in our lives.

Did you know that patience brings peace? I know that isn't what you may have wanted to hear. But there are scriptures that support what I am saying. Look them up for yourself:

Romans 5:2-5, Romans 15:4, 2 Corinthians 6:4, I Thessalonians 1:3, 2 Thessalonians 1:4, I Timothy 6:11, Hebrews 6:12 (in this particular one, it says through faith and patience you shall inherit the promises of God), Hebrews 10:36, and Revelation 14:12.

The last one – Revelation 14:12 - is the one I was wanting to get at, yet read them all they will help you greatly. It says, "Here is the patience of the saints; here are they that keep the commandments of God and the faith of Jesus." Those who have patience will keep the commandments of God. When we keep His commandments, we stay in peace. When you have the patience of God, you will overcome the devil.

But you need to remember the BIGGEST thing that we as Christians forget! When (not if) we don't keep the commandments, we need to confess our sins and receive forgiveness immediately. That way we stay in obedience at all times. It's not that we do everything right all the time, it's when we do something wrong we stay in right standing with God because we have applied the sacrifice Jesus gave for our sins! That is why there is a scripture that says we no longer sin. It's not that we are not sinners; it's that when we sin, we are immediately purified through receiving forgiveness, and no longer habitually sinning.

Peace and patience go hand in hand. If you don't have patience, you don't have peace. And if you recall, patience is a love virtue! As a matter of fact, if you read each virtue, patience is within each one. In order to have long suffering, you have to have patience to do so. In order to not be easily provoked, you have to have patience to not be provoked. Patience is weaved within First Corinthians 13. In some translations, the first virtue says that Love is patient. James 1:3-4 "Let patience have her perfect work, that you may be perfect and entire wanting nothing." If any of you lack peace, if any of you have wants, if anyone is discontented, then you probably don't have patience.

Let me explain with my seat belt story: I find that when I don't put on my seat belt, I am always watching for the highway patrol. So when I do see one, I'll put it on quickly. It only causes me to be edgy and anxious while driving. But on the other hand, when I simply put it on when I get into the car, I drive in peace. I'm not worried if a highway patrol pulls up next to me, because I've "obeyed" the law.

Peace comes with obedience to the ordinances of man (1 Peter 2:13) and obedience to the royal law found in James 2:8. We are to love one another and Matthew 22:38-40, we will be in obedience! As we take God at His Word and "do" what He asks, righteousness, peace and joy will come. But again, when we mess up, we are to go immediately to God and confess so that we stay clean before our Lord.

Then finally, an area that will produce peace is walking in truth. By staying truthful we won't have to remember what lie we spoke. By staying in truth, you please God. "I have no greater joy than to know that my children walk in truth" (3 John 1:4). You want to live in Righteousness, Peace and Joy? Then speak the truth with all men at all times (Ephesians 4:25).

Below lists some Scriptures to help you on your journey:

(John 14:27) Jesus came to give us peace, not as the world gives though. He came to give us peace within our hearts and minds.

(Isaiah 26:3) Perfect peace is for those whose mind is stayed on Him BECAUSE we trust Him. Many forget to read the rest of that scripture that says, a person who is in peace has their mind on God, but ALSO trusts Him. We cannot have peace without trusting the peace giver! It's like trying to get something from someone you are mad at. It won't work.

(Philippians 4:6-7) *"Be careful for nothing, but in every thing by prayer and supplication with thanksgiving let your request be made know unto God, and the peace of God which passes all understanding shall keep your hearts and minds through Christ Jesus."*

It goes on to say what we should think of. "Whatsoever things are true, honest, just, pure, lovely, good report, any virtue in it, if there be any praise, think on these things." (Boy that leaves a lot out of the things we DO think of!)

By thinking the way God thinks, will produce peace. My job as a minister is to help you "think" like God thinks. What a difference this would make in our lives if we did that. We wouldn't worry, we wouldn't fret and we wouldn't get anxious or frustrated, because we would "know" that God is working things out for good.

(Hebrews 12:14) Follow peace with all men, and holiness, without which no man shall see the Lord. (This looks like a criterion to see God)

(Zechariah 8:16-17) Speak the truth, exercise judgment that brings peace. If you are in fear, you will not have peace.

(Proverbs 2:1-5) Knowledge is very vital in living in peace. We are told in proverbs over and over that we are to seek knowledge, but with all our getting, get understanding. (I believe knowledge and understanding is breeding ground for peace to come.)

(Acts 2:25) David took his peace - always putting God before him caused him to be able to do this.

(Romans 26:3) To be carnally minded is death, but to be spiritually minded is life and peace.

(Revelations 3:10) Because you have kept the word of my patience, I also will keep thee from the hour of temptation, which shall come up on all the world to try them that dwell on the earth.

(Revelations 3:12) Behold I come quickly, hold that fast which you have, that no man take thy crown (patience). If you read the verses above, "thy crown" is patience. How many times have you heard, "I lost my patience again." That is what this is talking about. Patience IS peace.

(Isaiah 57:21) There is no peace for the wicked. Who is wicked? A person with an unbelieving heart (Hebrews 3:12). Do you have peace? If not, I would look closer at your heart to see if you are in unbelief and doubt?

Abiding in God Results in Peace, Peace creates Joy

(Psalm 91:1) He that dwells in the secret place of the most high shall abide under the shadow of the almighty. (And rest of the chapter)

(John 15:7) If ye abide in my and my words abide in you, ask what you will and it shall be done.

(James 4:8) Draw nigh to God and He will draw nigh to you, cleanse your hands ye sinners; and purify your hearts ye double-minded.

(Ephesians 2:14-16) Peace comes from Jesus, He reconciled us to our Father thereby making peace.

(Proverbs 3:1-8) Keep the commandments... for long life and peace shall be added to you.

What are the commandments of God? Jesus summed it up in Matthew 22:38-40. "We are to love the Lord our God with all our heart, soul and mind, and love our neighbor as ourselves."

(2 Timothy 2:24-26) A servant (teacher, minister) of the Lord must not strive,

but apt to teach, patient... so that those we instruct will recover themselves from the snare of the devil.

(Mark 5:34) Daughter, thy faith has made thee whole, go in peace, and be whole of thy plague." Peace comes when we are healed, healing comes by faith, faith is believing, believing brings peace.

(James 3:17) But the wisdom that is from above is first pure, then peaceable, gentle and easy to be entreated, full of mercy and good fruits, without partiality, and without hypocrisy. And the fruit of righteousness is sown in peace of them that make peace.

(Isaiah 54:14) In righteousness shalt thou be established: thou shalt be far from oppression; for thou shalt not fear: and from terror; for it shall not come near thee." Righteousness causes all fear to go!

Now we are getting down to the nitty-gritty. A person who has no peace or patience more than likely doesn't have a revelation about the Righteousness of Christ. It appears that a person who has peace, is walking in righteousness.

Okay, now this is the interesting part. I have found, in my own life, that until I trusted God, I had a hard time with peace and patience. Perhaps you say you do trust God yet you don't have peace. Let's take a deeper look within.

❑ Do you have fear?

❑ Do you doubt?

❑ Do you have any unbelief?

❑ Are you frustrated and confused at times?

❑ Are you stressed?

❑ Do you ask God "why " all the time?

❑ Do you lose your temper easily?

❑ Are you easily provoked to anger?

❑ Do you compare your life to other Christians?

Do the things listed produce peace? Not hardly. We need to be honest with ourselves. Because if you are any of these things (or more) then it is more than likely that you may not trust God.

(Isaiah 26:3) *"Thou wilt keep him in perfect peace whose mind is stayed on thee, BECAUSE he trusteth in thee."* This is a powerful scripture, so let's look at it closely.

God keeps us in peace; we don't keep ourselves. Scripture says, "He will keep us in perfect peace when our mind is on Him." We don't keep ourselves in peace, He does it when we do our part. As a matter of fact, if we do anything, we are to pursue it. We pursue it by keeping our mind on Him! He does the rest. But, we can't really keep our minds on Him as long as our minds are filled with other things that are robbing us of peace. And the reason we cannot keep our mind on Him is that we don't really "know" Him. We don't really "know" that He is with us in every breath we take, every move we make and that He's ever watchful of us. We don't really know His character, one of love and peace and compassion. Some still see God as very mean. We cannot trust someone we don't know. We cannot walk in righteousness if we don't really know the "righteous" One.

I'm not talking about Salvation, but perhaps I should, because a person who is saved has believed on the one who sent Jesus. Hebrews says, "We must first believe that He is..." First things first. Since I had a problem with doubt and unbelief. What I mean is that I would believe God was there in some of my situations, but not in all. I could believe God to get me up in the morning, but I couldn't believe Him to pay my bills. So then I took it upon myself to "do" something because answers weren't coming from God quick enough, or it seemed, not at all. This is where doubt sets in. We have to believe He is there ALL THE TIME, and He is good ALL THE TIME. We do this by getting a revelation on His Love, His Righteousness, and His Joy. "The Kingdom of God is not meat and drink (outer condition) but Righteousness, peace and Joy in the Holy Ghost" (Romans 14).

So far we have recognized some things about our own heart condition that pertains to peace, patience and righteousness describing all the ingredients for living the abundant life that is spoken of in the Word.

We do have a part to play here. Patience comes by trials. Patience produces peace. Peace results in righteousness. It all works together and not one without the other for completeness in God.

Jesus IS our peace. "My peace I leave with you, not as the world gives, give I unto you." He bequeathed us His peace. It's yours for the taking.

Take Your Peace! Nothing outside of you will give you peace. "Outside" peace is what the world wants to see. All beauty queens are asked what they would like to see in the world, and their candid answers are "World peace." When Jesus came, He didn't come to bring peace (worldly kind) but a sword (inner peace). Peace comes from your own thoughts. But know that with peace come trials of patience because they work together. By working together will result in you having contentment in all things. No stress, no worry, no anxiety ONLY PEACE. The kind that no matter what is going on around you, you cannot get upset.

If you'll notice, peace was something everyone needed to pursue. If you look in the Bible, many greetings and departures address this. For example, ending in the book of 2 Thessalonians says, "now the Lord of peace Himself give you peace always by all means." And the greeting in 1 Timothy:2 says, "Unto Timothy, my own son in the faith, grace, mercy and peace from God our Father and Jesus Christ our Lord." It's throughout the whole Bible! There is a reason we all need to remember to "take our peace."

Ministry

If you are willing to pursue peace, then follow along with this prayer:

"Father, I am not walking in peace like I want to. I know that I have caused much of my own upset by not trusting you. I confess my lack of patience Father. I confess my fear of desiring patience because I know that everyone knows what happens when we ask for patience! But, I will not fear, and I ask you now for more patience. I confess my distrust and my guilt. Forgive me for not trusting you in all things. Help me to trust you Father. Help me to believe you. Help me to know you. Help me to gain more understanding on the way you think. I know that to think like you, and the things you want me to think about will produce peace. Help me to get a revelation on your Love for me. Help me to receive your love every single day, no matter what I have done. Help me to get a revelation on Righteousness. That to be righteous is to believe. Help me to pursue peace and not fear having to go through trials for patience that will bring peace. I confess my doubt and unbelief. I confess my fear of what I may need to experience to attain peace. I am determined to hope in You Lord. Help me to put on my shoes of peace daily, and walk the talk, dying to myself daily that produces patience, which results in peace and relationship with you and with others. I receive healing and restoration now and give you permission to work things out in my life that causes patience to be tried, so that it produces peace. Help me to trust you more every day, help me to believe you have my best in mind, every day. In Jesus name, Amen."

Along with pursuing peace; be sure to continue forgiving. Forgiving keeps the way open for God to pour more peace and love into your life. Forgiving causes us to walk "peaceably with all men" as the scripture tells us to do. We don't have to "try" to be in peace, we will just "be" in peace.

CHAPTER SEVENTEEN

The Gate

The reason I call this "The Gate" is that it describes the hard times we've had to go through. Things like dealing with a person that is hard to get along with. Having to ask for forgiveness from someone you would rather not. Facing ramifications of our actions. Living through a hard and traumatic experience. The gate is a place of discomfort, but is quite necessary for our healing and growth in the Lord.

(Matthew 8:13-14) *"Enter ye at the strait gate, for wide is the gate, and broad is the way that leads to destruction, and many there be which go in there: because strait is the gate, and narrow is the way, which lead unto life, and few there be that find it."*

For years I thought that it said a wide "road," but it says a wide gate! If you take a look at a gate, you will notice it's not very wide at all. There is a hinge and it swings back and forth and normally big enough as an extra large doorway. So keeping that in mind, we need to understand that there are things we go through that we can't take with us through that gate. There's only enough room for you! So in my experience and through revelation of the Holy Ghost, He showed me that the gate is a place of purging. We can only take through the gate those things that are of him, all other stuff has to go, and that's when it gets uncomfortable. We start to squirm as we approach that "thing" (the gate) we have to do, and some never go through the gate but turn back and stay stuck where they are and its all because of emotional pain of some kind.

What's happening is that when you begin to approach the gate, all kinds of stuff that is inside you begins to surface, such as anger, resentment, fear, doubt, distrust, the "what if's," hate, confusion, feelings of unworthiness, failure, what will they think are thoughts that are causing the pain. Those are the things that have to go BEFORE you can get through the gate! So as you approach these feelings (sins) start to intensify, and you start to feel really uncomfortable. But good news... this a ALL GOOD! It means God is exposing things that you need to take responsibility for, confess and repent! See, these aren't "feelings" that come from an outside source they are coming from within. When we have to face a hard thing, it's helping us see what we are made of. It's like squeezing a lemon, when you are squeezed what comes out? Or do you want to stay in your stuff and not go through because it hurts too much.

The hurt is the Holy Ghost cutting between soul and spirit! Let Him do the work in you because that's what will make you free.

For example, let's say you have to face an audience because you have a big presentation to do. Before getting up there, you get a bit apprehensive, fearful, uncertain, but you still do the presentation. Once it's over, peace is restored, right? We come into the "liberty and freedom." But let's say at the last minute you said, "Oh, I can't go out there, someone else is going to have to do it." You leave the office and go sit in your car. You did not pass through the gate! And guess what, you have robbed yourself from a blessing and even feel guilty or ashamed. Or how about things like facing a person you need to in order to clear up a misunderstanding, or facing a fear that you have like flying, dentists, or traveling. Whatever the issue is you need to go through is "the *Gate*."

People shy away from discomfort and unfortunately don't realize they are losing a blessing. The gate that is straight and wide are individuals who choose the easier more comfortable way. However, don't know that they are putting themselves more and more in bondage to whatever they are shying from. Fear is the main reason people don't enter the narrow gate. The narrow gate only has enough room for you to go through. If we are carrying unforgiveness, bitterness, hurts, that we can't seem to let go of, we won't be able to "fit" through the narrow gate. And if we do attempt to go through the gate, we start feeling uncomfortable. That uncomfortable feeling is God pulling away the chaff from you, which can be painful, so you can "fit" through the straight gate and narrow way. But many, when they start to feel any discomfort or "emotional" pain, they turn back and stay in that "wide" area.

Many have used this scripture when teaching about salvation, but this scripture pertains to our every day life as a Christian. Now that you understand what is happening in your life when things become hard, if you choose to plow through, you will obtain your blessing.

So how do we do this? First of all recognize that fear is working at preventing you from entering that straight gate! Now that you know this is a good thing not an attack from the devil, you can go through and be victorious. Realize that the pain you will experience is only emotional. Then with eyes facing forward, holding onto the Word of God that He is with you "through" the fire, and plowing on ahead taking that "thing" head on. Hold onto the legs of your kitchen table if you have to so that you don't turn and run, you will experience the discomfort for a brief second, then you will pass on through that gate, and enter into "freedom and liberty."

Yes, it's that simple. The hard part is not knowing what is happening you to as these feelings start to emerge. But now that you know, it's God wanting to pull off the "stuff" that is hindering your walk, you can now go through with courage and boldness. (Hebrews 4:16)

As you face each thing in your life with this kind of insight, you will become freer and freer. You will gain confidence in God, peace, and able to help others go through their "gate." This will help increase your faith so as other "gates" come into your life, you can go through with ease and without fear of what is happening. It's always those first few at first that are hard because no one every taught you it's okay to "feel" uncomfortable.

To put in an extra word here. It's not always an attack from the devil when you begin to feel uncomfortable about something. Truly, it's God letting something surface that you need to see so that it can be purged out of you.

Many of whom I teach this to have said that it is a "squeezy point" for them. They actually "feel" being squeezed. They know it's not fun but when the commit themselves to go through, it's been a tremendous release for them.

I know that this will be true for each of you who decide to conquer your fears or whatever is hindering your walk. Take the Word with you and face each situation. Sure, it may not be a pleasant experience at the time, but the wonderful thing about it, is that once you have gone through that specific gate, you never have to go through it again, just new ones.

So once you have passed through that gate you enter into a place that is refreshing, peaceful and victorious. You feel like shouting and dancing and singing... well, um... some of you anyway, the rest just feel better. However, something to keep in mind, just around the corner is another gate with an entirely different issue. And each gate you pass through brings you into more peace and freedom. You will begin to hear God clearer, your time with Him will be more personal, things will be different.

Door of Entry:

Let me share a story that you may have already heard before, but it helps bring this section of teaching to a point.

My husband was in Vietnam and had experienced lots of shell fire. Some of the metal from the bombs penetrated into his body. Upon coming back to the U.S. he still carried this shrapnel in his body. From time to time, a piece would start to work its way back out of his skin. He would see something protruding out of his arm and not sure what it was, at first. So would try to put ointment on it to get it to go away. But it only got bigger and bigger. Until one day he had to go to the Dr. and found that a piece of metal was trying to come out. *It was trying to come out the same place it went in.* So the doctor removed it. By then, it was all pussy, festering, and hurt a bit as it was being removed and stitches were added to sew up the hole. The Lord used this as an example of what I'm sharing here.

That door - the place where the shrapnel went it, was painful for Tom. Same as a hurt, issue, fear that enters our heart. Sometimes we felt it, sometimes we didn't. But it's there nonetheless. But then, as the shrapnel in Tom's body was coming out, it came out with a little puss, festering, and some pain. Same as with what we are being purged from. The pain may come, a little crying, a little pain, but once it's out, it's OUT! It is no longer in you to hurt you or cause you discomfort any longer. Then God can mend the hurt and pain of your heart from that situation, just as the doctor stitched up the hole in Tom's arm from the shrapnel never to go back in again.

This is a tremendous revelation teaching and I pray that you receive this with complete understanding. Understanding why things hurt so much, why things are happening to you that you don't understand. It's that God's whole purpose is to get you through those "door points" (Gate) to get rid of those things that are weighing you down and preventing you from living the life He destines you to live! (Hebrews 12:1)

As we read on in Hebrews 12:2, this is a perfect example of Jesus entering an uncomfortable place (the *Gate)*, but if He didn't we would never be saved! *"Looking unto Jesus the author and finisher of our faith; who for the joy that was set before him endured the cross, despising the shame, and is set down at the right hand of the throne of God."*

In this scripture, Jesus saw the other side of that "squeezy point." He saw the joy that was set before Him, but also knew in order to get there he would have to "suffer." So He "endured" the cross, despising shame (which was the *gate*), and is now sitting at God's side, which is the liberty and freedom He attained because He "went through."

We are no greater than our master, what He went through, it is certain we'll get to experience some of the same things (Matthew 10:24; Hebrews 4:15).

Be at peace when "fiery trials" come your way, they are there for you to exercise your patience, faith, trust and hope in God (1 Peter 4:12).

Tests and trials will come to all - this is a promise! But these tests and trials are for good, they work the truth in us and work the junk out of us. When you get bent out of shape, that shows you what you are truly made of. We want to get to the place that when things happen, we stay in peace!

1 Peter 4:12: *"Beloved, think it not strange concerning the fiery trial which is to try you as though some strange thing happened unto you; but rejoice inasmuch as ye are partakers of Christ's sufferings; that, when his glory shall be revealed, you may be glad also with exceeding joy."*

The trying of your faith works patience.... patience produces peace (James chapter 1). Isn't that what we all want? More peace? Medically proven - when we are at peace our bodies work at full optimum!

❑ Tests are used to see if you are going to trust God and love Him no matter what. I see it as being on a 100 year job interview. The whole purpose of this life is to prepare us and set us up for what is coming to this earth and prepare us for the next. This life is a vapor - a short span of time. The real life is the one to come, new heaven and new earth... all these things shall pass away, behold all things will become new. This is a shadow of things to come... so if this is a shadow, wow the things to come must be amazing! (Colossians 2:17; Hebrews 10:1)

❑ Life is like an obstacle course. There are so many things to jump, go through, weather, and the one who wins this "game of life" is the person who stayed in faith. "He who runs the race shall obtain the prize." It doesn't matter if you make it to the finish line just as long as you are in the race.

Ministry Prayer for You to Pray:

"Father I have to admit that I have turned from going through things because it just seemed too hard and painful. I ask you to help me face these things Lord, not turn away, but "go through." I know you are with me, let me not fear the emotional pain that I may experience or fear you cutting away stuff that needs to be cut away from my life. I give you full permission to get rid of anything that hinders my walk, causes me to stay in the wilderness. I want to live in the joy of the Lord, enter Your rest and the abundance You have promised. I know that I have prevented good things from coming into my own life, and now I'm ready to get with the program. Now that I know it's a good thing to be uncomfortable, I will not fear because it's you bringing things up that need to be confessed and purged. I know that by facing it and going through any discomfort will bring me out to the other side, full of liberty and freedom. I choose life Father. Give me strength and boldness to "endure" as Jesus endured. Giving me "staying" power to allow you to do the work in me.

Help me to go through "fiery trials" knowing that I'll come out as gold on the other side. Forgive me for any fear I have had, fear of pain, fear of what others will think, fear of failure, or whatever the fear is. Release me from all fear and fill me with your love and truth. Cleanse me from all the dross that is weighing me down and as you begin working in me, help me to remember the principle of "the gate" so that I won't run away from what I need to go through. I want to go through the narrow gate Lord. I give you all the glory and praise for what you are doing in my life. In Jesus name, Amen."

CHAPTER EIGHTEEN

Spirit of Anger

The Bible teaches that the wrath of man works not the righteousness of God (James 1:20). This is the type of anger that is sin. It depends on the motive of the anger. If you are angry and standing in the gap for others, then this is righteous anger. But if you are angry because of something that happened that affects you personally, then you are in sin.

Don't let the sun go down on your anger. (Ephesians 4:26) Reconcile to each and every person in your daily life so that when you go to bed you go to bed without anger. Anger can cause you to lose sleep, have bad dreams or if not dealt with can cause relationship problems and even health issues.

If you have anger toward another or if you know someone is angry with you, go to them and reconcile before making requests to God or offer anything - even praise! (Matthew 5:24) "Leave there thy gift before the altar, and go thy way; first be reconciled to thy brother, and then come and offer thy gift."

Righteous Anger

So what about anger that is good? Even Jesus got angry at the merchants when he saw them selling and buying goods in the temple. So when is it right for us to get angry? Let's take a look at Nehemiah. He showed righteous anger. He wasn't angry for himself, he was angry at the king for causing the people anguish. He went to the king and represented the people. He didn't get angry because of what he wanted or what he saw that affected him, it's only righteous anger when we are representing others needs. But truthfully, more than not, we get angry because of injustice done to us.

So, if you have the wrong anger, what do you do?

The first thing we do is find out what is behind the anger. Anger is NOT the problem, it's a result of the problem(s). The second thing we do is make a choice today to get rid of anger not co-exist or manage it. Jesus came to eradicate not put a program on it.

There could be circumstances that cause you to become angry, or even anger passed down through your family line.

Anger can be produced because of things happening around us, but the truth is, its not really what is happening around us but what is going on inside of us. Like the teaching called "The Gate" when we are "squeezed' we will see what we are made of. So when things happen, what comes out? One can be anger. And yes, your anger can stem from your ancestor passing it down to you, but you are still responsible for what comes out of you.

The following are areas that can produce anger:

Not feeling loved = (#1 issue behind anger. Fear is the direct opposite of love - and fear is the main root behind anger.)

☐ Anger is a result of not feeling loved. We are angry because we see others being blessed when it should be us being blessed.

☐ Anger is a result of fear that could also produce one or all of the following manifestations:

Feeling ignored	Feeling embarrassed
Self-hatred	Being confused
Being frustrated	Being unnoticed
Feeling rejection	Having been abandoned
Abused	Ashamed
Hatred	Depressed

If you identified one or more of these listed, don't get condemned, count it all joy knowing that what is being revealed are things God wants you to see so He can purge. Take each thing you recognized in yourself before our Father in Heaven and first John one-nine 'em: receive forgiveness, healing and restoration.

Impatience: As described in the "Peace" session, patience brings peace so therefore, impatience doesn't bring peace. What it brings is anger because we don't have peace! People don't want to gain patience because it means they'll be losing something. Impatience is a killer, and will cause us to fall into self-pity, guilt, and shame.

Justice: People want to see justice done for the wrongs done to them. This will keep a person stewing in their juices, resulting in anger and strife. Justice is a killer, and will cause us to fall into self-pity, guilt, jealousy, fear, and comparison.

Betrayal: This causes a lot of anger, but this kind of anger produces "rage" that comes from having been lied to or stolen from. The longer it is in there the harder it is to identify. I shared the story about the rage and anger that I had in the "Abandonment and Rejection session. The rage and anger I had came from a past relationship that popped up 30 years later. But thanks be to God, He freed me.

Jealousy and Envy: This causes much anger. "Why oh Why can't I have what they have?" I'm "doing" all the right things, going to church, etc., yet I'm not being blessed. Coveting other people's stuff falls into this same category. Being discontent also falls into this category. Jealousy causes us to "feel" left out, causes us to be angry about our lives.

Fear: We respond to fear with anger. When we get scared, or abruptly alarmed, the end result, most of the times, is anger.

Unforgiveness: Anger comes when we don't forgive or RECEIVE forgiveness.

Being controlled: Others trying to mold you into what they think you should be and not accepting you as you are.

Ephesians 4:26 says you can be angry if you don't sin. People use this to justify their anger. They tell me it helps them be strong so that others won't step all over them. But in reality, anger is causing people to put up blocks and self-protecting mechanisms instead of relying on God to do that. Anger is a contradiction to God's love. It will block the flow. Nehemiah displayed righteous anger, the kind that is acceptable. He became angry when he saw the injustice done to his people. He went to the king in his anger to defend them. Anger helps us "move" to do something. However, what I find is that most of us are angry because of what has happened to us, not what has happened to others and that is the wrong kind of anger. Even when we are angered because of what happened to another, are we allowing sin to reign?

Romans 12:19 describe anger as wanting revenge. And we know that we are not to revenge anything or anyone.

Addressing generational anger: Anger can also be passed down from the parents to the children. It could go all the way back 10 generations or more. How do you know if this is the case with you? Perhaps it's a reality for all of us who have anger because more than likely some of it was passed on to you. But again, no matter where it came from, we are responsible for our own lives.

To be rid of generational anger, you need to identify which parent or both or grandparents were angry. Were they jealous? Perhaps un-loved? Perhaps impatient? Perhaps victimized? Nehemiah 9:2 says to confess the iniquities of our fathers. So, in doing that, those iniquities will not pass on to the 3rd and 4th generations. You may be that 3rd and 4th generation now! But you can stop that cycle today (Deuteronomy 5:9).

See by identifying our own sins, we are only half way home. By identifying the iniquities of our fathers, we are now digging into the deeper things. Iniquities come partly by unconfessed sins of the Fathers, AND sins we have never dealt with.

Ministry

First of all, I will not send you to anger management classes. This is just a way to "justify" your anger, keep the anger, and go into "works of the flesh." This is all bondage. Jesus came to set us free. He set people free by removing that which was tormenting us.

A note of caution: As you know, when you pray for something, it ends up manifesting. Remember if you pray for patience you get trials. It's the same thing here, so don't be concerned because you are feeling "more angry," because the very thing sometimes manifest before it can come forth. So during this time, I pray God's sovereignty over you.

If you want to be on your way to freedom FROM anger, then pray this prayer and allow God free reign to get the anger out. Remember, it's not the "anger" it's what's behind the anger. When we are angry, we are not believing God loves us enough to take care of our specific situation. We may even be angry at Him! If you find yourself in this situation you will need to repent your blame and accusation as discussed in an earlier teaching.

Ministry Prayer for You To Pray:

"Father, you never tire of me coming to you. You enjoy hearing from me. As a matter of fact, you tell me that you want me to pray without ceasing, so I will take you up on that. You know that I'm dealing with the issues of anger. I know it is not from you. I know that we are to be angry and sin not, but that is hard for me to comprehend, so I choose not to be angry at all and make no excuses for it when I am. I want to be free from anger Lord, it doesn't produce any good fruit. I don't want to go to "anger management" classes, I want to be free from it. I know that I may have other roots behind anger, so help me deal with each one of those things specifically. Help set me free Lord, show me what is causing my anger and help me see each one. If I need to forgive, show me how. If I need to love and accept and have more patience, teach me. I want to be free from all anger. I confess the sin of anger my mother and father had, along with ten generations back. I ask you to forgive them and thereby releasing me and my family from all dis-ease related to it. I know that if I get angry, you are there to forgive. Help me to confess to you each and every time and receive forgiveness quickly for myself and help me to forgive others. Restore peace to my heart Lord, help my unbelief. In Jesus name. Amen."

It's important to go over the session on God's Love, Forgiveness, Fear, and Peace for further study, to get at the roots which result in anger.

CHAPTER NINETEEN

Co-dependency

What is Codependency? The Webster's Dictionary says it perfectly, "A psychological condition or a relationship in which a person is controlled or manipulated by another who is affected with a pathological condition." Pathological means: altered or caused by disease, the structural and functional deviations from the normal that constitute disease. Its deviation from an assumed normal state of something nonliving or nonmaterial.

Soul-ties is not listed in the dictionary, but it means we have tied emotionally to another. Soul-ties can be good or bad. We can have soul mates with our spouse because we have become one flesh. But soul mates and soul-ties are different. Soul-ties are detrimental to a relationship, which allows others to control us. We can even have soul-ties incorrectly with our spouse. How do you know? When they can control you with a word, look or action.

So in layman's terms: To be codependent (or have soul-ties) means we allow someone else (a person who is sick or unstable) to control and manipulate us to do things we would rather not do.

We can be codependent to people we know or with people we don't know. It can be anyone who uses actions, words or gestures to get us to do what they want. We can actually become codependent to about anyone and any thing.

Let me share some examples:

We hear of codependency with people who are addicts to alcohol and drugs. People who are co-dependent tend to protect, lie, and enable the one to stay in their junk by not being honest and truthful with them or those around them. We often take on the responsibility of these individuals to clean them up, but what we are doing is taking on their "junk" which causes emotional destruction in our own lives.

Codependency can also be with people you don't know. For example, we can become codependent when we drive our cars. If you see someone behind you tailgating, some of us would respond to that. Either we will go faster or slow down. Either way, their actions caused us to respond incorrectly. We've made soul-ties or became codependent to them. To not be codependent is to allow others the freedom to do whatever they want without it affecting us to make decisions one way or another. (If we respond in retaliation, we took the bait, and now we've become codependent to that person.)

I suppose you can think of many areas in your life where you have codependency. I had it with my son. I felt responsible for his happiness and was trying to do everything in my power to make him happy. However, it didn't work at all. It only caused more hurt and frustration and even pushed him away further. I'm no longer co-dependent with my son. He has a life to live.

Decisions to make, and results to bear. My job in anyone's life is to pray that God lead and direct them in all truth. My job is to love people regardless of their sin or sins toward me, or even their thoughts toward me. My job is to forgive all those who offend. My job is to have compassion to all men, with patience and long-suffering.

Codependency does not do this, it takes on this person's "stuff" for themselves and it becomes theirs. We stay connected emotionally to a person, even when they are long gone. Sometimes we may think of them and feel bad, angry, controlled, hurt, fearful and bitter. We are still "tied" to them emotionally.

So what is the answer? We need to break the soul-ties or codependency. It doesn't mean that we will not have the person in our lives any more. It means we will not allow them to control us any more. Isn't that freedom? And you do this by forgiving them from your heart.

When you are finally free, you can actually forget to call someone on their birthday and not feel "guilty" or feel "bad" that you didn't call them.

Question: Can you think of anyone you have soul-ties or co-dependency with? Make a list of them.

How to break the ties:

- ❏ If you had at least one name, it's for certain you are tied to them emotionally.

- ❏ Pray God break the codependency and soul ties off you in Jesus name.

- ❏ Pray God replace it with love and peace and dependency on you, no other, and restore the relationship correctly.

- ❏ Forgive the person you are feeling co-dependent toward, and receive forgiveness for your own part in it. Be sure to forgive from your heart - refer back to the forgiveness teaching if needed to forgive from your heart.

- ❏ Then cast OUT the spirit of control, manipulation and defilement. Ask for God's love to fill you with His love and truth, and release you from any codependency and soul-ties.

Ministry Prayer For You:

"Father, this dear saint (and yes, you are a saint) and I come before you recognizing the need to sever all wrong soul-ties. We are not to be controlled by another's actions, facial expressions, words, or manipulations. We desire to respond to individuals the way you desire us to, not because of codependency. So Father, I break my soul-ties with _____ (name them) and ask you to restore our relationship properly. I release them and I ask you to release me from them as well. They are free to be and do all they desire, hope or ask for, just as I do. Help us to be free from each other's control and manipulation. I break the ties now in Jesus name. I thank you for forgiving me, I forgive them. I thank you for restoration and healing in my heart. I thank you for giving me a healthy attitude toward them. I ask you to help me have proper love and compassion toward this person, but no longer take on their "junk" to cause me to respond in a way they desire. I want to respond in your way Lord, yours and yours alone. I thank you for showing this to me. Help me to continue to forgive those who tend to control and manipulate me, this way I will remain free from wrong soul-ties. Thank you for your love, I ask you to flood my heart right now with love and compassion for them and for myself. I forgive myself now in Jesus name for allowing things to have gone on so long. But I receive forgiveness today. I give you all the praise. In Jesus' name, Amen."

Further Resources:

Pick up my book called "Do You Have an ImBIBLICAL Cord?" It goes into greater detail on this topic and many have found freedom!

CHAPTER TWENTY

Frustration

Galatians 2:21 *I do not frustrate the grace of God: for if righteousness come by the law, then Christ is dead in vain.*

Frustration comes when we try to keep some sort of law. It's trying to do something we simply aren't able to do. It's not that we haven't tried, it's that we are trying to "do" something only God can do. We cannot keep the law, it is not in us, that is why God sent Jesus to "fulfill" the law for us. And from my own experience, those who try to keep the law may not just be about the law of God, but their own laws they have made and are putting on others and themselves to keep. See, when we become Christians we have a desire to perfect. Perfectionism causes frustration because we can never be perfect. We have the desire to be perfect because the Bible continually talks of being perfected in Christ. The problem is, we forget about the "IN" Christ part and try to be perfect in our own strength.

If we look at the things that frustrate us, it always has to do with someone not doing what we want them to do. That even includes ourselves. Not being "perfect" the way we think "perfection" is. So let's take a minute and see what the Bible says.

Romans 13:10 *"Love worketh no ill to his neighbor: therefore love is the fulfilling of the law."*

Galatians 5:14 *"For all the law is fulfilled in one word, even in this; Thou shalt love thy neighbor as thyself."*

Simply put, to be perfect is to love. When you love, frustration is nowhere to be found because love is tolerant, forgiving, kind, and affectionate one to another.

Let's look at an example of a situation that manifests frustration. Let's say that you want your kids to clean their room. You have harped and harped and you cannot get them to do it but only once in awhile. You are totally frustrated at them. The truth here is that you are trying to get someone to do something, trying to make someone conform, instead of giving that person/situation to God for Him to do His will in their lives as with this situation. We are to train up a child in the way he should go. We aren't to make the child do things that we want them to do, but to train them in the things of the Lord like truth, honesty, forgiveness, courage, fearlessness, etc. Let's say they don't like cleaning their room. Just shut the door. Stop fussing over that "one" thing about your kids. Let them be free to make decisions. You can guide and direct, but we need to allow them the freedom to make decisions. This will reduce your stress and frustration and also the kid's. Because truthfully, by trying to "get" them to do things you are pushing them out even farther. I found that when we release them to be, they will do the very thing you wanted from them in the first place.

They'll do it now because they want to. I'm not saying you don't enforce rules in your home, but if you want to see things turn around, give them some space.

I know some parents who told me that when they asked their kids to clean their room up, they would respond with "I did." Some kids think that what they are doing is perfect, but you don't think so. So this may cause a child to strive to be perfect but can never make that mark because whatever they do will never be good enough — for you. This causes kids to stop trying. The more we push as parents, the more they fight back, or digress. We are to walk peaceably among all men. That even means our children.

There is a scripture that says not to provoke your children to anger it can result in the child being discouraged (Colossians 3:21). Discouragement causes depression, self-hatred, hopelessness, rebellion can cause physical and emotional problems.

Disciplining a child is different than what I'm talking about. But even in discipline, take these things into consideration. We discipline a child so that they don't do the thing they just did that caused them to be disciplined. But be careful that you aren't disciplining them for not being "you." What are the things we are to train the children in? Yours are the things of God?

I don't know why I began talking about children, but I supposed someone needed to hear this.

Other forms of frustration are that things just go wrong. You may have lots of errands to run and all day one thing after another keeps getting in the way. Frustration begins to get the better of you.

All frustration comes as a result of trying to do what YOU think you need to be doing to be okay. But the truth is, if we truly trusted and believed God we would never get frustrated because we would know that whatever is happening at the moment. God is in complete control and nothing is a surprise to Him. We can trust in that, knowing God knows everything and is working things out regardless of what it seems like. We can stop struggling with things and we can rest in that "knowing."

As said earlier, by trying to keep the law that we put on ourselves, we are causing most of our own frustration. Jesus came to fulfill the law so we don't have to put the law upon ourselves. And I believe that we put laws on ourselves to be more "perfect" so that we'll be right with God. The truth is you ARE right with God whether or not you keep the laws. As long as you are hid in Christ (have Him as Lord and accept His sacrifice for sins on the cross). So when we don't do something we think we should do, we're still okay. We can still go on without any frustration. We make amends, do what we are lead to do by the Holy Ghost for restoration or whatever the case may be, and move on.

Others who push out ahead of God also get frustrated. Trying to do what only God can do. Or when we see something that someone else is supposed to be doing, but they don't, we find ourselves wanting to do it for them. Yet, in most cases it's things that we can't do. For example: If you want someone in your family to change in an area but you don't see it happening, you can get frustrated with that person because they aren't changing according to your ideals and timing. We are then crossing over into the Holy Ghost's job and also bordering on control and manipulation, which is a form of witchcraft. I'm not saying you are a witch, but what is the basis behind spells and incantations? To control and manipulate other people in doing what they want.

When you begin getting frustrated by "trying" to make something happen, you are stepping on God's toes. You are moving out of the "shadow of His wings" where peace and safety is. We are stepping out of God's covering and into our own selfish means. We need to understand where the fine line is between our "doing" and God's "doing." When we cross that line, frustration sets in. This is a good indicator to regroup at that moment. When you begin to feel the frustration set in, stop and ask yourself these two questions:

- ❑ Am I trying to make something happen I have no control over?

- ❑ Am I trying to change someone?

For example, you cannot control traffic. You get frustrated in traffic because it's slow and you have many errands you have to run. You need to stop and regroup, and regain your peace. No amount of frustration is going to change the situation, get your errands done any quicker, it'll only make you angry, feel guilty later, and be exhausted. And truthfully, in a few days those things you thought were important to do won't even be remembered! Why lose your peace over things that won't matter later.

So how do you stop getting frustrated? First by recognizing you have no control over things around you. You have no control of other people's lives. You cannot make anyone do anything.

Personal Account: I recall having this at one time especially in ministry. I pour out my heart, life and energy as I minister to people. But frustration can set in when I don't see the people "doing" what I shared. Some just want a blue pill to make it all better and don't want to do anything for themselves. But I had to let all that go and only do what I can do, and that is share God's love in truth, and pray for them to receive. Now I'm free to be.

When you recognize that you are frustrated confess to God what you are frustrated about. Frustration is caused by trying to make something happen that you have no control over. So by confessing your need to control and asking for forgiveness, that is a good start. And confess to Him that perhaps when you want things to happen, you get in there and try to make things happen instead of waiting on Him. Receive forgiveness for playing "Holy Ghost Jr." and ask for His peace, contentment, and trust in Him alone. Ask Him to help you recognize when you get frustrated to stop and back off, and acknowledge Him. "*In all they ways acknowledge Him and He will direct thy paths*" (Proverbs 3:6). As we do this, we will become less and less frustrated. You will begin to experience more peace. Others around you will begin to experience more peace. Isn't that what we all want?

There is also frustration in your self. Not being able to do the things you "think" you should be doing. Let's say you've been a Christian for a long time but you don't think you are coming along as quickly as you think you should. You begin getting frustrated and even angry, ashamed and embarrassed with your self. The truth is, you are changing, if you are a Christian. The enemy is an accuser and wants you to believe you are not. Your thoughts are your own enemy, because the mind is where the enemy fights his battles. The way to stop getting frustrated with yourself is to start loving yourself, accept yourself, forgive yourself daily, have compassion on yourself and give yourself a break.

The next time you get frustrated pray something like this:

"Father, I'm frustrated again, I ask you to forgive me for stepping out and trying to make _____ happen. (Use your own words for the situation/person involved.) I know that I cannot make anything happen, or change anyone, or change situations around me or even change me. But I can allow you to change my heart in that situation. I ask for your peace to come in. I confess my sin of control and fear, and I will step back and wait on you. I am sorry for crossing the line and trying to do "your" job. I will trust You, I will not be afraid. Thank you for your love and truth penetrating my life right now. In Jesus name, Amen."

CHAPTER TWENTY-ONE

Vision

I understand now why people can perish without vision. (Proverbs 29:18) Not only because the Bible says so but because I've seen it first hand personally. When there is no vision, there is no hope, no purpose to continue living, no self-worth, and so on. But I discovered something that I find that many have done when choosing a vision to focus on, it's short termed, therefore, short lived.

I discovered that the true vision is the ultimate final prize that we are all after as Christians. Eternal life. But I found that people don't want to think about that because then they'll have to think of death. More and more people fear death. The enemy has us blinded by the truth because death is the doorway to the life-eternal. It's not to be feared. The reason we fear it is that: 1) We're afraid to leave people behind; 2) We're afraid it will hurt; 3) We're afraid we don't really know where we are going; 4) We may secretly think it's not real. So the more we don't think of dying, the better off we are. However, then our life is not living to its fullest because we are keeping our mind on things on this earth that are short-term.

What I mean is that by focusing on the farthest thing from today, which is eternal life, the journey along the way doesn't become a hindrance. It's when we look at our feet on our journey that we stumble and fall over that journey. But looking out beyond our feet - which represents the daily life situations to the ultimate prize, and watch the peace that will come. If we set our sights on things above (as the Bible teaches us to do continually) the things all around us won't cause us to stumble. Nothing can get us down when our eyes are SET on the final destination.

Let me share a personal account. I have to get up and go to work everyday like most people. I had focused on this life and going to work as my means of provision and motivation. However, after a time of the same old thing, I found myself looking for other means of motivation. Just getting up and going to work wasn't enough, I had to put other things into it to get me going. Things like making lunch plans, working on a fun project, wearing a new dress, or getting my hair done. I continued looking for something else to satisfy and give motivation. However, now that I got this revelation and have set my eyes toward Heaven and the ultimate prize of transformation to eternal life, my job or earthly responsibilities no longer are a burden or a stumbling block. I'm not looking at them any longer to satisfy and motivate. I'm looking far beyond them, and because of that they have become dim in His presence. (Genesis 15:1) My joy and hope only comes from God. And by keeping my eyes and mind and vision on Him, will satisfy my daily life and the things of this world will not distract me or cause me to fall. The daily things I do now are just stepping stones to the final destination. And when I look at life that way, the steps I take aren't that difficult.

My vision is eternal and not made by flesh and blood. Anything that causes me to stumble is because I've taken my eyes off the final destination.

The Bible continually talks of keeping our thoughts on things above, keeping our eyes toward the hills from whence comes our help (Psalm 121), Looking up for the returning of Jesus Christ, and pressing on toward the mark, the final mark of the gift of eternal life. Each of these scriptures talks of looking PAST this life and into the next.

I know that when I plan a trip somewhere, I don't always look forward to the "getting there" part, but think of what I'll be doing when I get there. Enjoying the sun, sight seeing, shopping, whatever. And it helps me get there with ease, without fear, without distraction. I look forward to the "good" that awaits there. And that's what God showed me. To keep my eyes on the prize, the reason we are saved in the first place is for our eternal home in heaven. (Of course, I also got a revelation on living in the moment, and even in the journeys now I enjoy each step taken.)

That's the great prize, the final hope of our calling. Our eyes are to be fixed on this vision. If Peter didn't look down when he was walking on water, he never would have sunk. But he took his eyes OFF His redeemer. This will cause every person to fall in one way or another. But no more. I ask the Lord to remind me when I begin to look upon this world instead of keeping my eyes fixed toward the eternal, invisible Kingdom. I find this is affecting everything I do and think now. Shopping is no longer a desire, because by shopping I'm keeping my eyes on this world and what it has for me. TV is becoming less and less attractive because it's keeping my eyes fixed on this world. I'm changing the company I keep and choosing to be around people with vision and hope. I needed to separate myself from things that tempted so I could keep my eyes focused God. Because truthfully, even my ministry is not the end of all ends, it's my journey to help me grow more and hear from God in ways unimaginable to REACH that end. So that if one day I don't have this ministry, that's okay, because it was being used to bring me in closer relationship with Him, preparing me for my final destination with Him. Along the way I'm helping people find their way as well, so we stay ready for the coming of our Lord Jesus Christ.

The Bible talks of those looking toward Jesus' return as truly the blessed of this earth. I've heard the saying, "Too heavenly minded is no earthly good." But I think that is a lie. To be heavenly-minded causes us to be of earthly good.

Prayer for You to Pray:

> "Father in Heaven, I am so pleased that my home is with you in Heaven. I want my focus to remain steadfast on you and your Son Jesus. I want to live in this world with vision and hope of you so that others may come to know your glorious love. I know that what I keep my eyes on reflects in my life, so help me to keep my eyes and thoughts on things above, not on things of this earth. I know that by doing that, by seeking first the Kingdom, all these things - the things of this earth - will fall into place. The things on this earth are only a shadow so help me to hold on loosely to them, but tightly onto you.

Let me not look at the waves of life that will cause me to fall, but on my redeemer. I know in so doing I will remain calm in the midst of storms and peace will be a constant. I thank you for continually teaching me how to stay focused - keeping my thoughts on you, on what is good, right, perfect, lovely, and virtuous in everything I do, and everywhere I go. In Jesus name, Amen."

By adjusting your focus on God, you are making your journey through life a pleasant one.

CHAPTER TWENTY-TWO

Riches and Wealth

This is such a controversial subject. Here's an insight that is worth considering if you are in a dilemma about wealth, prosperity and "pursuit of happiness" in what the world can offer.

Let's keep things simple, basic, and to the point. First of all, recognizing that "the good life" as described in the Bible is from a spiritual standpoint. The Bible is a spiritual book to help us live in the invisible Kingdom. The Bible says, Flesh and Blood cannot enter the Kingdom, so neither can substance.

1 Timothy Chapter 6 goes into what the riches really are. Let's look at that chapter starting in verse 5, last part "...supposing gain is godliness; from such withdraw thyself." Verse 6 - "But godliness with contentment is great gain. For we brought nothing into this world, and it is certain we can carry nothing out. And having food and raiment, let us be therewith content."

This scripture looks really clear to me that "wanting" riches of this world is not godly but being content is.

So to me, being at peace with what we have, not focusing on what the world has to offer is how we become rich.

The Bible talks clearly about wisdom and understanding being far greater than rubies and gold. It talks of the "attributes" of God being the wealth we are to seek after, not the earthly riches, which we cannot take with us to the life ever after.

As we read onto verse 9 *"But they that will be rich fall into temptation and a snare, and into many foolish and hurtful lusts, which drown men in destruction and perdition. For the love of money is the root of all evil; which while some coveted after, they have erred from the faith, and pierced themselves through with many sorrows."*

It's not that we can't be rich, it's that it causes many to stumble who are rich. And we know that many of those in Hollywood who are rich have said that they realized that riches can't bring them peace. And riches also keep them away from seeking God because they don't think they need Him. So there can be a stumbling block when being rich and especially seeking to be rich.

Verse 11, *"But thou, Oh man of God, flee these things; and follow after righteousness, godliness, faith, love, patience, meekness. Fight the good fight of faith, lay hold on eternal life, whereunto thou art called, and has professed a good profession before many witnesses."*

This is what "great gain" is all about. This is what is priceless. The attributes of God. And the ultimate richness is eternal life!

The Bible tells us to seek those things that are above, not of things on the earth where moth and rust corrupt and where thieves break through and steel. It says to lay up for ourselves treasures in heaven, where moth and rust don't corrupt and where thieves don't break in and steal, for where our treasure is, there our heart is also (Matthew 6:19-21).

Verse 14, *"That thou keep this commandment without spot, unrebukeable, until the appearing of our Lord Jesus Christ."*

It is clear to me that when we seek the riches and good things of this world, we are actually being disobedient to the Word! When we "seek those things above" we are keeping His commandment. We may be causing our own demise and poverty. Because if we "seek first the Kingdom" God will give us what we need to live a life pleasing to Him and us.

Verse 17 talks of those who are rich, *"Charge them that are rich in this world, that they be not high-minded, nor trust in uncertain riches, but in the living God, who gives us richly all things to enjoy; that they do good, that they be rich in good works, ready to distribute, willing to communicate."*

This tells me that rich people have a tendency to become high-minded and forget that it was God who blessed them with the riches in the first place. He wants to give us richly all things to enjoy. But when He does, He wants us to be able to use it for others too, not just keep it for ourselves, which most rich people do. I think the part that says, "ready to distribute" may be hard for some to grasp. Perhaps they won't want to listen to God, He may say to sell it all and give it to the poor. Hmm... isn't that what Jesus asked the rich young ruler to do but he couldn't because he had great wealth?

It's not that we can't be rich in the things of this world, it's all a heart condition. I know that God will provide all I need, and He has certainly blessed me with enough to give away, that is why I have this ministry. Freely I have received so I freely give. If rich people did this, they wouldn't be living in extravagant homes that look like museums, they would live modestly, share what they have and give away a whole lot more. I also believe this world would be a lot happier with more "richer" people besides.

This is a point of view God is using to help me to be more content with what I have and not "hoping" to be wealthy some day, because truthfully, I am wealthy. I have the wealth that counts. I can't say why people prosper more than others; that's not mine to decide. But what we do have, we need to be content with without comparing ourselves to others. Especially when we "think" others don't deserve it.

Then the final outcome of all this is the great prize – that of salvation. Throughout this scripture it talks of trusting God and gaining eternal life. Truly, those are the two main things we are to keep our minds on. So many scriptures talk about keeping our eyes looking up for the return of Jesus. Press on toward the final prize, which is eternal life. I realized that to be rich is to have my eyes focused on the "real" prize, the real wealth, the real riches, and that is having eternal life. "What does it profit a man if he gain the whole world but lose his own soul, or what shall he give in exchange for his soul?"

When we have eternal life, we have the richest gift of all.

Revelation says that we will receive a crown of life. And it goes on to say, *"Let no man take thy crown"* (Revelation 3:11). A crown represents authority, ruler ship, and wealth. I think having that crown is of more value than anything on this planet, don't you?

If you are thinking, "What about being prosperous now?" I can tell you truthfully, if you seek those things above as I just shared, you will have what you need, and perhaps more to give away while on this planet. But if you seek after those riches (and God knows your heart), you will never attain them, and if you do, they will ensnare you because you gained them with wrong motives.

Ministry Prayer:

If you want to cut free from the "desire" for wealth, yet able to receive all that God wants to give you because you are heirs to His Kingdom, then pray this prayer.

"Father In Heaven, help me to focus on what the true riches are. I don't want to be deceived, I only want to seek what you want me to seek. Help me to let go what I think will make me happy, what I think I need to make it through another day. You are all I need. You are my "exceeding great reward" as spoken in Genesis. I am having a hard time accepting that Lord, help me to accept that Lord and get my focus on things above not on things on this earth. I confess my sin of "want" and "wrong desires" to bless my flesh. Help me to understand that prosperity is not a sign of doing well in the Kingdom. Godliness I have discovered is contentment with what I have. I want only those things that you want for me: truth, peach, long-suffering, kindness, and love. I want a revelation on those as being riches, and that whatever I need to live on this earth, you will provide. Let me not fear that I will be in lack, because you are my God and will not suffer me to be in want. For you Lord, are my Shepherd, I shall not want. I will trust and not be afraid. Help me to believe and trust you more Lord in the area of provision and having a cup that runneth over. Let me understand what the "runneth over" stuff for me is and help me be content with what I have now. And whatever I do get in abundance, I distribute to others to bless them. Thank you for helping me see these truths in my heart. Thank you for setting me free from bondage of wrong thoughts toward wealth. I pray this in Jesus name, Amen."

Poverty

Before we can really conclude teaching on riches and wealth, we need to address the spirit of poverty. It could be that all your life you've had to struggle because your parents struggled, that is a generational poverty familiar spirit that has to be cast out. Then there is the poverty mentality that you will never have enough. And because of that you are "cheap" in everything you do. But if you look back, you will find that by being cheap you spent more. So that "cheap spirit" also has to go.

So my prayer for you is this:

"Father, you want us rich and wealthy in you, but our cheap and poverty mentality has been blocking your flow. I pray that each person who has this issue be free now in Jesus name and that all assignments against them from the kingdom of darkness be broken off. I ask for restoration and healing now, in Jesus name."

CHAPTER TWENTY-THREE

Holiness

Holiness is ours when we receive Jesus Christ as our Savior because the Holy Ghost takes residence in us. It's the job of the Holy Ghost to shed truth to us about what is in our hearts revealing what is of God and what is not of God.

Before we were saved, we lived by our conscience at best, but when the Holy Ghost takes root in our lives, we live by our conscience what the Holy Ghost teaches you. That is why things seem to be hard at times to be a Christian because now you get to "see" all that stuff God sees. Now we need to get to work. This is where the rubber meets the road. This is when the flesh begins screaming. But really, it's the sin in us screaming because it doesn't want to leave. But, as you allow the purging to take place (as discussed in other sessions), you will be made freer - resulting in being made more holy.

Holiness is of the Lord. This is what I read over and over in passages regarding Holiness that it's "His" Holiness, it doesn't say anything about it being us. However, we are made holy because of the righteousness of God in Christ Jesus. We need to realize and understand that righteousness causes us to be Holy. But, the Bible says there is none righteous. So how then do we become Holy? By believing in Jesus and His life. We "put on" righteousness as a robe when we "believe" and "receive" all that Jesus is. That is what it means to be "hid" in Christ. Another scripture says, *"To live is Christ, to die is gain"* (Philippians 1:21).

This is why many Christians struggle. They are now seeing what is unholy in them and it makes them feel condemned which results in anger, self-hatred, and the like. But we have to realize that it's "His" Holiness and will always be His. So you need to know that you will never be completely holy until you are resurrected into life everlasting. We need to understand that our lives are hid in Christ, and it's His Holiness that we live in. We need to understand that our righteousness is as filthy rags and there is none righteous, no not one (Romans 3:10). Once we understand this, we will find more peace, we will be able to forgive ourselves easier, and love ourselves, others and God because we are no longer "driven" to be perfect.

Perfectionism doesn't lead to holiness. I minister to so many who want to be perfect. The Bible does say "Be ye perfect even as your Father in Heaven is perfect." But you need to read what that perfection is – it's loving unconditionally. It doesn't say anything about "doing" everything right or having others do things right. Perfectionism comes from legalism (rules and regulations for holiness), and is not of God! We are not made holy because of what we do, we are made holy because of His Holiness in us shining the light on that which is not holy so we repent. That's what we do. We repent for what we see that is not of God, and when we do that, more of His Holiness shines in us. When that begins to happen consistently, our lives begin changing into His image. We begin doing things right, we begin making better choices.

It's important to get it down in your hearts once and for all. Holiness doesn't come by what you do but whom you believe. Because Holiness only manifests in us when we "know" we are righteous - right now.

Romans 6:22 - *But now being made free from sin, and become servants to God, ye have your fruit unto* **holiness,** *and the end everlasting life.*

It's clear that when we are cleansed from sin and submit to God, our fruit is holiness.

In ministry, most of the people I work with are Christians who have anxiety and stress related problems. I discovered one main theme in each one - they have a desire to do what is right but they find themselves messing up. Because of this they can't seem to forgive themselves, they think they have to punish themselves, they think they aren't worthy to be loved by God, they are filled with regrets, doubt and unbelief toward God, guilt, shame, unforgiveness and depression. These individuals don't know that holiness was imparted to them when they received Jesus Christ and that when they sin, they can go directly to God and confess their sin to be restored to holiness again. Holiness isn't perfection, Holiness is "in" Christ Jesus. Holiness is a clean heart. Holiness is not perfectionism, nor is it keeping all the rules and regulations. I may not do everything right, but I'm still a Saint! A Saint is a holy person, and regardless what you think about yourself, if you are a believer (even if you are an unbelieving believer) you are a Saint, which makes you a partaker of Holiness.

So then why do things seem to get worse when we become a Christian if we have the Holy Ghost in us to make us holy? Because the Holy Ghost sheds light on what is in us that doesn't belong to God. This is where we get uncomfortable in our own skin. Now that we have been given a desire to be Holy we now expect our flesh to be PERFECT. So we get mad at ourselves when we don't say things right, do things right, make a perfect cake, have perfect hair, perfect size, perfect kids, and perfect husband. We wonder what is wrong with us How can I be a Christian and think and do these things? We have to understand and believe this truth. The Holy Ghost living inside us gives us a desire for holiness, I am right in God's eyes because I have accepted His Son. I may not DO everything right, but that's not what makes me righteous and perfect. Because no flesh will ever be made perfect no matter how long we live on this earth. We fall short of God's perfectness. If we understand that "It is not I that does it but the sin that dwells in me doing it" (Romans 7) we then will be able to move on in our life without guilt and condemnation. We will love ourselves, we will understand ourselves, and we will not be disappointed in ourselves, we may even laugh at ourselves knowing that we are loved, forgiven and perfected by God's love.

See, we are "being perfected" which is a process. So by God's grace and mercy, He sent His Son so when we didn't do everything right, we have a Savior to redeem us.

The Bible says to cleanse our flesh AND spirit. So this tells me that our spirit could be dirty too. Where does the Holy Ghost live? Within our spirit man.

And because He's in there along with all those other creatures, the battle is on! That is why things seem to get worse when we become a Christian (after the honeymoon is over) because the Holy Ghost is shining a light on the junk. And since we have a desire to be holy now and yet we see all that junk, we get condemned! But that's where we need understanding. We aren't to let ourselves fall under guilt and condemnation, but rejoice that God showed you what is there so you can be purged. We need to separate ourselves from the sin inside knowing that we are "Free" from the bondage of sin. Our flesh and spirit needs to be transformed, and that is a process. And in that process we need to exercise forgiveness. Receive forgiveness from God, forgive ourselves, and forgive others.

In order to exercise forgiveness, we need to have the manifestation of Jesus in us to be able to do so. We are saved through the forgiveness of our own sins, and we will continue to stay free and become freer the same way. The # 1 block to unrest in our spirit and enmity with God is unforgiveness.

As the Lord begins to expose sin in your life it may be something you never knew was there. Some people have said to me that it just jumped on them. But I have to tell them the truth. The stuff was in there all along, it just took the situation they are in to bring it to the surface. God is orchestrating everything in your life for one reason only, to bring you into relationship with Him. And in order to do that, you have to be holy. God cannot fellowship with darkness. So He made us a way to be holy in the midst of our unholiness... through Jesus Christ.

God doesn't show us everything at once because we won't be able to bear it. So as He shows us something like self-righteousness, we may even be shocked. But after we see it, we can repent. Then He shows us another thing, then another, then another. After awhile, we could start to get depressed because of all the junk we see in us. It could cause us to become fearful thinking that others saw what we see. I remember one day when God showed me -- me... I was almost embarrassed to go outside thinking others saw all that junk. But God reassured me that He had mercy on me and caused me not to fear.

During the purging, we could get a bit uncomfortable. The flesh begins to scream and say, "I don't like it, stop, this hurts, it's uncomfortable, I don't think I can bear this pain". So instead of allowing God to go THROUGH with the purging, we shut down, we turn away, we go and call a friend, we eat, we watch TV, we shop, we avoid it, at any way possible. This reminds me of the scripture, "Be not weary in well doing for in due season you will reap if you don't faint" (Galatians 6:9).

So as things get a bit hard, rejoice knowing that you are just about on the other side of things. Because unfortunately, it doesn't leave any other way, so the best thing to do is to ENDURE the pain for A LITTLE WHILE and it will be done with. This is called "long suffering" which is one of the fruits of the Spirit. You will need to know that if you choose to not allow God to purge you, because He doesn't do anything against your will, it will visit you again another day. So just take the purging when it's happening and get it over with once and for all.

Holiness is the manifestation of knowing you are righteous. If we knew we were righteous, our actions will follow - which is doing things right (holy). It's not the other way around. And so if you make a mess of things, confess them to God and as you do this, you will become more holy!

As I began running references in the Bible on Holiness, I discovered something quite interesting. In the Old Testament, holiness always accompanied "His" holiness, or the "Lord's" holiness. Then as I read the New Testament, holiness was something we could have. Why? Because in the OT the Holy Ghost wasn't imparted to every person (only a select few at times) but in the NT, all those who received Jesus Christ also receives the Holy Ghost!

I want to share some of the scriptures that talk about holiness. I think the Bible does a much better job than ever could.

Romans 6:19 - *I speak after the manner of men because of the infirmity of your flesh: for as ye have yielded your members servants to uncleanness and to iniquity unto iniquity; even so now yield your members servants to righteousness unto **holiness**.*

When we yield to righteousness - only found "in" Christ Jesus, the manifestation is **holiness**.

1 Thessalonians 3:13 - *To the end he may establish your hearts unblameable in **holiness** before God, even our Father, at the coming of our Lord Jesus Christ with all his saints.*

Holiness is something that comes from a heart condition. By dealing with your heart issues you become more holy. Remember, holiness is the manifestation of righteousness within.

Titus 2:3 - *The aged women likewise, that they be in behavior as becomes **holiness**, not false accusers, not given to much wine, teachers of good things;*

In this passage their actions display holiness because they aren't speaking badly against each other. Again this is a heart condition. When we confess our sins because we understand we are free from sin, our "behavior" begins to display holiness. Again, it starts in the heart.

Hebrews 12:14 - *Follow peace with all men, and **holiness**, without which no man shall see the Lord.*

Restored relationships are required to experience holiness. Love and forgiveness is holiness and holiness is the "ticket" to seeing the Lord.

But don't get condemned. We have an advocate, Jesus Christ. We will see the Lord because we have "put on" Christ through salvation. Becoming Holy is the process we now live on this earth. It's a process, process, process. This has nothing to do with your salvation! You think you are saved one minute and because you see something in you that is not of God, you aren't saved the next.

The truth is, you are sealed by the Holy Ghost of promise (Ephesians 1:4) the minute you accepted Jesus Christ into your heart and trust Him to forgive you and cleanse you of all your sins.

Romans 12:1 - *I beseech you therefore, brethren, by the mercies of God, that ye present your bodies a living sacrifice,* **holy***, acceptable unto God, which is your reasonable service.*

We are holy people, we just don't know it. Holiness is being pure before God within our heart. Holiness is of the Lord when we take on His righteousness. It's called "imputed" (Romans 4:24) (Dictionary meaning for imputed: to ascribe to or charge (a person) with an act or quality because of the conduct of another over whom one has control or for whose acts or conduct one is responsible.) Jesus is the responsible one and because of His conduct, we are made righteous.

Romans 16:16 - *Salute one another with a* **holy** *kiss. The churches of Christ salute you.*

A holy kiss means to love and receive love from each other with a pure heart.

1 Corinthians 3:17 - *If any man defile the temple of God, him shall God destroy; for the temple of God is* **holy***, which temple ye are.*

Very clearly put, we are the temple of God which is holy! I urge you to pray God give you revelation on holiness so you can find your peace with Him, with others and with yourself.

1 Corinthians 7:14 - *For the unbelieving husband is sanctified by the wife, and the unbelieving wife is sanctified by the husband: else were your children unclean; but now are they* **holy***.*

Interesting that holiness doesn't come by what we do, but what He has given us if we are in the Lord.

Ephesians 1:4 - *According as he hath chosen us in him before the foundation of the world, that we should be* **holy** *and without blame before him in love:*

Colossians 3:12-13 - **Put on** *therefore, as the elect of God, holy and beloved* **(us)***, bowels of mercies, kindness, humbleness of mind, meekness, longsuffering; forbearing one another, and forgiving one another, if any man have a quarrel against any, even as Christ forgave you, so also do ye. Above all these things put on charity, which is the bond of* **perfectness***.*

I read in these verses that holiness is manifested in our lives when we walk in love. Love is holiness, and when we walk in love we are walking perfectly!! But the truth is, we are holy because the Holy One lives within us. As you read in some of these scriptures, God puts holiness upon on because of His holiness... Just believe it so you can receive it!

Are you still not convinced you are holy? 1 Thessalonians 5:27 - *I charge you by the Lord that this epistle be read unto all the holy brethren.* YOU are the holy brethren!

To bring this home, for holiness to be a reality to us, we have to understand that we are forgiven of all our sins. And when we do sin, we have an advocate, Jesus Christ that cleanses us from all sin. We need to know that by being Christ's we are no longer bound to sin, even though sin is still there. Paul says it eloquently, "Who can save me from this body of sin? Thanks to God, Jesus Christ can" (Romans 7).

Ministry:

"Father, I come before you with this dear Saint who desires to be holy. Let them know they are righteous right now and to accept all that Jesus has done to bring that holiness upon them. We discovered that holiness is the manifestation of righteousness. Help them to know they are righteous right now even in the midst of their mess. Let them confess their sin of doubt and unbelief and begin to be the person you created them to be. Let them see past their own noses and see the glory you have for them. We are changed from glory to glory, and with that we become more holy. Let them be at peace with you Father and find their joy again, release them from all fear by pouring your love into them. Remove all condemnation from their lives and replace it with acceptance and forgiveness. Help them to understand the truth of who you are and who they are. In Jesus Name, Amen."

CHAPTER TWENTY-FOUR

Onion Principle

One of the teachings that impact many who hear it is the "Onion Principle." It's a good description of a life that has layers and layers of pain, unforgiveness, broken relationships are wrapped around their hearts. Have you heard the saying, "Hard-hearted" or "Cold-hearted?" Well, this is the reason. Over the years many hurts and offenses took place and after a time this person begins to protect themselves from further harm forming a casing around their heart. What they don't realize is that within this casing are the very things they don't want to have. Bitterness, anger, fear, resentment, rejection, abandonment represent these layers. The layers represent pain, they are a result of taking on sins that came out of a relationship or situation. These are the very sins that have separated you from yourself, God and others.

As like an onion, the outer part is easy to peel off, but when it gets closer to the core, the tighter the onion rings. So is it with the "junk" around your heart. That stuff closer to the core has been there a very long time, fermenting all these years. This "junk" is what is causing your illness and emotional pain. No one else is doing this to you. It is what you have allowed to encase you! John 20:23 says, "Whosoever sins ye remit, they are remitted unto them; and whosoever sins ye retain, they are retained." Clearly this tells me that if I do not forgive someone of their sins, their sins fall upon me and I take them in. But if I forgive them, the sins return to them and I'm not affected and no pain or layers of sins are added to my life. This is a choice that every person makes every single day. Whether to forgive someone or not. Walking in love is walking daily in forgiveness.

For example: If someone pulls out in front of you in traffic and you become irritated with them, you were just offended and took on a stranger's sins, adding them to what is already in you, causing your onion to grow. Yes, it's just that simple. And look at all the layers that are there because you didn't know that forgiveness removes the layers of pain from your life.

An interesting thing I found is that as I face each layer in my life the harder it gets to face because I'm now getting to the core. Those are things that have been there for a long time that I may not even know are there. My husband would tell me to "Just flush it" when I come home and share an experience I had with someone. But I know that just flushing it isn't going to do it, it has to be rooted out and only done through forgiveness. Well since I was never taught this principle those many years back, I have a lot of forgiving to do! As we get closer to the inner layers, we may feel a bit of pain and discomfort as we face each one. But regardless, all that stuff has to go.

I've shared the story many times so far about my husband's experience in Vietnam with the shrapnel penetrating into his body. This is a good example of that. Because each layer is like one of those pieces of shrapnel. The way that it went in is the same way it's gotta come out. Once we have recognized we have a "piece of metal" under our skin (as the old saying goes, "they are getting under my skin" - is not far from the truth!) it's time to let God dig it out.

The Holy Ghost divides rightly, between soul and spirit (Hebrews 4:12), and He's the only one that can cut away the layers without *killing* us. Our job is to recognize the "metal pieces" (sin or hurt) in our lives and agree with God to get rid of it.

Be sure to follow the teaching on forgiveness because it will deal with each and every one of your layers. By going through that teaching, you will be purged one layer at a time. As the layers are removed by God through the prayer of confession, you will find yourself feeling lighter, treating people differently that you were having problems with, and developing a better relationship with God, yourself and others because all the "JUNK" is no longer there to pollute your mind. You are no longer living through this junk, but free from it. Many make choices in life because of the "filters" they live through. Get rid of the filters, and you will be free to see the truth.

Exercise: Draw layers around and around forming a circle. This represents an onion. How many layers do you think you have? Every hurt, offense or unforgiveness is a layer. Take a moment to reflect on this. It's not to bring you into guilt or depression, it's to help you to see how much God is there waiting to help you remove each and every layer so the REAL You, comes forth. These layers have caused us to become someone we aren't. Let's remove those things that are NOT you, so you can see You. Many don't even know who they are, it's because of these layers.

Ministry:

"Dear Heavenly Father, I pray for my dear friend that they would look at this principle as a blessing. To know that all that junk they see inside of them is as a result of some kind of an offense. Don't let them feel bad or get angry, but simply deal with each one. Help them to recognize the individual(s) involved and forgive them. As we forgive Lord, you purge and cleanse us from all unrighteousness making us righteous! Help us to remember to come to you in confession not depression. I ask for you love to penetrate their lives and fill them with your presence. In Jesus name, Amen."

CHAPTER TWENTY-FIVE

Knowledge and Understanding

With all your getting, get Understanding (Proverbs 4:7).

Hosea 4:14 *"The people that do not understand shall fall."*

I can't tell you how much I want to just "know" everything. I would say to my husband, "What are you thinking?" I just want to know what he is thinking. I would overhear a conversation and want to "know" the details, which is none of my business. I want to "know" where I'm going at all times. I want to "know" everything! And since I'm a teacher, that is rightfully so, but even in that there has to be a balance. Knowledge alone can cause so much grief. The Bible says "knowledge puffs up" (1 Corinthians 8:1). And if I look at that in the spirit, I would see a big inflated head trying to stay on top of a body. It's wavering back and forth, tipping from side to side because the head is too big. This is an unstable person, wouldn't you agree? Because all that knowledge is making them top heavy. That is why so many of us feel confused, afraid, angered, especially when we have to make decisions. We find ourselves second guessing ourselves because though we have a head knowledge, we don't have a heart knowledge.

Then on top of that, the more we "know" the more we are responsible for. Ecclesiastes says that with much knowledge comes much sorrow (Ecclesiastes 1:18). But that didn't stop me from wanting to "know." I think we get that (ladies) from our mother, Eve. She "had to know" what God knew and so ate from the tree of knowledge. I think we have been on that road ever since, but it doesn't have to continue. If you are ready to get off that treadmill of "having to know" everything, then, this article is for you. Let me share a story.

My husband and I had just retired to bed when he said, "Oh, I forgot to do something." So he got up and went out into the kitchen. Well, I forgot to do something too, so I got up as well. He saw me coming and said, "What are you doing up?" He was standing there holding a bag of something. I said, "I needed to set up something to record on the TV." With that I went to bed. He came into the room and I asked him what he was doing. He told me he wasn't doing anything. I was persistent. I wanted to "know" what he was doing. I started getting ugly. I was becoming suspicious, and mad, and felt left out of whatever it was he was doing. Then all of a sudden I was snapped out of it when I heard the Holy Ghost say, "Tomorrow is Valentine's day." I couldn't believe what I had done. I spoiled a surprise! I turned to Tom and said, "Oh Tom, tomorrow is Valentine's day, you were putting something out for me so I would be surprised in the morning." He said, "Well, no surprise now, you just had to know didn't you?"

That is an example of what we do when we need to know everything. We cause our own grief! Perhaps you can think of a time you nosed around for some information and all it did was cause you upset and grief and you wished you didn't find out. There is a reason we aren't to know everything. I realized that when we "know" some things, we tend to use it to control our situation and other people. For example, when I know that someone at work is having a party, I want to find out if I'm invited, who all is invited, so that I can decide if I want to go or not. I want to control the situation.

And you may know someone that is a "know-it-all." They talk about all that they know, and they use it to tell you what to do. I think those having to listen get tired after awhile, wouldn't you think? But people who think they know everything would rather listen to themselves speak than listen to anyone else. A person who "knows" a lot tends to be self-righteous, full of pride, arrogant, controlling, manipulative, and full of fear. They are driven to talk because they think it will cause them to be loved and accepted. But as you know, it does the complete opposite.

I would like to set the record straight now. I don't want to "know" anything! I think Paul says it quite nicely, "I know nothing but Christ and Him crucified." If I would keep that kind of mentality, I wouldn't get into so much trouble!

The need to know comes from a spirit of witchcraft. Not that we are witches but that the spirit behind that craft is present. It uses control and manipulation through "knowing" for selfish purposes.

So what do we do about this? The Bible is clear about us gaining knowledge, right? As stated in the scripture referenced at the top of this teaching "The people that do not understand shall fall" Hosea 4:14. I've seen this happen first hand! You will notice that when knowledge is present in a passage of scripture, so is "understanding." Knowledge without understanding will cause a big mess. Knowledge - truth; understanding - revelation of that truth. Revelation is what changes people's lives.

I've listed scripture references below for your convenience, but please take a look yourself to read the whole context.

Proverbs 2: *My son, if thou wilt receive my words, and hide my commandments with thee; So that thou incline thine ear unto wisdom, and apply thine heart to understanding; Yea, if thou criest after knowledge, and liftest up thy voice for understanding; If thou seekest her as silver, and searchest for her as for hid treasures; Then shalt thou understand the fear of the LORD, and find the knowledge of God. For the LORD giveth wisdom: out of his mouth cometh knowledge and understanding. He layeth up sound wisdom for the righteous: he is a buckler to them that walk uprightly. He keepeth the paths of judgment, and preserveth the way of his saints. Then shalt thou understand righteousness, and judgment, and equity; yea, every good path. Then wisdom entereth into thine heart, and knowledge is pleasant unto thy soul; Discretion shall preserve thee, understanding shall keep thee.*

Exodus 31:3 *And I have filled him with the spirit of God, in wisdom, and in* **understanding**, *and in* **knowledge**, *and in all manner of workmanship.*

Exodus 35:31 *And he hath filled him with the spirit of God, in wisdom, in* **understanding**, *and in* **knowledge**, *and in all manner of workmanship;*

Nehemiah 10:28 *And the rest of the people, the priests, the Levities, the porters, the singers, the Nethinims, and all they that had separated themselves from the people of the lands unto the law of God, their wives, their sons, and their daughters, every one having* **knowledge**, *and having* **understanding***;*

Proverbs 2:3 *Yea, if thou criest after* **knowledge**, *and liftest up thy voice for* **understanding***;*

Proverbs 2:6 *For the LORD giveth* **wisdom***: out of his mouth cometh* **knowledge** *and* **understanding**

Proverbs 9:10 *The fear of the LORD is the* **beginning of wisdom***: and the* **knowledge** *of the holy is* **understanding***.*

Proverbs 15:14 *The heart of him that hath* **understanding** *seeketh* **knowledge***: but the mouth of fools feedeth on foolishness.*

Proverbs 17:27 *He that hath* **knowledge** *spareth his words: and a man of* **understanding** *is of an excellent spirit.*

Proverbs 19:25 *Smite a scorner, and the simple will beware: and reprove one that hath* **understanding**, *and he will* **understand knowledge***.*

Proverbs 28:2 *For the transgression of a land many are the princes thereof: but by a man of* **understanding** *and* **knowledge** *the state thereof shall be prolonged.*

Isaiah 11:2 *And the spirit of the LORD shall rest upon him, the spirit of wisdom and* **understanding**, *the spirit of counsel and might, the spirit of* **knowledge** *and of the fear of the LORD;*

Hosea 4:6 *"My people are destroyed for lack of* **knowledge***: because thou hast* **reject***ed* **knowledge**, *I will also* **reject** *thee, that thou shalt be* **no** *priest to me: seeing thou hast forgotten the law of thy God, I will also forget thy children.*

Isaiah 40:14 *With whom took he counsel, and who instructed him, and taught him in the path of judgment, and taught him* **knowledge**, *and shewed to him the way of* **understanding***?*

Jeremiah 3:15 *And I will give you pastors according to mine heart, which shall feed you with* **knowledge** *and* **understanding***.*

Jeremiah 4:22 *For my people are foolish, they have not known me; they are sottish children, and they have no* **understanding***: they are wise to do evil, but to do good they have no* **knowledge***.*

Daniel 1:4 *Children in whom were no blemish, but well favored, and skilful in all wisdom, and cunning in* **knowledge**, *and* **understanding** *science, and such as had ability in them to stand in the king's palace, and whom they might teach the learning and the tongue of the Chaldeans.*

Daniel 1:17 *As for these four children, God gave them **knowledge** and skill in all learning and **wisdom**: and Daniel had **understanding** in all visions and dreams.*

Daniel 2:21 *And he changeth the times and the seasons: he removeth kings, and setteth up kings: he giveth wisdom unto the wise, and **knowledge** to them that know **understanding**.*

Colossians 1:9 *For this cause we also, since the day we heard it, do not cease to pray for you, and to desire that ye might be filled with the **knowledge** of his will in all **wisdom** and spiritual **understanding**.*

Proverbs 3:19 The LORD by **wisdom** hath founded the earth; by **understanding** hath he established the heavens. *(Isn't it interesting in this scripture that when God is talking of himself, he didn't need to mention the Word "knowledge" because He is knowledge.)*

There is always a balance in what is taught, and that's the part I had been missing. With knowledge we also need understanding. That then takes that "big head" syndrome and eases it into our hearts through understanding. Now we can find that balance and peace we desire. I use that now as an indicator of being out of balance. Am I getting irritated? Am I getting frustrated or angry? Am I getting upset at all? If so, it's an indicator I'm not "understanding" what is going on. I'm not saying we need to know why... that is different. What I'm saying is that we need an understanding of the situation.

When someone is in pain and wants to share it with you, all they want to hear from you is, "I understand." It seems to make all the hurt go away and they find peace. But when we come back and say, "Well, if you would have done this or that..." It only causes strife, and doesn't ease any pain and may make it worse for them. Understanding is the "key" to wisdom. The Bible is clear when it says that we need wisdom. We get wisdom *through* knowledge and understanding. And then we have what we need to make sound decisions.

So after realizing this about me - because the Bible says we are to know our own heart - I began to name off all the things I "knew." Let me share some with you.

I know God has called me into ministry. I know God loves me. I know there is a plan for my life. I know I love to eat. I know I need to eat better. I know I love to shop. I know I need to restrain myself while shopping. I know I like to watch TV. I know I need to cut back watching TV. I know I need to exercise. I know I need to get closer to God. I know I want to be all God wants me to be. I know Tom (my husband) is right about many things even though I don't like it. I know I have a long way to go in my walk with the Lord. I know I have a desire to retire so I can work Full-Time in ministry (by the way, this has come true.) I know I want to plan more conferences and seminars. I know I want to travel. I know I want to buy a new Harley so Tom and I can ride together (this too has come true). I want to know the Word more. I know what I don't like. I know what I like. I know, I know, I know.

Many of these areas cause me grief because I haven't asked God for understanding as it pertains to each and everything I know. All this can cause anyone to fall off the wagon and make goofy decisions that could come out all wrong. I've been there, done that, and I'm through. How about you? I want to not only "know" some things, but I also want understanding in those things so I can make good decisions. Even saying that causes me to feel at peace.

So what I did was take each thing I listed above and then added to it something like this: Lord, You love me, help me to get a full understanding of your love. Because getting a full understanding of your love will plant it in my heart. It won't just be head knowledge but life changing knowledge.

God loves me and has my best in mind. See, that is "knowledge" and "understanding" working together. I "know" God loves me (knowledge) He has my best in mind (that's understanding). They have to work hand in hand. Many know God loves them, but it stops there, and they still live in fear, unbelief, doubt and stress. Why? Because the understanding isn't there. When we understand, we are able to "receive." Many haven't received the Love of God for themselves, all because of lack of understanding.

The Bible says that the fear of the Lord is the beginning of wisdom. Remember, knowledge and understanding produces wisdom. So if you want to fear the Lord biblically, then gain knowledge and understanding in that area and wisdom will come. Then your relationship with God will greatly improve because you indeed acquired the mind of Christ.

Another area that I didn't have revelation and understanding in was that I "knew" I was supposed to quit my job and work in full-time ministry. I just didn't know when. It's not on the list above because that has actually come to pass but wanted to share my accounts on that situation. See, during this decision-making my husband seemed to be a stick-in-the mud. I felt that he was preventing me from fulfilling God's call on my life. But the truth was, he wanted me to see the big picture and to see clearly before making the decision to quit. He said that he sees me doing great things in this ministry but that I wasn't thinking things through, as I needed to. I hated waiting, but even in that I asked God for understanding. Sometimes we want things now because we are in fear of it not ever happening. I had to confess my fear to God and receive forgiveness. Because the truth was I was in fear of running out of time, not doing what I thought I was supposed to do before leaving this planet. That decision was made and 8 months later I retired. As I look back on this, I had submitted to my husband and in the end, he supported my decision and we haven't looked back once and God has been faithful to our necessities ever since.

I encourage you to begin asking God for understanding in the situation you find yourself in today. I guarantee you He will respond! He said, "Ask and you shall receive, He will hold nothing back." And believe me, that is the truth! Just since this morning when I asked for understanding, it's coming to me like a flood. So much so, I don't need to "know" so much any more. The need to know is diminished, and the only thing I truly need is to "know" more of God.

Whew... all that to get to that... which is what I needed all along. And the cool part is God knows everything, so why not put our confidence in Him and trust the knowing to Him.

I do have to add here that the Holy Ghost that dwells within you "knows all things." So truthfully, you do have at your fingertips everything you need to know.

A Personal Testimony:

As I mentioned, I had thought Tom was preventing me from doing God's will. After all, I have a vision for ministry; I want to do God's work! I feel like I can't do the things I desire to do. Does this sound familiar to anyone?

Even though it seemed like Tom was the one preventing me from going forward, it wasn't him, it was God speaking through him. Tom would say to me that it has to be in God's timing. I would get infuriated at him when he would say that but I knew what he was saying was true, but I just didn't want to wait. That's where understanding was lacking. So I began asking God for understanding in the area of timing. That's when God gave me this revelation: "If you work through your husband as it relates to your ministry, I will establish you, and keep you. If you circumvent him, you are also circumventing me, and it will be you who orchestrates it, not me, and if it's not me, you'll then wonder why it failed." Then what happens is that we blame God for our failure; after all, we were doing this "thing" for Him.

Remember the rule of thumb: God is first in our personal lives - having an intimate relationship with Him; then our Husband, then our families, then our work, then our ministry! I think what happens is that we don't have "understanding" in this area. We think that since God is first, so is everything we "do" for Him. Not so. God is first in our hearts to live after the examples of Jesus. To love all those we come in contact with, to fellowship with God, to acknowledge Him in all our ways. This has to do with our walk and our heart, not what we are necessarily doing. The doing comes "after" our family, work, etc. I believe that's why families in ministry suffer so, there's no understanding in this area so everything falls apart - even Christian marriages! Hosea 4:14 "The people that do not understand shall fall."

I have another story to share: One day Tom was in the kitchen making a sandwich. I came up behind him and when I would try to look over his shoulder he would lean that direction. When I would try to look around the other side of him, he would lean the other way. Then he turned to me and said, "You want to see what I'm doing so that you can tell me how to do it." Boy, he was right! Sometimes we just want to "know" so that we can tell others how to do it our way. From that day on I've stayed away from his sandwich making and would catch myself when I would want to "know" what he was doing. Boy, there is so much peace in that. After all, he's over 60 years old and more than capable of making his sandwich the way he liked it.

Ministry Prayer

"Dear Heavenly Father, what a wonder you are. You have all that we need to live, breathe and just be. I pray Father that each person reading this prayer agrees with me not to only "know" things but with that knowing a desire for understanding. I pray that each person seek both, not just one without the other, so that they can begin to walk in wisdom. Thank you for revealing this Lord, and I pray that each person gets a deeper revelation in this area and shares this truth with others who are missing it. I ask you to cleanse us and purge us from our own selfish thinking that if we knew everything, we would be okay. That is not true. Help us to only "know" those things you want us to know and leave the rest. We confess our "need to know" to you Lord as we also confess our control or manipulation that resides in our heart as a result from that need. You are all we need. Help us to understand YOU more Lord in a way that will change us forever so we are filled with you and you alone. Thank you for your love, we receive more of it right now into our hearts and lives. Help us to gain more understanding about your love for us personally. Help us to ask for understanding in everything we "think" we know. I thank you for all you are showing to us and doing in our lives, in Jesus' name, Amen."

CHAPTER TWENTY-SIX

Discernment

Hebrews 5:14 says that Discernment is knowing the difference between good and evil. You must not only know what is "good" but what is "evil." If you don't know who the enemy is, how can you resist him?

This is a list of some of the Devil's wiles (wiles = ways): Galatians 5:20

- ❑ Devourer (Malachi 3:11)

- ❑ Tempter (Matthew 4:1 and Luke 4)

- ❑ Dumb Spirit (Matthew 9:32-33)

- ❑ Accuser of Brethren (Revelations 12:10)

- ❑ Betrayer (John 13:2)

- ❑ Perverted (Acts 13:5-10)

- ❑ Liar, thief, hateful, unforgiving (Ephesians 4:24-32)

- ❑ Unclean Spirits (Luke 4:33)

- ❑ Murderer (1 John 3:15)

- ❑ Rebellious (1 Samuel 15:23)

- ❑ Devilish (James 3:15)

- ❑ Sorcerer (Acts 13:8) Elymas means False Prophet

- ❑ Idolatry (Isaiah 14:12-15) Idolatry begins with an "I"

Following is a list of some of the enemy's characteristics (manifestations) (2 Corinthians 2:11)

Note: If you are not clear of their meaning, just look the word up in the dictionary.

Rebellion	Depression	Obsessive
Jealous	Guilt and Condemnation	Insulting
Envy	Dishonest	Opinionated
Strife	Rude	Sharp
Impatient	Judgmental	Wasteful
Fearful	Merciless	Worrier
Angry	Hateful	Gossip
Sorcerer	Fortune Teller	Distrusting
Inconsiderate	Blame Others	Revengeful
Self-Righteous	Proud	Self-centered
Insubordinate	Denial	Discontent
Offended Easily	Murder	Defiant
Lustful	Greedy	Cold-hearted
Liar	Complainer	Childish
Disobedient	Man Pleaser	Bitter
Self-pity	Confusion	Sluggard
Lazy	Distrusting	Unbelieving
Controlling	Insecure	Evil Communication
Idolatry	Stubbornness	Covetousness
Suspicious	Accusation	Retaliation

Mark off any that you manifest. Did you know that these are YOUR sins? You've been defiled. Now take your list (rap sheet) to God and confess your sins and receive forgiveness for them, forgiving yourself as well. You won't just do this once or twice, this is a continual thing if you want your heart to remain clean before the Lord, as we are all sinners and have need of daily renewal.

Personal Testimony from Linda:

I want you to know that everything that is listed above were things I found in me. The night that I learned that "I" was responsible for my life God was able to introduce me to me. I sat down and simply asked Him, "Lord, what sins can I possibly have?" Well, with that it opened the understanding of my heart, and that's when I wrote down these things listed above. Since then, of course, more has been revealed and now I know to take all my sins to the Lord and receive forgiveness. I practice what I preach. The truth never fails. I had to see the truth in my own heart before I could go further. See I had seen all these things in others, so I believed others were to blame for my problems. But of course, I learned that wasn't the case. I could only see in them what I myself had! "Take the beam out of your own eye and then you can see to take the beam out of your brothers." But the truth was, once I got my own beam out, I couldn't see it in my brother - or it wasn't a big deal any more and didn't even have the need to say anything to them. That was the night a flood of teaching came forth, and as a result I created this teaching to share with others what God has done in me. I was so self-deceived for over 18 years (as a Christian) and didn't know that I had the keys to unlock my cage.

We are to "KNOW" our enemy, otherwise we won't know how to defeat him. The Bible says many are punching in the air, and the enemy isn't even there. We have to discern our thoughts, our heart, and our words. What is coming out of your mouth? What are you keeping your mind on? If any of these "wiles of the devil" are still working in your life, that is a GOOD thing... Not because it's "working in your life" but because you are admitting it. Now you can do something about it.

Don't go around saying, "That's just the way I am." No, that is not. Just as we learned in the "Onion Principle" teaching, these things come from layers of brokenness, relationship breaches, pain, trauma's and more. The enemy wants you to think like him so you won't be free, nor be productive as a believer. Choose today to pay attention to what the enemy is doing. Not to give him credit at all, but not to be afraid to see it either. That saying that goes, "What you don't know can't hurt you" is a lie. The Bible says that God's people perish for lack of knowledge (Hosea 4:6).

Ignorance is no excuse any longer. With the web, TV, and places that information is put out there, we can no longer say, "I just didn't know." Did you know there is a clause in copyright laws that say this?? So we need to know our enemy, just as much as he knows us and how to push our buttons. Let's get rid of those buttons in our heart, so that when he comes along to try to push us around, we will push back.

Another thought here, we have to stop being so afraid of the devil. God is greater than He is, so why do we cower down? It's because we don't really know the power that God has placed in us. So if you have ever been afraid of evil, darkness, what the devil is doing, or even afraid to talk about him, then repent right now for making the enemy greater than God. Repent for fearing the devil. You will be amazed at that one confession how the power the enemy had over you will disseminate.

Ministry:

"Father, I pray for this individual reading through this teaching. They are searching, but what they are searching for is an intimate relationship with you. By recognizing the things in us that prevent that, we are "doing" the Word. I ask you for you to help them see the truth in their own lives and what is in their heart that does not belong to you! Help them look at each area fully and not fear what they see or feel bad or guilty for what is there. But to rejoice that they see it because it's the beginning of their freedom from it. I ask for your infinite mercy to flood their hearts right now and that no matter what is there, they remember that all their sins have been forgiven over 2000 years ago and to just receive what Jesus did on the cross for them. All guilt and shame removed from them, and they can enjoy you even more. It's not that all our sins are gone it's that all our sins are forgiven and covered! We give you permission to reveal these things in our heart but most of all reveal your Son in our lives focusing on what He's done so that all these things we see in us and around us won't burden us or overwhelm us. Let me not be afraid to see the truth of what is going on in my heart, because until I see it I won't be freed. So today, I believe I'm on a pathway to restoration. I thank you, in Jesus' name, Amen."

CHAPTER TWENTY-SEVEN

Abortion Recovery

This teaching is designed for individuals who have had abortion(s) and still experience pain and guilt whenever the memory comes to mind.

I want to share my story to give you an idea where I'm coming from so that you know that I know exactly what you have been going through. I was very active sexually as a teenager and young adult. During a three year span I had eight abortions. I used abortions as a means of birth control; after all, it was free at the clinic! These were done during the late 70's. However, I did have two more and a miscarriage in the mid 80's. And during that time I was a Christian! Of course I can justify why I had to make these choices. I can put the blame on those around me or on my situation. I have done that for years, but when I stopped doing that, that was the first step to my healing.

The first thing that I had to come to grips with is that I made the decisions and to take responsibility for those decisions. I knew it was wrong to have those abortions but that was the only thing I knew to do at the time. I was sad about having them but nothing compared to when I became a Christian. The guilt and shame intensified. And that confused me because I thought coming to Christ was freeing, but I found myself in more bondage and pain. My mind would wonder thinking how old the children would be and if I'd have any grandchildren. These thoughts not only affected me, but all my relationships as well. I felt like I had nothing to offer anyone so all my relationships were destined to doom. I lived as a "victim" who was full of self-pity, self-hatred, guilt and shame. How can anyone have a solid sound relationship with all that going on inside? It even affected how I responded to children or to young families with young children. Some of you know exactly what I mean without me having to go into details.

We cannot do anything about changing the past. The past is the past. But we can do something about where we are right now. And that's what I want to bring you to. This information is based on the Word of God and it's the only place you'll find what you are looking for, restoration, peace, stability, and a sound mind. Hey, I know many drugs that can give an illusion that we're okay, but when the drug would wear off, we are right back where we started. I know that some of you have turned to alcohol. But we all know that isn't the answer. But I found the answer. And if I can be healed in my heart to where those thoughts and remembrances don't burden me or fill me with guilt, then you can be free too. See, we aren't free from what happened, that is part of our memory, but we are free from the pain of what happened! This is what it means when we are free - we are free from the sin.

I now help others who are in the middle of their crisis and pain without "feeling" the pain of my own past. I can be compassionate to others without falling apart myself. I am equipped now to help others without the emotion that comes out in memory of my own experiences. See God doesn't necessarily remove the memory but He does remove the pain. It's the pain that is keeping us in torment. Some of you have even developed physical illnesses, not even knowing they are connected. But they are. What a man thinks, so is he. Whatever has been going on in our mind WILL eventually manifest in our flesh. It's medically proven and personally I have seen this to be the case.

I want to get right down to the truth. There are 6 principles:

❑ Identify - acknowledge where you are in your heart right now.

❑ Admit - whatever happened in the past, today, begin taking responsibility for your life.

❑ Confess to God why you are feeling guilty.

❑ Receive God's Unconditional Love

❑ Receive forgiveness from God for yourself

❑ Forgive others

I'll go into each step thoroughly to help you understand what they mean.

The **first** step is to Identify. Before anyone can be healed within, you have to admit where we are. We need to recognize that abortion was not the right answer to our problem, that it is sin. Don't be afraid to admit this. The Bible says that "The truth shall make you free" (John 8:32) We have to admit that we had the abortion and not be afraid to speak the truth. I believe many of you reading this do acknowledge this in your heart but it has sat there and sat there causing you pain and grief. But there is HOPE for you.

Second step to take is Admit – take responsibility. We need to get back our lives and begin taking responsibility for all our actions. We need to stop blaming others or our circumstances for our choices. Simply accept the truth that you made the decision and that is that. Those who are alcoholics need to acknowledge they have a problem before they can get helped. It's the same with abortions. It could have been the spouse or boyfriend that made us feel like the abortion was the only choice. It could have been a parent or guardian. It could have been a nurse at the school. It could have just been your own fear of how you would take care of a child. It could be ignorance, like I had, to use the abortions as a means of birth control. I had to stop blaming the people who told me abortion was okay because the baby wasn't real yet. I simply stopped all that blaming and took the responsibility upon myself for those decisions. But it doesn't stop there. I know this one is a hard one to grasp, but keep on reading.

The **third** step is to Confess. I'll bet many of you have been so sorry all your life. Acknowledge the sin before God and confess it to Him. Receive His forgiveness and forgive yourself. (I believe this is the place where many can't get past because we can't forgive ourselves or even think we should be forgiven for the things we did - this is what I'll be covering in detail. I believe that you have already done steps 1 and 2 to some degree, now it's time to get past all that and move into a new phase in your life. I understand that you may have been grieving for that child (or children in many cases) for so many years. You have difficulty parenting the children you do have because of your guilt and shame. It's time to be healed. It's time to take back your life. It's time to move on. It's time to stop grieving. It's time to get out of your grave clothes and walk in the land of the living. If you are ready for this, then continue.

The **fourth** step is to receive the unconditional love of God and <u>believe</u> you have been forgiven. Many are stuck in this position because they simply can't understand how anyone could be forgiven for their horrific sin. This person is correct, they don't understand, otherwise they would be free today from guilt and shame. We need to allow God to love us.

I have known many Christian women who had abortions early in life but are still tormented by those thoughts and other past regrets. But it all boils down to not receiving the Love of God personally. We think, "How can God love me, look what I've done?" But the truth is, He does. This acknowledgment is very important for your restoration and healing to occur. God's love is unconditional. And let me set the record straight, this is NOT the unpardonable sin. The unpardonable sin is to reject Christ as Savior. I know that my past and my relationship with my earthly father (or men for that matter) were not very good. As a matter of fact, this is my fourth marriage and I can't count on my feet and hands all the men I lived with before, in between and after each marriage. I was seeking love, but I wasn't getting the right kind of Love. What a mess my life was! In my case, I had been a Christian for 18 years before I truly received the love of God unconditionally for myself. That's when my heart and life began changing.

The Bible tells us that Jesus is the healer of a broken heart. So let's start at the beginning, which is a pretty good place to start. He receives anyone who calls upon Him, no matter WHAT we have done. I'm speaking from experience because if there was anyone who lived a "wild" life, it was I. God is the only one who can heal. So be sure to start by asking Jesus into your heart. And as the prayer says, asking for forgiveness for ALL your sins, even those you think shouldn't be forgiven.

The Bible says that perfect love casts out all fear because fear has torment (1 John 4:16-18). If we are sad all the time, in pain about our memories, if we are fearful, if we have doubts and worries about our future, then we are not receiving His love. If you are not receiving the love of God you are probably in fear, self-hatred, self-rejection, and always feeling guilty and condemned about something. You may think that you don't deserve to be happy because of what you have done. You may even suffer from stress, anxiety, phobias and panic attacks as I did for 30 years. I heard a doctor say something that I believe pertains to us. "If my mental patients knew they were forgiven, they would walk out of this hospital within a week healed." I believe this is true for us too. We have a hard time forgiving ourselves let alone receiving forgiveness from God. We think we have to carry that pain as "penitence" but to tell you the truth you are trying pay for something you can never repay! When you do this you are putting yourselves on the cross saying that Jesus wasn't enough.

Remember, that is what Jesus did so you won't have to.

The **fifth** step is to <u>receive</u> forgiveness from God and forgive yourself. Of course you and I both know that this one is very hard. Until you begin receiving the Love of God for yourself, it will be literally impossible to forgive yourself. So how do we do this? By confessing your sin before Him. This is an example of how God began restoring me. I prayed, "Lord I had many abortions. Each one was a child Lord. I admit my sin and I thank you for forgiving me of my sins. God, you said in I John 1:9 that if I confess my sins, You are faithful and just to forgive me of all my sins and to cleanse me from all unrighteousness. By faith I receive the forgiveness for the abortions. In Jesus name, Amen."

To know God's love will help you forgive yourself. See while we were yet sinners Christ died for us because of the Love of God toward us. "We love Him because He first loved us" (1 John 4:19). We cannot even love God correctly without His love in us first. The problem is not with God the problem is with us believing He loves us and has a good plan for our lives NO MATTER what our choices were. The problem is us not receiving that love. When we receive that kind of love, nothing is impossible. We begin to love ourselves properly, WITHOUT condition. See, our love is human love, it is full of conditions. There are flaws and ultimatums in our love with ourselves and with others. Sometimes we think we have to "do" something to be loved. But with God, HE IS LOVE, He cannot do anything else, nor are we to do anything else but receive it. (I John 4:16) He loves you RIGHT now even with all the past mistakes. He saw you do them, He was right there watching. Nothing was hid from Him. Yet He loves you. Yet He wants to heal your heart. Why? Because you are His daughter. The children that were conceived are with Him right now. He beholds their face every day. He wants you to join them someday in Heaven. He wants you to look up toward the heavens not down to the ground. By allowing the truth to penetrate your heart, and recognize the things that you have done point blank, will bring healing! It's "knowing" the truth, which sets us free. Don't be afraid to see the junk in your life. Once you see it, then it's God's job to clean it out and heal you!

So now that He knows I mean business, He wants to clean up everything in my heart and help me forgive anyone and everyone that was involved in these decisions. Because, from the abortions we have had, we take on other sins. For example because of the abortions, we may have became fearful, angry, hopeless, helpless, uncertain, unstable, hurt, painful, depressed, suicidal, addicted to drugs or alcohol, bitter, resentful, man hater, self-hatred, self-rejection, abandoned, offended easily, ashamed, embarrassed, jealous and envy, condemned, liar, distressed, to name a few. These are the "sins" that you retained, they have to be confessed. Not just the abortion, but all the "junk" that goes along with it. It's these sins that are keeping you from being set free in your mind and allowing you to receive blessings from God. See the "abortion" is a result of a sinful thought. So even though we confess we had an abortion, we also need to see what the roots were behind that decision. If they aren't dealt with they will remain and continue to torment you in other areas of your life.

The Bible says in Isaiah 59:1-2 and Jeremiah 5:25 that it's our sins and iniquities that prevent good things from happening to us. These things that you just named need to be confessed as well.

So take your "rap sheet" to the Lord and confess these sins to Him. Thank Him for forgiving you of these sins and believe that He WILL wash you clean. God never goes against His Word, He said that IF you confess your sins, HE will cleanse you from them. Our job is to confess and His job is to cleanse and restore us. Let's take Him at His Word. Let's not make it more complicated than it really is.

Let me explain what is happening here. By identifying YOUR SINS that you became because of your past you are now at the brink of a breakthrough. See when you receive forgiveness for those sins they are removed once and for all from your life. You are FREE from these sins. Jesus is the only one who can cover our sins. By His death on the cross, He carried them all for us so we won't have to anymore. If this is true in your life, then what we confessed is no longer there. Once we confessed these things, we are MADE free. Now we can truly forgive ourselves because there is nothing left to keep us from doing so. It's like we never committed the action of sin in the first place!

The **sixth** step is to forgive anyone that has hurt you. In the case of the abortion(s) we need to forgive the father of the child and anyone else that was involved in the decision you made. This is not always easy, but is required for you to find the peace you need. The Bible says that "If you don't forgive your brother (people who hurt you) then I (God) won't forgive you either" (Matthew 6:14). We have to reconcile first to our brother before coming to God. That is why our prayers aren't being answered. There is too much unforgiveness toward other people and it hinders our prayers to God.

So, how do we forgive someone we can't forgive? If you follow these steps, you will find out. Get out a piece of paper and draw a line down the center of it making two columns. Place the name of the individual at the top of the page. Begin writing down things on the left column they did that hurt you. This may take some time, but that's okay. Ask God to help you. Don't be afraid of the emotional pain, it's all part of the healing process. Then on the right column, write down things YOU became because of that person. For example, you may have become fearful, angry, bitter, resentful, ashamed, etc. It may be some of the same sins you confessed earlier. Sins are piled upon sins, that's why we are so sick, emotionally and physically. The sins you just recognized are the sins you have taken on from that person.

John 20:23 says that *"Whosoever sins ye remit shall be remitted unto them, and whosoever sins ye remiss, shall be remissed."* What it's saying is that when we don't forgive the person from our heart immediately their sins jump on us. Now we are carrying not only our own junk, but also all the other person's too! How heavy that becomes in our spirit! No wonder we are so sick and tired. We are carrying stuff that our bodies weren't meant to carry. Jesus was the only one who was meant to carry these sins...

Once you have identified these sins of yours, first John 1:9 'em! Yes, take them to God in confession and thank God for forgiving you - that is how you receive forgiveness for them. This will cause God to remove them from your life, allowing you the ability to forgive the person needing forgiveness. You are now free to forgive yourself.

Another area is in the area of accusations. We have inadvertently blamed God for not intervening in the situation, whether it's having the abortion or someone hurting us. We have secretly doubted Him, this is what is keeping us from our restoration and healing. We have to restore our relationship with God in order for the rest to fall into place. After all, He's the blessing giver, He's the restorer, and if we have a breach with Him, how can we be healed? How can we receive anything from someone we don't trust, or have been disappointed with, or are mad at?

The process of forgiving yourself is not a long process if you have the pieces. We have a hard time forgiving ourselves because of Guilt and Condemnation. Receive forgiveness for yourself once and for all and let GOD do the healing and watch Him move in your life.

As God began healing me, He also showed me that I never grieved over these children. So one day, I did. Along with that grieving I named each one. The Lord helped me to see them as people, but all I ever referenced them as were "them," "its" or "abortions." I never placed a name or even a face on them. But I have now. I put all their names in my Bible. They are alive and well, and I am celebrating the fact that I had a part in bringing them into this world, if not for this life but for the life after. A huge healing took place in my heart.

This was how the Lord helped me to heal. This way may not be the way God wants you follow. I remembered sharing this story at a ladies seminar and one of the ladies began crying profusely. She just couldn't even comprehend doing this because her pain was so great. I do know that it allowed God to reach down into her heart and begin churning up things that needed to be brought to the surface for healing to take place. I don't know what has happened to her since, but she remains in my heart and I'm believing God's restoration and healing for her life.

I would like to take a minute to talk about the enemy. As we take responsibility for our actions, I also had to realize that there was a spirit at work as well. It was the spirit of fear and the spirit of death. I had to confess that I allowed the spirit of fear to manipulate me in making the decisions to have abortions. As I thought about this, I realized that most of the decisions were made out of fear - fear of not being able to take care of the child, fear of loosing my freedom, fear of a birth defect because of all the drugs I've taken, fear of what people would say about me, and the list goes on. So my decisions were made out of fear. And the spirit of death is present any time death is involved and not dealt with in a godly manner. For example: Fear came first then the spirit of death comes in to cause me to get the abortion. Then other times we can be with a loved one that just passed on, there is a spirit of death there too. And if our hearts aren't processing that death properly, that spirit of death can play havoc on our lives.

So in order to get past this, I prayed this prayer. "Dear Heavenly Father, I have taken responsibility for my actions, but I also recognized that I was under the influence of fear. I confess that I submitted to it and repent for having had fear. I cast out that spirit of fear now and will no longer bow down to it. I also recognize that the spirit of death took root in my life. I ask you to forgive me for entertaining that spirit and cast it out in Jesus name. Thank you for filling me with your love and forgiveness. I realize now that fear killed my children. That is the plain fact, and that you have forgiven me for being ignorant and fearful. Thank you for forgiving me and loving me even in the midst of this. In Jesus name, Amen."

After I exposed the enemy and prayed that prayer, more healing too place in my heart. Fear was no longer preventing me from seeing truth, and death was nowhere to be found tormenting me.

What are the results of doing all this? Well, my life with my husband has completely transformed. Where there wasn't much intimacy, we are now very intimate. Where I had problems with relating to babies, those thoughts and feelings are no longer there. Where I was jealous of young families with children, these thoughts and feelings are no longer there. I'm FREE from the pain of those memories. I can speak of the abortions without gripping pain in my chest. I can now help others, like you, who need to be set free. I can see others and have relationship with others without my past hurts causing my response. What I mean is that for example: When I saw a family with children, I wouldn't be very friendly to them because my jealousy was manifesting. When I started to have a relationship with anyone, I was always full of suspicion. These responses are from what was still in my heart that hadn't been purged yet that related to these abortions (or sins that haven't been dealt with in general).

Look at the choices I made, I had numerous abortions and many sexually transmitted diseases. I committed fornication and adultery, have been married several times, I gave my son up at age two-and-a-half to be raised by his father. I lied and cheated. I had a fowl mouth that only spoke cursing. I can go on and on, but I think you get the picture. I'm someone who never though she could ever be blessed with anything. Yet today I am. I am happier than I could have ever dreamed possible. I have a wonderful husband who loves me. I have a beautiful home on a plot of land in a retreat setting besides a beautiful rushing river. I was given a wonderful job (from which I was able to retire early) and great friends. I have a ministry God has entrusted to me to help others, like you. I write and produce musicals and plays. I sing and have opportunities to put together concerts and community outreach events. I'm helping establish other ministers in their ministry. God has given me a desire to help teenagers, not to mention care for small children. My son and I are great friends; he's an adult now with children of his own. These are the blessings God has given to me IN SPITE of my decisions that I made in my life. I have peace in my heart and mind. There is no pain left in me. It's the PAIN in us that prevents us from moving on.

I won't ever forget that I had those abortions. I won't ever forget the many men I lived with. I won't ever forget the problems I caused my family. But I also won't forget how much GOD loves me and has forgiven me and washed me clean of it ALL and removed the stain AND pain from my life. It was coming to the acknowledgment of His love and receiving His love along with forgiving myself and others, that has afforded me all these blessings. It's not that I do everything right, I don't, but its that I confessed my heart to God and allowed Him heal me and set me free.

Ministry:

"Dear Heavenly Father. Standing with me is this dear loved one who has accessed this teaching because of their personal decisions for having abortion(s) or for someone else going through pain and suffering because of abortion(s). You know their situation. You know when it happened and who was involved. Yet you still love them. Let them get a revelation on how deep your love really is. There is nothing they can do that will separate them from your love. As they face each area discussed, I pray you give them mercy and grace to deal with them accordingly. I ask you to fill them with your unconditional love and allow them to receive it as well. Help them face their sins and confess them and "receive" completely forgiveness for them. They are no longer to carry this weight any longer. Yes, what they did was wrong and they know it, but you forgave it already. Help them forgive and love themselves. Spirit of fear, go in Jesus name. Spirit of death, go, in Jesus name. You have played havoc in their lives for too long and they are no longer going to allow you to use them as your puppet. They fall out of agreement with everything you stand for. You are no longer welcome here, so go. Father I ask you to flood them with your presence and love and forgiveness. Release them from all guilt and shame and mend their broken heart. Help them forgive all those involved, and confess any sin of blame they have against you too. Thank you for loving them Lord and helping them find their peace. Because you know Lord where I was and where I am now and if it wasn't for what I'm teaching these individuals I wouldn't be free. You are no respecter of persons so what You have done for me, you will do for them. Thank you Father, in Jesus name, Amen."

CHAPTER TWENTY-EIGHT

Sex and the Bible

In order to be "one" with God, "one" with yourself, and "one" with your spouse, we need to get rid of all the other wrong connections to our soul and spirit.

Inordinate Affection: (wrong soul-ties)

Colossians 3:5; Lists "inordinate affection" among many other sins such as fornication and idolatry and lying. Inordinate Affection is also known as "soul-ties" to wrong relationships. It can mean emotionally or physically, we are allowing others to have control over us. It means we are tied to the other person's wrong behavior, activities and other relationships. Soul-mates and soul-ties are different - one is Godly and one is not. An inordinate affection can be between two friends and of the same sex. They aren't sexually active with each other but they have tendencies of control over one another. Discussed further in this teaching.

Many of us have soul-ties that we are not even aware of, and that brings us to the issue of Sex and the Bible, Fornication and Adultery. The word fornication comes from a Latin word meaning "to visit a brothel." This is the word the King James Version translators used to translate the New Testament Greek word *porneia*. *Porneia* is used throughout the New Testament and refers to any type of heterosexual intercourse, which takes place outside the marriage. Promiscuity is the modern word for casual sex among many partners.

We all know fornication is sinful, but learning why may help us understand why it's talked about in I Corinthians 6:13, 15-20.

If you have had sex/intimacy with one person all your life, then you are only exposed to that one person. If the other person had more than one partner, then you are not only exposed to them, but all their partners as well. See chart below:

# of Partners	Total Exposed to
1	1
2	3
3	7
4	15
5	31
6	63
7	127

No wonder we cannot have intimate relations with the one we are with, there are "too many involved" in that "one" relationship.

To be healed in this area, confession of all relationships is to be done (as discussed in the forgiveness teaching) and then receive forgiveness breaking soul-ties to each and every individual involved. I find that when we truly forgive someone, soul-ties are cut automatically. I know when someone hasn't forgiven another is when they are still being controlled and manipulated by them.

Pray for healing and restoration from God into your lives to restore you to yourself. Forgive those who have caused pain during these relationships, and receive forgiveness for hurting others.

We can have inordinate affection (soul-ties) without having sex, especially with the same sex, which is called "Situational Homosexuality."

It looks like this: Two friends can create an unclean relationship. Jealousy and envy of seeing them have friends, not including you. Unnatural bonds go from friendship to control. These HAVE to be severed.

How the Body reacts:

Our bodies were designed to become "one flesh" with a mate - one mate. It is very literal too if you take a look at how a sperm and egg become "one" flesh in the womb. I was reading through the Bantam Medical dictionary and read something quite astounding. We are all made with a specific number of cells. The sperm carries half of these cells and the woman carries the other half so that when the baby is born, they have the exact number of cells! This is God's divine creative abilities at work. Now, what we also know is that DNA can change, and we discuss this more when dealing with fear, and that is why we have birth defects. Some of the building block cells of human life were compromised in some way.

The relationship with a man helps boost the women's immune system. His sweat even helps to regulate her menstrual cycles (Clinically proven)

If a woman exposes herself to another's sperm, while she is with child, it can have an adverse reaction on the fetus, depleting that child's immune system from birth.

When we become "one" with our mate - we mingle our blood streams. Since "life is in the blood" (Leviticus 17:11). this is where the enemy wants to come and mess with our blood stream.

Kissing on the mouth also transfers viruses from one body to another, be it a common virus or sexual virus such as herpes, mono, etc. You are exchanging blood cells, viruses, bacteria and perhaps unknown infectious agents yet to be discovered. Now I understand why Hollywood has so many relationship issues, with them kissing each other during their acting, they are transferring viruses and other agents to one another, chemicals and DNA that are supposed to be for a married couple, and let's not forget transferring spirits... Yikes!

We receive our blood streams from our parents. If they were disobedient and living wrongly, we will inherit everything they took into their own lives. We can receive a virus that will affect all the generations after.

"Flee fornication, every sin that a man doeth is without the body, but he that committeth fornication sinneth against his own body" (1 Corinthians 6:18).

This type of living also affects our minds. It causes alienation in our thoughts - with others, ourself, and God. Read all of Ezekiel Chapter 23, it talks of two women having inordinate affection.

"Know ye not that ye are God's temple, and the Spirit of God dwells within you? If anyone corrupts the temple of God, God shall bring corruption to him; for the temple of God is holy, which ye are" (1 Corinthians 3:16-17).

If we do not heed this scripture as it relates to sexual issues, we will receive corruption. Our health will deteriorate! Simple as that.

How to Be Restored

By recognizing the truth of your own situation, regardless of how hard it is to see, you have made a step in the right direction. Do not go into guilt or condemnation, but go to God for healing and restoration.

Pray something like this:

"Father, I recognize and take full responsibility for the choices I made in my life with regard to sex. I have had more than one partner, and I take this to you in the Name of Jesus for healing and restoration. (Talk to God about this, tell Him of those you were with, etc.) I break all soul-ties, wrong affections toward them, and ask for you to heal my life and their life. I ask you to heal my body and cleanse any defilement that I brought upon myself. I ask you to restore my spouse, that no defilement from me is placed upon him/her. I pray for cleansing and purifying of our hearts and lives from our bad choices, and ignorance in this matter. I pray for healing of any viruses or transmitted diseases to one another. I forgive those whom transferred diseases to me knowingly or in their ignorance. I forgive myself for doing the same with others. (Talk to God and be specific).

I ask you to reveal any relationships that are inordinate, any soul-ties and co-dependencies that I have so I can be free from them. I ask you to reveal too me if I'm someone who others need freedom from as well because I'm causing that soul-tie to continue. I ask you to release me from them all right now, exposing each one so that I can be freed.

I thank you for working this out in my life and restoring my body, mind and heart in cleanness to you Lord. I cast off every unclean and defiled spirit in Jesus Name!"

Note: If you have had multiple partners, be sure to name each and everyone off to the Lord and receive forgiveness for each and every act with them. Pray for all soul-ties to be broken and that God restore you to wholeness in Him.

CHAPTER TWENTY-NINE

Spirits Revealed

This topic can be controversial. There are many Christians who don't believe they can possess any other spirit than the Holy Ghost. This was my belief for many years until I saw what I'll be showing you in this teaching. You decide for yourself. Mark 7:21-23 says that these things come from "within" the man.

Some believe that there are no evil spirits at all. Some believe that there are spirits but that they only "oppress" us and cannot inhabit us. That means that a spirit can come along and torment them, but not get inside. Well, let me ask you a question. When you "feel" fear, is it on our insides or on your outside? When you are angry, does that feeling of anger well up from inside or outside? You decide. Because until we realized there is a possibility that these can be "inside" us, we won't get free. The enemy wants us to believe this so that we won't be free. So instead of trying to convince anyone, let's take a look at what the scriptures say.

I ran a reference on the word "spirit" and was amazed to find so many listings, both of God and of the enemy. So if you see any of these areas manifested in your life, then take them to God. Let Him deliver you from these spirits and be restored once and for all. It's not time to fall into fear about what you see, but rejoice at what is being exposed. Once the spirit has been exposed it looses is grip on you. Then you have the authority to tell it to take a hike.

Then as you recognize and cast them out, open your heart to more of God and His love. By replacing those areas with more of God, the evil spirits will not be able to return. And we simply fill up with God by loving Him and staying clean before Him through confession. It's actually easy... we have made things complicated.

Spirits from God		Evil Spirits	
Spirit of God	Gen 1:2	Anguish of Spirit	Exodus 6:9
Spirit of Wisdom	Exodus 28:3	Spirit of Jealousy	Numbers 5:14, 30
Spirit of Understanding	Job 20:3	Sorrowful Spirit	I Sam 1:15
Contrite Spirit	Psalm 34:18	Evil Spirit	I Sam 16:14-23, I Sam. 18:10, 19:9,20; Acts
Free Spirit	Psalm 51:12	Lying Spirit	I Kings 22:22
Broken Spirit	Psalm 51:17	Haughty Spirit	Proverbs 16:18
Humble Spirit	Proverbs 16:19	Broken Spirit	Proverbs 17:22

Excellent Spirit	Proverbs 17:27; Daniel 5:12; 6:3	Wounded Spirit	Proverbs 18:14
Contrite Spirit	Isaiah 66:2	Perverse (Stubborn, turning from what is right) Spirit	Isaiah 19:14
Spirit of Grace and Supplication	Zechariah 12:10	Spirit of Judgment	Isaiah 28:6
Poor in Spirit	Matthew 5:3	Spirit of Deep Sleep	Isaiah 29:10
		Spirit of Slumber	Romans 11:8
Spirit of Truth	John 14:17; 15:26; 16:13	Spirit of Heaviness	Isaiah 61:3
Spirit of Holiness	Romans 1:4	Vexation of Spirit	Isaiah 65:14
Law of the Spirit	Romans 8:2	Spirit of Whoredoms	Hosea 4:12; 5:4
Spirit of Adoption	Romans 8:15	Unclean Spirit	Zechariah 13:2 (Idolatry) 2 Corinthians 12:20
Love of the Spirit	Romans 15:30	Residue of the Spirit	Malachi 2:15
Fervent in Spirit	Romans 12:11	Unclean Spirit	Matthew 10:1; 12:43; Mark 1:23,26; 3:11,30; 5:2,8,13; 6:7; 7:25; Acts 5:16; 8:7; Rev. 16:13
Spirit of Meekness	1 Corn. 4:21	Devils	Matthew 12:28; Rev. 16:14
Spirit of Faith	2 Corinthians 4:13	Dumb Spirit	Mark 9:17
Fruit of the Spirit	Gal 5:22	Foul Spirit	Mark 9:25; Rev. 18:2
Spirit of Wisdom	Ephesians 1:17	Deaf and Dumb	Mark 9:25

Spirit of your mind	Ephesians 4:23	Spirit of an unclean devil	Luke 4:33;36; 6:18; 9:42
Holy Ghost	Ephesians 4:30; 1	Seven other Spirits worse than the first	Luke 11:26
Sword of the Spirit is the Word	Ephesians 6:17	Spirit of Infirmity	Luke 13:11
Spirit of Jesus Christ	Philippians 1:19	Spirit of divination	Acts. 16:16
Ministering Spirits	Hebrews 1:14	Spirit of Bondage	Romans 8:15
Spirit of Grace	Hebrews 10:29	Spirit of the World	1 Corinthians 2:12
Spirit of Prophecy	Revelations 19:10	Anti-Christ (unloving)	1 John 2:18,22; 4:3; 2 John 7
Meek and Quiet Spirit	1 Peter 3:4	Another Spirit	2 Corinthians 11:4
Spirit of Truth	1 John 4:6	Spirit of disobedience	Ephesians 2:2
		Seducing Spirits	1 Timothy 4:1
		Spirit of Fear	2 Tim. 1:7
		Lusting Spirit	James 4:5
		Spirit of Error	1 John 4:6
		Sensual	Jude 19
		Drunkenness	Jeremiah 13:13; Ezekiel 23:33

Prayer for you to Pray:

Father, I recognize some of these things within me. I repent for those I see (name them off) and fall out of agreement with them. I give my life to you, no longer under the snare of these spirits. They must leave now in Jesus Name.

Prayer for You:

"Father I pray that every evil spirit exposed in this Saint's life GO by the power of the Holy Ghost! I ask for your unconditional love to flood them in these areas that were riddled with torment and heal them Lord. In Jesus name, Amen."

Note: Study these scriptures. Learn about them, the more you discern, the faster you will be able to keep yourself from the snare of the devil.

CHAPTER THIRTY

Departmentalizing God

Have you ever been stressed? Well, that is a silly question for most of you... of course you have from time to time. You have families to take care, you have schedules to keep, bills to pay, plans to make, etc. Stress is a part of your make up. But... is that from God? I think you know the answer, but just in case, "Stress is not from God."

Why do you think we have stress, anxiety, fear or worry?

Because we departmentalize God.

Have you ever found yourself saying, "Boy, I've gotten off track somewhere." And you can't figure out what went wrong? You've been feeling "bad" and even guilty but not know why. I can tell you it's because you departmentalized God.

Let me share a story to explain what I mean.

I went on a 2-day trip with my mom and three sisters to Reno, Nevada for Hot August Nights. For those of you who don't know what that is, it's where old vehicles rally there for a big car show. It's set in a 50's environment with that old music, dance, hop, etc. I've never been to one before and this was also a chance to visit with my family.

I took God everywhere I went, even when I sat down at a slot machine. I took Him in the bathroom with me and outside to look at the old cars. And do you know what I discovered even when I knew being in the casino wasn't the place I was supposed to be? I still took God with me. What happened was short of a miracle. Since I brought Him IN those areas, He let me see those things through His eyes. Instead of putting the money in the machines, I noticed hurting and sad people all around me. They're all looking for that big jackpot to end all their problems. But these were ordinary people. Many looked like they were spending their food money or bill money. I wandered around and even took time to say hello to a few that were alone and sad. Even though I knew that I wasn't to be in the casinos, I still took God with me. The Bible says that even though I make my bed in hell, He is there.

I used to think if I left God at the front door, that's where He stayed, and I would be okay to go in. But the truth was I became guilt ridden the whole time I was in there. But this time I noticed I wasn't feeling guilty or shameful at all. I went in there and took God with me, He let me see the situation through His eyes and when He did this, I found myself staying outside or in my room. I didn't feel any guilt at all, only His love, peace and His joy. He didn't judge me or condemn me, He loved me "through" it.

I used to departmentalize God based on what was going on. For instance, when I went to work, I left God outside the door. What I mean is that I wouldn't "think" of Him once during my workday. I would get so wrapped up in my work that I wouldn't even acknowledge Him in it. Then when I would leave to go home, I would pick back up with Him from the morning. Of course, you and I know, God was with me all the time, the issue was that I didn't "acknowledge" Him being there so to me He wasn't.

I just thought He was there waiting for me and we'd drive off together. I departmentalized God and now I know those times I didn't take Him into my job with me, things weren't so peaceful. The joy of the Lord wasn't there and I began disliking my job and what I was doing. I couldn't wait to get out of there every day, and looked forward to weekends, and dreaded Sunday's because work was just around the corner.

If I took God into my job with me "acknowledging Him in ALL my ways" I do believe things would have been better. I did take Him in the last few years before I retired because I finally saw what I was doing. Because you and I know, He was there all the time. It's that I didn't acknowledge He was there that my puny little mind assumed He wasn't. And the Bible says, "Whatever you believe, so let it be done to you." If I didn't believe God was there at my job, then He wasn't. If I believed God was there, then I would see Him in everything I did.

Another area that I departmentalized God in was while shopping. I would get frustrated, exasperated with people, impatient, and angry realizing now it was those times I left God out of that moment. I would have Him in some moments, especially when I would spend time in my chair reading the Bible. But I now know I can have Him even if I'm not sitting in my chair; like ironing or cleaning my house. I would say, "When I get done with this laundry I'll read the Bible." But the truth is, I can spend time with God WHILE doing my laundry. If we don't departmentalize God, then we won't have that yo yo effect in life nor get off the beaten trail. The result would be developing a constancy that cannot be moved when something hard comes your way. You don't have to seek God for hours and hours to hear your prayer because you never let up praying. The Bible says to pray without ceasing. What does that mean? Simply acknowledging God in all your ways!

So next time you have a list of things to accomplish, put God after every item to remind you that He wants to go with you, no matter where you go! He's there any way you might as well acknowledge Him. I found something even more amazing. I remember watching a movie called "Armageddon" with Bruce Willis. They were tasked to land on a meteor, plant an explosive device inside the center of it and then detonate it, destroying it. But they didn't get deep enough within the core of the meteor and so the explosion didn't even phase it. The Lord showed me that's what was happening in my life. If I take Him into those places where I would normally not acknowledge Him, He is going to expose the truth to me from the inside out. And that's what we want. We want all those things we try to keep from God brought out into the light. He can only do this if we let Him in those areas deep inside. If you only let God touch the surface, like with that meteor story, the same thing will happen for you... and nothing will change.

If this describes your life, if you are hiding parts of your heart from God thinking it's too hard to face, too embarrassing or not important, or it's sin you cannot face, or if you leave God at the door when you go someplace you really shouldn't be, then I want to pray for you.

See, no matter what you think you have done that may have caused you to get off track a bit, remember, Jesus paid for it all. He is the restorer. But if you don't go to Him, how can He restore? Be restored dear Saints. Go to Him with everything, and in everything, and while doing everything, then and only then will you truly understand the relationship He wants with you. This relationship of "knowing God" is really "knowing His heart." That's what we all desire, and that's what we all yearn for. Knowing His heart means He loves you no matter what! You cannot earn it, you cannot even stop it, God is love, He can do nothing else.

If you want to get off the "rabbit trail" you may have been on, or running from something within your heart you don't want to see, I want to pray for you.

Ministry Prayer for You:

"Father, when we make our bed in hell you are there, when we live on this planet, you are there, no matter where we are, you are there. Help us to remember you IN ALL OUR WAYS, so that you can direct our paths. Let us not be afraid to take you with us even when we go where we shouldn't. I ask you to help us see our hearts clearly at these times and see what you see so that it will set us free and help us make good decisions where we go. Help us to run to you with our issues, or disappointments, our anger, our confusion, our questions, our relationships with others and be completely honest with you. After all, you are in there too. You see it, so why do we think we are hiding anything. Let everything be exposed Father that is not of you. Remove what is not of you and replace it with more of You. I confess all fear, dread, doubt and unbelief. I confess my sins of _____ (name them) and ask for your forgiveness. I ask for you to heal my broken heart. I thank you for restoring me to you, myself and others as we continue to walk out this life time together. In Jesus name, Amen."

CHAPTER THIRTY-ONE

Potential Blocks to Blessings

In this session, we will address several blocks that were in my life that were key in preventing the blessings of God to fall upon me. It's not that God was not wanting to bless me, it was that I wasn't able to "receive."

The main theme to every block listed is the absence of love. You can also look at it this way, if love is not received for yourself, or love is not given out to others, then that is a major issue in your life. Jesus came to show us the Father's love. If that was Jesus' main objective, then what should ours be?

The Bible says that "If ye forgive men their trespasses your heavenly Father will also forgive you; but if you forgive NOT men their trespasses, neither will your Father forgive you your trespasses." (Matthew 6:14) In order to have a good relationship with your Father in Heaven, you need to have relationships restored at this level. The Bible says "Whatever you do to the least of these my brethren, you do it unto me." (Matthew 25:40) If we don't forgive others, what does that say about our relationship with God? If we don't love others, what does that say about our relationship with God? The Bible says that people will know us by our love one for another (John 13:35).

Jesus came so that we could have a relationship with our Heavenly Father. He came to cleanse us from all sin. However, if someone does not recognize this and apply the sacrifice Jesus did on the cross for that sin, but keeps it because they think that sin is unpardonable, that person stays in that state of guilt and shame, then that will be a major block from having fellowship with God. And a result of not having fellowship with God is not having healing and blessings come your way. Remember that SIN SEPARATES us from God. We put a BLOCK before God to work in our lives because of our stink in' thin kin'. Isaiah 59:1-2 clearly states this. He can heal and deliver, but He chooses not to because of our sin! Jeremiah 5:25 says, "Your sins and iniquities prevent good things from happening to you."

So keep in mind if there is any unforgiveness or sins that have not been confessed as you go through these blocks at that moment, stop and bring it before the Lord. Don't fear or get condemned because they are there, but rejoice that the Lord has shown you so you can be free! These spirits are using you as a puppet, you need to get your life back today. 2 Timothy 2-23-26 says that a minister is to help you identify what is there and help you recover yourself from the snare of the devil and loose you from those bands that bind you (Isaiah 53).

There are many blocks I am sure, but the following are the main blocks I had in my own life. Once recognized, God was able to begin the healing in my heart, which then healed my body, changed circumstances in my life, and brought me peace.

Once I dealt with a block, I was no longer tormented by it. I may have had tests along the way but they were no longer preventing me from living my life and being close to God. When we get rid of blocks, they are no longer before us but behind us, and so we are able to see clearly. I've been teaching this stuff for many, many years and I myself have been healed in many areas and I never have to go back over an area where I was stuck because whom the Son has set free, is free indeed. Believe me, there will be plenty of new areas to cover as the days press on. That's what Jesus meant when he said, "Anyone who puts his hand to the plow and looks back is not fit for the Kingdom of God" (Luke 9:62). It doesn't mean you can look back onto things you haven't dealt with, it means you don't need to keep rehashing over things you have dealt with. If you keep rehashing, then there is unforgiveness or other blocks preventing you from moving forward.

Each day should be a new one with new exciting things. It could be a new direction in your ministry, it could even be a new health issue that presents itself. Regardless of what it is, things should be new all the time. Jesus said He wants to do something "new" in us. But if we are stuck in our junk of yesterday, we are unfit for the "Kingdom of God."

What are blocks? Blocks are emotional, spiritual and/or physical issues that prevent you from:

> a. Receiving God's love
> b. Having Healthy Relationships
> c. Healing
> d. Blessings and Promises of God
> e. Seeing truth

Identifying blocks will help you find peace within. These things can be emotional, spiritual or physical and can even cause dis-ease in our bodies. It's proven medically that guilt causes mental breakdown, fear causes stress and many diseases derive from that. Shame causes insecurity and fear., and worshipping idols or statues or symbols can cause bodily injury. The Bible is full of dis-eases that manifest in our bodies based on our thinking.

Below lists a few of these blocks to help you see where you are. Again, not to bring you condemnation, but to bring you to a place of surrender, repentance, and total restoration.

❏ **Unforgiveness** - Unforgiveness is the #1 block to all healing, It interwines in every area of our life. When we have fear, there is unforgiveness somewhere. When we have relationship issues, there is unforgiveness somewhere. When we are feeling guilty, there is unforgiveness somewhere. That is why it's so important to take care of this one first and foremost. During ministry, the first thing we do is get individuals to repent for any and all bitterness towards themselves, others and even God. Scriptures are clear that if we don't forgive others, neither will God for Christ's sake, forgive us. Here are a few of those scriptures:

Matthew 6:12 *And forgive us our debts, as we forgive our debtors.*

Matthew 6:14-15 *For if ye forgive men their trespasses, your heavenly Father will also forgive you: But if ye forgive not men their trespasses, neither will your Father forgive your trespasses.*

Matthew 18:20-22 *For where two or three are gathered together in my name, there am I in the midst of them. Then came Peter to him, and said, Lord, how oft shall my brother sin against me, and I forgive him? till seven times? Jesus saith unto him, I say not unto thee, Until seven times: but, Until seventy times seven.*

Matthew 18: 34-35 34 *And his lord was wroth, and delivered him to the tormentors, till he should pay all that was due unto him. So likewise shall my heavenly Father do also unto you, if ye from your hearts forgive not every one his brother their trespasses*

Mark 11:25 *And when ye stand praying, forgive, if ye have ought against any: that your Father also which is in heaven may forgive you your trespasses.*

When we forgive, we open up channels of God's blessings that you may never have dreamed possible. Jesus died on the cross to show us His Father's love THROUGH forgiveness towards us. We also need to forgive one another. But we need to learn to forgive from our heart, not just with mouth service as saying, "I forgive you but...." We have to remove that but (which is unforgivness), so that we are made clean in our hearts unto the Lord.

Many are dying in their sin because they dont' know how to forgive compeltely. Did you know that a victim needs to be forgiven too? For more information on this topic, plesae be sure to pick up my booklet called "Forgiving from Your Heart" or "Bitterness and Unforgiveness, the deadly duo." Both go into the "how to forgive" exercise that can change your life and those around you.

❑ **Fear** - Lack of God's Love "Perfect love casts out all fear and torment." If we have fear, then we aren't being made perfect in God's love. There are hundreds of thousands kinds of fear, but we first need to get rid of the "spirit of fear" in order to be victorious over the fearful thoughts. Fear is a manifestation of something that we experienced, saw, heard, felt, or believed that the spirit of fear plays on. It starts in our thinking! The Bible says that perfect peace comes when our minds are stayed on God BECAUSE we trust him. (Isaiah 26:3). This is the real ticket! Trusting God because in doing that, we stay in peace, and there is no fear because there is no fear in love. (Refer to the in depth teachings on fear).

I discovered that fear was a spirit and I was a puppet on a string to him to do whatever he wanted with me. But after casting it out - yes as a believer - my life began manifesting amazing things - I was no longer controlled by fear, I was now free to keep it off WHEN it tried to return because it will try to "tempt" me to fear again – that's his "MO" (Method of Operation).

2 Corinthians 10:5 says to cast down all imaginations... this is where the enemy attacks us, in our thoughts. James 1 teaches that we are tempted (to fear) when we are drawn away by the lust inside of us. So it's important to release the spirit of fear from your life and to begin basking in God's love. For in doing so you will be keeping yourself from the snare of the devil (2 Timothy 2:24). Submit yourself unto God, resist the devil and he will flee (James 4:7).

❑ **Lack of God's Love**. I just spoke on the area of fear, but without God's love we can never overcome fear. I had to get a deep revelation on God's love for me because the fear was so M in my life. Some people can receive God's love effortlessly, but I had to fight for it. I was in a fight for my life for so many years just keeping my head above water. But when I realized it's God's grace, love and mercy that will hold me up and place me upon high places because of His love, things began changing. My heart was being renewed and I was building a trust toward God because I was finding time to get to know Him. We cannot trust someone we don't know. As I began understanding His love, the love Jesus gives, and the power the Holy Ghost gives and visited with all three, I was being made whole. I needed to restore my relationship with all three... after all, they are all God. I had a lopsided relationship because I was only talking with Jesus. I didn't pay much attention to God because I didn't think He was paying much attention to me. I didn't even know He really existed!!! So as I began my relationship journey with the Father, the Son and the Holy Ghost, my life began changing. (Read more about this in the love of God teaching session.)

❑ **Doubt and Unbelief** (John 6:28-29) We are to believe! Believe on the one who sent Jesus. Do you feel stuck? Do you lack peace and stability? James 1 says that a double-minded man in unstable in all his ways. When we have doubt, believe, doubt, believe, we are double-minded. We need to remain constant in belief no matter what is going on.

For believers Jesus is a stepping stone.

For doubters Jesus is a stumbling block.

Remember, this scripture is talking to the Christians! We need to decide if we are believers or doubters. Recognizing this will help God restore your faith in areas you are stumbling. Do not be ashamed to confess this to God, it's between you and Him.

❑ **Pride** is the original sin - it's behind every sin, that's where it started with Lucifer and that's where it starts with us.

Pride is what caused Satan's fall. He was thrown down with such force from heaven that in his wake there was a lightening bolt! (Luke 10:18) That was pretty hard, don't you think? Pride comes before a fall.

So we have to look at our lives and see how many times we have fallen. But the bible says that a righteous man may fall seven times, but he can get back up. (Proverbs 24:6)

Satan fell and he can never get back up! He is trying to keep you down when you fall, it's up to you to get back up. It's not a time to get under guilt about it, it's time to just face it and address it. Then after he fell, love was removed from him leaving him alone which resulted in fear. Now he works day and night to get you to fear so you are separated from the Love of God. Pride is behind every type of sin imaginable.

Indicators of pride:

- When we do what we want out ahead of God
- Frustrated with others because they don't do it our way
- Irritated by others
- Rebellion
- Control and Manipulation
- Fear
- Needing to be needed
- Needing approval and acceptance
- Get embarrassed easily
- Sensitive and hurt easily
- You say, "I'm a good person" but you don't feel appreciated
- "I can do it better than them"
- Don't they know who I am and what I have to offer?"
- You think everything that happens is because of you
- You think everything that happens is about you
- Offended continually
- Feeling guilty
- Self-exaltation - Bragging and exalts own achievements
- False Humility - looking for someone to see their humility
- False sense of responsibility (false burden bearing) - you are not Jesus

A person who is humbled manifests the following:

- Nothing anyone says hurts them, they are never offended and if they are, they repent
- Submits to authority
- Forgive quickly and unconditionally
- Esteem others over own self and desires
- Trust God in every area of their life

- Peace, stability and soundness
- Teachable
- Admits when they are wrong
- Sees the good in everyone

While going through this teaching, and other areas of teaching, you may start to get a bit uncomfortable. You may want to run or question God on what is going on, but the truth is, He may just be cutting away the pride in your life that is attached to your soul. Let Him do the work. Buckle your seat belt and go for the ride. I had someone ask me what it meant to "buckle your seat belt and go for the ride?" It's like getting in a roller coaster and Jesus is the buckle. He holds you in and keeps you safe so you can have fun!

Exercise 1

From the list above, do any ring true for you? Is so, check them off. This is not to bring you under condemnation but to help you see where the root causes are behind your issues. Pride is a hidden enemy but once he is exposed, you are well on your way to freedom. This is an area people don't even know they have because it is so hidden. We are self-deceived with pride. It's identified as a major block to our blessings.

Exercise 2

Since pride is the root of all sin, take tie to seek God on the matter. Ask yourself what your motive is behind issues. Anything you do to make yourself look good, feel good, or appear good is pride. If you have a need to be needed, that is pride. If you think things can't get done without you, that is pride. When you are dealing with a sin or area in your life that you struggle with, ask God where the pride is? Then as the Lord shows you, take what you see and confess your sin. For example, getting your kids to sit still in church. Are you wanting them to be quiet for "their" good or so that "you" look good?

- **Shame** (I Peter 2:4-7) Close kinship to pride. Whoever believes that Jesus is the chief cornerstone (and all that it represents) we will never be put to shame. There are several references to "shame" in the Bible so it tells me that there is a real problem here and if not dealt with can lead to other problems. And whoever doesn't believe this truth, that same rock becomes a stumbling stone. And this reference isn't talking to non-believers, but to Christians! How many Christians are stumbling around in their life?

  - Shame is an inherent feeling that no one can feel for me. It's produced by our own thought process. If I don't know who I am, that I've been chosen by God, that no one else's thoughts about me matters, then I will be shamed (embarrassed) and set up for rejection and abandonment.

- **Guilt and Condemnation** (produces shame), unworthiness which leads to a lack of courage or boldness. (Be sure to go through the Guilt and

Condemnation teaching in depth.) If you continually live under any kind of guilt or condemnation, you have not applied the forgiveness to your sins that Jesus sacrificed His life to give. When you are under guilt, you believe that you have to "pay" for your sins, or that your sins are so bad, they could never be forgiven. That is a lie! Jesus was enough - it's up to you to believe that. You need to understand "repentance" and what salvation really means.

List your guilt and regrets here:

_____

_____

_____

_____

Take these to God and confess your part in the guilt. You should never be under any guilt, ever! Guilt is an indicator something is not right in your heart. Don't let guilt stay, recognize it, go to God with it and be set free. Conviction is from God, letting you know of something you did wrong. But guilt is put on you when you don't deal with that conviction.

2 Peter 1:5-9 Says that whoever lacks these things cannot see and he is blind, and has forgotten that he was purged from his Old Sins!! Remember, we are recognizing things that we struggle with, which is a tell-tale sign we have not "received" the forgiveness of your old sins (or new ones for that matter).

Staying clean before God is our main focus. In every area of our life. We do that by confessing everything we see to God that is not of his nature and character! It's not that we are perfect, we'll never be perfect, but we can stay clean before God in our heart when we take everything to Him in prayer.

❑ **Accusations** (blame) One major block! Bitterness and disappointment toward God. Blame and Guilt comes from accusing. Judging is very close to accusing.

  • Romans 2:15 "accusing or excusing one another"

  • I Thessalonians 5:23 "preserved blameless"

  • Revelations 12:10 "accuser of the brethren is the devil"

Strong's concordance: Against one in the assembly; i.e. a complaint of the law. Satan offered complaint about a believer who was not obeying the law.

Satan's nature is to accuse - he turns the truth into a lie: (Romans 1:25). The following scriptures describes how Satan accuses:

  ❑ Accused God of withholding good – (Genesis 3:5-6)

  ❑ Accused Job to God – (Job 2:5)

- ❑ Accused Brethren (Rev 12:10)
- ❑ Adam and Eve took on the characteristics of accusation - blaming each other (Gen 3:12-13).

Practical application: Satan actually accuses you - sometimes - of something you actually did! For example if you were impatient with someone at church, he will continue to remind you all day and make you feel bad that you were impatient. So, how to deal with this is:

- ❑ Agree with your adversary quickly (Matthew 5). This means receive what they say, and if it is correct say, "Hey Devil, yep, you are right. But guess what, I'm forgiven!" And if it isn't correct it wouldn't bother you in the first place... Selah.

- ❑ When you see a sin associated with that accusation, confess it to God. Don't keep it, come clean before God about it, don't dilly-dalley around. Take responsibility and repent and receive forgiveness.

Manifestations of accusation:

- ❑ Suspicious - always looking for evil intent Num 16:3 Matthew 9:34
- ❑ Bitterness - keeps record of wrong done
- ❑ Easily Offended
- ❑ Envy and Jealousy
- ❑ Murder - gossip/slander
- ❑ Scrambling thoughts - misunderstandings - this is NOT an accident - Kingdom of Satan wants to separate us and if he can do it by causing misunderstandings, then so be it.

Results of Accusations:

- ❑ Makes one feel unworthy, guilty, not pleasing to God
- ❑ Works against, self, God and others
- ❑ Blames God for evil happenings. "We call evil good when we do this."
- ❑ Keeps record of wrong done when God has forgiven

- ❑ Co-Dependent, burden bearing, plays Holy Ghost over another's sin

- ❑ Falsely charges others with your own sins (we accuse others of things that we ourselves have done.)

Exercise:

Write down any disappointments, wishes, dreams or desires that have NOT been fulfilled

_____

_____

_____

_____

If you look at each of these carefully, you will discover that God is at the root of each of these. We are disappointed with God because since He is God, why haven't these things come to pass? Why didn't He stop things from happening. Why, Why, Why?

The truth is, behind every thing listed above, there is blame and disappointment toward God. You don't want to feel that way, but that is the truth.

Now take each one of these to the Lord and tell him how you feel about them. Be honest with Him. Tell Him you blame Him, that you don't think He's been fair, perhaps you feel He's withholding good from you, perhaps you feel He doesn't love you like He loves others, etc.. Repent to Him for thinking these things about Him.

The truth is; God didn't cause any of these things in your life to happen. We are reaping what has been sewn. God is not mocked, whatever you sow, that you shall also reap (Galatians 6:7). I heard someone say once, "This world is a place of reaping and sowing." What we have today is what has been sown in our generations before us or what we ourselves have sown! Sometimes for good, sometimes for bad. It's up to us TODAY to decide what to do with this sowing thing. Choose today to start sowing good seed into your life so you reap a harvest later and break the curse from your generations by confessing their sins. (We cover more later in a chapter called "Generations.")

We need to stop blaming God for our circumstances and related issues. We have been given freedom to choose our path, God is not going to tell you what to do but what He does do is that whatever choice you make He is there to help you through it. He does not drive or even lead, he guides and prods, but you still have to make the choice.

God is not evil and by blaming Him, we are calling Him evil. Repent this to Him along with any other areas where you accuse Him of not being the God you expected Him to be (James 1:17).

Sample prayer:

"Dear Heavenly Father, I realize that I have been blaming you for not fulfilling my life the way I believed it should be. I realize that you are good and can only give good, so the junk in my life didn't come from you, it came from my own choices. Forgive me for not seeing. I take responsibility for my life and ask you to cleanse my heart and fill me with your love and peace. Cleanse me from all unrighteousness and restore our relationship. In Jesus' name, Amen."

❑ **Abandonment and Rejection** - (For more in depth study, pick up my book called "Abandonment and Rejection.) These two areas are most common in people's lives. But I discovered that these two areas would block my relationship with others, God, and myself. If I feel rejection, I will also reject others. I discovered that in order to "feel" rejection, you first have to have been abandoned, physically, emotionally or spiritually. In order to truly understand abandonment and rejection, you first need to know their definitions.

1. Look up the word Abandonment in the dictionary and describe:

2. Look up the word Rejection in the dictionary and describe:

3. Write down the names of individuals who abandoned you. (Could have been a family member who left you, an emotional or spiritual abandonment.)

_____

_____

Take these individuals to God and forgive them. (Refer to the "how to forgive" section). The truth is, people will abandon you and when they do, what are you going to do about it? Remember, no matter who abandons you, God will never abandon you. The reason you may think He has is because you have a breach in relationship with Him somewhere in your life and you seem to be far away from Him.

The truth is, He is as close as a breath, but you have put up a block between you and Him because of possible blame and accusation toward Him.)

4. Receive God's love - for He has not abandoned you - He is your Father. He is not silent to you. He does not ignore you. You need to understand God's relationship with you as Your true Father. He is not like your earthy father at all who is imperfect. God's love and relationship with you is perfect. When we finally get this in our hearts, our whole life will change. We will no longer need the "approval" of others once we "know" we are accepted and loved by God.

❑ **Lack of Patience** – (Romans 5:3)"And not only so, but we glory in tribulations also, knowing that tribulation works patience, and patience experience, and experience hope. Hope makes us not ashamed because the love of God is shed abroad in our hearts by the Holy Ghost which is given unto us." (1 Peter 2:20-24) "When we suffer patiently for wrong done to us, this is commendable to God!"

Pay close attention to how we suffer - with patience!!! We are no greater than Jesus and look how he took no offense to wrong done, he didn't even defend Himself, and he was given a place most honorable of God, to sit at His right hand. Jesus endured with patience didn't he???

In order for us to obtain the promises of God, we need to have patience. But patience comes through tribulation, that is why we are to "rejoice" when tribulations come because it creates in us patience. (James 1: 2) Patience is worked in us by experience. Then when we begin to live in patience, we have peace that restores all Hope in God.

Are there any areas in your life where you lack patience? Confess them to the Lord and allow Him to develop patience. Patience is the root of Peace! You have patience, you have peace. And isn't that what you want? Peace also balances out your system so your body works properly. Don't be afraid of asking for patience, it will actually help free you!

❑ **Thanklessness** - Be thankful every day. Thank God for His mercy and Grace. Thank Him for your life. Thank Him for your situation. Yes, thank Him IN all things! If you keep asking you are still climbing a mountain. But once you begin thanking Him, you are sliding down the other side of the mountain. You have begun to "Receive." Psalm 100:4 "Enter into his gates with thanksgiving, and into his courts with praise: be thankful unto him, and bless his name." Colossians 3:15 "And let the peace of God rule in your hearts, to the which also ye are called in one body; and be ye thankful." 2 Corinthians 9:12 *"For the administration of this service not only supplieth the want of the saints, but is abundant also by many thanksgivings unto God."* (You want to be supplied and abundantly filled? Then be thankful to God!) Romans 1:21 "Because that, when they knew God, they glorified him not as God, **neither were thankful;** but became vain in their imaginations, and their foolish heart was darkened." (When we don't thank God, our hearts grow hard and darkened with sin.)

Proverbs 10:28 Hope comes when we are thankful (glad). We need hope to continue to seek and serve and love others, self and God. Our hope comes from God. "Hope in God." Nothing else!!! As we focus on God, all the rest will follow that we need to hope in.

❑ **Hopelessness** - Hope deferred makes the heart sick. (Proverbs 13:12) We are saved by Hope (Romans 8:24).

When we Hope, it should only be in God. What are you hoping for?

Are you hoping that someone helps you? Are you hoping the doctors figure out what is wrong with you? Are you hoping that your job offers medical coverage? Are you hoping you get a new car? Are you hoping that the weather cooperates? Are you hoping in things???

If you are relying on God to deliver what you are hoping for, then you are doing wisely. If you are hoping in fear, then you are setting yourself up for more pain and suffering.

❑ **Approval and Acceptance** - When we constantly need approval from people, this will block our peace and relationship with God and man. (Psalm 23) The Lord is my shepherd I shall not want... so why do I need approval?

I need to be needed is rooted in pride. A person who feels that no one is paying attention to them is someone who is needy. This very thing will cause people to reject you - the very thing you don't want. The only way to be freed in this area is to confess your self-righteousness and pride and seeking approval from man.

The Bible says we are already accepted, we are already approved of and to seek man's approval is the sin of "people pleasing."

❑ **Ungodly Grief** - Having a sense of grieving over a long period of time (years and years) will block your peace and rob you of the present. Self-pity glues us to the past. Regret glues us to the past. Guilt because of someone's death, glues us to the past and opens the door for the enemy to keep you down. If you are **suffering** long-term due to a loss of a loved one, or even loss of a job or relationship, etc., and it's keeping you from moving forward with your life - this is ungodly grief. Jesus is the only one who carries our pain and grief, but when we keep it, we are trying to take His place. It's time to take off your grave clothes and come out from among the dead and into the living.

Grief can even cause your eyes to have problems. Psalm 6:7 *"Mine eye is* ***consumed*** *because of grief; it waxeth old because of all mine enemies."*

Grief can cause other health issues - Psalm 31:10 *"For my life is spent with grief, and my years with sighing: my strength faileth because of mine iniquity, and my bones are consumed."*

Grief can cause us to have anxiety - Jeremiah 45:3 *"Thou didst say, Woe is me now! for the LORD hath added grief to my sorrow; I fainted in my sighing, and I find no rest."*

One of my favorite verses is found in 2 Corinthians 2:5-11 *"But if any have caused grief, he hath not grieved me, but in part: that I may not overcharge you all. Sufficient to such a man is this punishment, which was inflicted of many. So that contrariwise ye ought rather to forgive him, and comfort him, lest perhaps such a one should be swallowed up with overmuch sorrow. Wherefore I beseech you that ye would confirm your love toward him. For to this end also did I write, that I might know the proof of you, whether ye be obedient in all things. To whom ye forgive any thing, I forgive also: for if I forgave any thing, to whom I forgave it, for your sakes forgave I it in the person of Christ; Lest Satan should get an advantage of us: for we are not ignorant of his devices."*

There may be someone in your life, a neighbor, friend, or relative that causes you so much grief! According to this verse, that person who causes grief are they themselves full of pain. They are filled with sorrow, and aren't being comforted. To forgive the person of causing you unnecessary grief and discomfort because as Christ forgives, so we must also, so that Satan won't get an advantage over us! So we not only help that person who is perpetrating our problems, but if we don't forgive them, it opens the door for the enemy to come and make things worse! So if you have been grieving over a loss, or if someone is causing you grief, in both cases forgiveness has to be administered. Confess where your grief is because when we keep on grieving about it, we are trying to get back something that was lost, and only God can replace it or heal your broken heart. But He can't unless you go to Him with it. And for those causing you grief, forgive them and go the extra mile to comfort them.

❑ **Judging** (I Corinthians 4:5) *"Therefore judge nothing before the time (which is when Jesus comes back to judge the World on the last day) until the Lord come, who both will bring to light the hidden things of darkness, and will make manifest the counsels of the hearts; and then shall every man have praise of God."*

Paul said that he didn't even judge himself! 1 Corinthians 4:3 *"But with me it is a very small thing that I should be judged of you, or of man's judgment: yea, I judge not mine own self."* Paul didn't listen to what others said about him, and he didn't even judge himself! We are not to judge others or even ourselves. With judgment comes sentencing. But Jesus pad for our sins and took on our sentencing so why are we continuing to do it to each other? We need to realize that when we judge, we always judge in an area where we "think" we've arrived! We have to understand that when we do something "good" it's not us doing it but God. (John 15:5) And when we do something "bad" it's not us doing it either, it's sin within us. (Romans 7:17). We are a vessel that holds something, we are ALL vessels holding something. How can we think ourselves so highly that we can even judge another?

1 Corinthians 5:13 *"But them that are without, God judges. Therefore put away from among yourselves that wicked person.* Selah

But judgment is the manifestation of pride and fear. If you want to be free from judging others, criticizing or complaining, then confess your pride, impatience, anger, frustration, self-righteousness and fear to the Lord. This isn't to cause you guilt or condemn you, it's to help you see the truth within yourself so you can come clean before the Lord. As long as we hide from these issues, we will remain in bondage to them. But once they are exposed, freedom is just around the corner.

❑ **Dishonesty** - It's the truth that makes you free, so the opposite is true. Lying and deceit put you in bondage. God's son's name is Jesus, who is truth. Satan had a son too, named "lies." Everything that the Lord created, Satan corrupts. He is the exact opposite of everything that is good. So when we are dishonest, we are following after that other kingdom. Many are in fear of telling others the truth, but we HAVE TO!!!! There is no other way around this. God can only bless us when we are honest. I know for a fact that if we have been lying about something long enough, it will bite us in the behind! We might as well come clean now. Today! So that you won't have to reap what you are sowing. I love how the Lord gives us TIME. He doesn't allow the manifestation of something to come for awhile, He's waiting us to make some changes. But if we don't then, He does have to allow chastisement to come. Lying will keep you in bondage. It's a destroyer. Lying is the enemy's attribute. I've often said this, "We lie almost every day of our lives about something, so we don't lose a friend or look bad." Unfortunately, it's true. To the color of your hair, to our age, from holding in a secret, to gossiping. We do it almost every day! We tell each other things that we don't mean, because we think we may "hurt their feelings." We need to be more concerned about hurting God's!

You shall know the truth and the truth shall make you free. We have to learn what that truth is, and walk in it. But in order to that, we have to be honest with ourselves. That is why this book is so valuable. It helps us see where we are being deceived. We are actually lying to ourselves when we don't see the truth about ourselves. Sometimes we start to blame others for our problems, but he truth is, we've done it to ourselves. When we can be honest in these areas, we are 1/2 way to our deliverance!

❑ **Communion** - *"For I received from the Lord what I also passed on to you: The Lord Jesus, on the night he was betrayed, took bread, and when he had given thanks, he broke it and said, "This is my body, which is broken for you; do this in remembrance of me." In the same way, after supper he took the cup, saying, "This cup is the new covenant in my blood; do this, whenever you drink it, in remembrance of me." For whenever you eat this bread and drink this cup, you proclaim the Lord's death until he comes. Therefore, whoever eats the bread or drinks the cup of the Lord in an unworthy manner will be guilty of sinning against the body and blood of the Lord. A man ought to examine himself before he eats of the bread and drinks of the cup. For anyone who eats and drinks without recognizing the* *body of the Lord eats and drinks judgment on himself. That is why many among you are weak and sick, and a number of you have fallen asleep."*

There are several things to see here. The main issue is that if you drink the cup and don't believe in the sacrifice for sins or if you eat the bread and don't believe in healing, then you are causing your own health issues. Then to go one step further, before taking communion we are to examine our own hearts and confess any sins. If we have to lay the cup down so that you can reconcile to someone, then do so. It's better to not take the cup than to take it unworthily - that is why so many among "us" are sick unto death.

❑ **Idolatry** - Sometimes we don't even realize we are committing idolatry. So instead of me telling you what it is or if you have it, let's take a look at what scriptures say.

1 Samuel 15:23 *"For rebellion is as the sin of witchcraft, and stubbornness is as iniquity and **idolatry**. Because thou hast rejected the word of the LORD, he hath also rejected thee from being king."*

Not only was Saul rebellious and stubborn, but was into himself - which is idolatry. And what is the result of this? Causes us to reject the word of the Lord and if we reject the Word (without you even knowing it because of idolatry) this will block your blessings. He desired power and leadership and was against David because he felt he was a threat to his throne. But the truth was, God made Saul king, not a man and God can remove the king, like He Did with Saul.

Colossians 3:5 says what Idolatry is: *"Mortify therefore your members which are upon the earth; fornication, uncleanness, inordinate affection, evil concupiscence, and covetousness, **which is idolatry**:"*

Again, it's all about "us!" Our pleasures, our satisfaction, our needs being met, our desire for more, wanting what others have, etc. It's all idolatry. It's not just setting up an image and bowing to it, yes, that is part of if and some do that. But it's the hidden idolatry in the heart that can trip us up and we don't even know it.

If you find yourself in this category as I did, confess this to the Lord and receive forgiveness. Make a stand today to not allow even yourself to get in the way of God's will in your life. When we make that kind of proclamation, things will start to happen. But you will be tested to see if you have fled from idolatry or if you still need to be purged. Keep on keeping on because I found that the hardest issue is to remove self out of the equation of life. We want to be comfortable and enjoy ourselves, but sometimes it's at other people's expense. Keep your heart pure toward God by checking your motives when you do this or that. Is it for the glory of God or for your glory? Simply repent...

❑ **Oppression:** The enemy can also oppress you without you even knowing that is what it is. We can be so busy getting at all the junk in us, casting off spirits, confessing everything we can confess, even addressing generations, and many of you have been doing this for some time, but there just doesn't seem to be a breakthrough to the degree you want to see it. It could be a spirit of oppression from your ethnic background. When you recognize this, you may find there is a familiar spirit that has been hiding out. Recently I ministered to several people who have been "doing" what they know to do to get free. But something just stays, or the feel "stuck." In looking at their background, many came from England, Germany, Africa or other countries. We took a look at each of these areas that pertained to their life and addressed the familiar spirits. For example, with a German background. There was mayhem, torture, death, betrayal, murder, that came from the holocaust. That spiritual condition was passed through the lineage. So we would address the spirit of death, health, destruction, insanity, suicide, division, hate, disobedient, self-mutilation, rebellious spirits, unloving, and others as the Lord led. And sure enough, that's what it was. Many even stated that something left them laughing or screaming. Oppression could come from a spirit that is hiding in your generations.

Closing Comment

There are many "blocks" preventing healing, health and blessings, I have come to the conclusion that when we walk in "Love and Truth" with God, ourselves and our fellowman, there will be NO blocks! Matthew 22:37-40 sums it up: "Love the Lord thy God with all thine heart, soul and mind, and love your neighbor as yourself, upon these hang all the laws and the prophets." If we did this one scripture, we would be a whole lot happier and freer.

Matthew 22:37-40 37 *Jesus said unto him, Thou shalt love the Lord thy God with all thy heart, and with all thy soul, and with all thy mind. This is the first and great commandment. And the second is like unto it, Thou shalt love thy neighbour as thyself. On these two commandments hang all the law and the prophets.*

Be not weary in well doing, for in due season you shall reap if you don't faint. (Galatians 6:9)

The Truth surely makes you free. (John 8:32)

Ministry Prayer for You to Pray:

"Father, thank you for this insightful teaching. I see that I have several blocks that prevent us from the blessings of God. Scripture says that I prevent good thing from happening to me. So I choose today to repent for these things that I'm allowing in my life, and I renounce them in my life and in my generations to follow. Purify my heart from _____(name them from the list) and cleanse me from all unrighteousness. Thank you for forgiving me and filling me with your love, compassion and forgiveness towards others and myself. In Jesus name, Amen."

Ministry Prayer for You:

"Lord, I agree with this dear Saint. As they recognize what is going on in their lives that is preventing them from finding their freedom, I thank you for showing them they simply need to acknowledge and repent. Receiving forgiveness for what they see. Now I cast out the spirits of fear, oppression, idolatry, ungodly grief, bitterness and unforgiveness, thanklessness, needing approval, accusations, judging one another, doubt and unbelief, hopelessness, lack of patience, abandonment and rejection, not discerning the Lord's body, dishonesty, pride, shame and not receiving God's love. I ask that each area be reconciled to You Lord, and that they would not fall under any guilt or condemnation for what they see, but to rejoice that they have an opportunity to be restored. I ask for healing in their bodies through their minds being renewed in the Word. In Jesus name, Amen."

CHAPTER THIRTY-TWO

Religion vs. Relationship

It's important to understand the meaning of: Religion and Relationship.

Religion defined in the Webster's Dictionary dated 1956: Piety, consciousness, to bind together, to gather, to collect, making the primary meaning a collection, and then more specifically a collection of religious formulas. 1) A system of rules of conduct and laws of action based upon the recognition of, believe in, and reverence for a superhuman power of supreme authority. 2) Specifically, a particular kind of faith and practice entertained and propagated by its devotees. 3) The essential observances and practices of a religious people or of a sect. "Pure religion and undefiled before God and the Father is this, to visit the fatherless and widows in their affliction and to keep oneself unspotted from the world (James 1:27). (Yes, it was in this edition of the Webster's dictionary!) 4) Spiritually pure, as distinguished from intellectual and social characteristics. Pure religion breathing household laws. 5) Devoted to consistency (i.e. its against my religion to do this or that.) 6) A religious order or state. 7) Practice of sacred rights and ceremonies.

The following are types of religions, still studying out the word:

- ❏ Established religion: a form of religion recognized and approved officially by a state or government

- ❏ Natural religion: religion derived from the teachings of nature alone.

- ❏ Revealed religion: religion based upon positive revelation.

- ❏ To experience religion: to have personal conscious evidence of the favor of God in the forgiveness of sin and a change of heart to the converted. (To get religion is the same)

- ❏ To profess religion: To make publicly with the church, to make monastic vows.

Now if we look at the modern version definition in the Webster's Dictionary it says: "The feeling of reverence which men entertain toward a supreme being; the recognition of God as an object of worship, love and obedience; piety, any system of faith and worship. (It also goes into the forms of religions as stated above.)

What does the Bible say Religion means?

Religion in the Bible: "Pure religion and undefiled before God and the Father is this, to visit the fatherless, and widow in their affliction, and to keep himself unspotted from the world." James 1:27. Interestingly that old version of the dictionary even quotes this! But as I looked in the current dictionaries that most of us use, nothing closely relates to the description above!

It's interesting that the meaning has changed in time about the word "religion" in the world, but HAS NOT changed in the eyes of truth. Let's start by discussing Religion, and close with a discussion on Relationships.

According to the meaning in the first definition of the word, it in a round about way talks about relationship. But it also talks about the need to have formulas that govern them. Jesus came to do away with the "law" thereby bringing freedom and peace. So, which one do you live under? Religion or Freedom? I want to ask you some questions to help us begin with this study. It's important that you answer them honestly to yourself, and if you aren't sure about a certain question, stop and ask God to help you with that question. Remember, the truth sets people free! Even the truth about your own feelings, no matter the answer!!!

❑ Do you want to belong to a religious organization?

❑ Do you desire to be involved at a high level of recognition?

❑ Do you have the need to be appreciated?

❑ Do you want to be heard and seen?

❑ Do you desire glory? (Now a religious spirit will automatically say no, but really think about it and confess the truth. Let's all get free OK?)

❑ Do you desire "How to" instructions to achieve your goals, including healing, etc.

❑ Do you fear man?

❑ Do you have the need to be controlling?

❑ Are you concerned about money?

❑ If in ministry, do you look for ways to bring in dollars?

❑ Do you have pride?

❑ Are you arrogant?

❑ Are you a respecter of persons? In other words, wanting relationships with people who have something to offer you.

❑ Are you judgmental? Critical about people, especially those who seem to compete with you?

❑ Do you require justice for injustice done to you? Do you desire to have laws and rules to govern you?

❑ Do you want to tell others what to do?

❑ Do you want a road map of your life?

❑ Are you selfish?

❑ Do you want more even though what you have is enough?

❑ Do you want others to do things that you aren't willing to do yourself?

❑ Do you care about how you look to others? Self doting, conceited

❑ Are you jealous and/or envious? (Look up the definition of these words to help you answer - they don't mean the same thing.)

If you answered yes to any of these, it is more than likely you have what is called a "religious spirit."

Let's see what Jesus says about it. Speaking to the Pharisees and Sadducees, "Woe unto you scribes and Pharisees, hypocrites@ for ye are like unto white sepulchers, which indeed appear beautiful outward, but are within full of dead men's bones, and of all uncleanness." Matthew 23:27.

As you study that passage of scripture, Jesus recognized that the religious people caused people to carry heave burdens of keeping laws and accordance yet they themselves don't keep them. They wear good apparel on the outside, but inside are full of death - there is no life or liberty in them.

If you are feeling "bound" when you go to your church meetings. If you don't feel free to say the things you want, or raise your hands in prayer and praise. If you are "afraid" what others will think of you if you don't go to church one Sunday. Ask the Lord if there is a religious spirit there. It sounds something like this, "I didn't see you at church last week." But it wasn't being said because they cared, it was being said to condemn and judge to make themselves look "religious."

I choose to release myself from that spirit by recognizing first if I have it, then recognizing if my church has it, and then I can make some choices on becoming free.

I too had to recognize if I had a religious spirit. I didn't think I did, but the evidence of my actions and thoughts proved different. So I began to investigate. Of course, I can only teach you now because I finally got free from it so I can clearly recognize what was going on and what I did that set me free.

All those questions that I asked you, I actually asked myself! And one of those that stood out the most for me was telling people (my husband especially) what to do, and wanting recognition, which is the same as desiring glory! That one last statement is what was the downfall of all the religious leaders in Jesus' day, and I believe is still the same today.

Religious people want to be heard and seen! That's what I desired. To be heard and seen, by people that are being heard and seen! Get it? What a cycle! The need for this is so that "we" receive appreciation, which as I said a moment ago, is the same as desiring glory. And you and I both know that all glory is to go to God, but if we are true with ourselves, we want a piece of it too!

Now it's not that I can't continue in ministry that is being heard and seen, but my heart condition is different toward it. My motives are different. I've removed the wrong soul ties to people and ministries that was motivated by my own desires, needs and wants. I'm still in relationship to these same people, and same ministries, but they are free and I am free to do what God has called me to do, not man!

This is hard people. For those who are like me, it's hard to make a decision to let go of the very thing we desire to achieve the goals we have for ourselves.

My goal in life is to work full-time in ministry. I had a "plan" of achieving that goal and it involved becoming connected closely to a well-known ministry. God cut that idea short, and with that came emotional pain. Within minutes, however, after realizing God had other plans for me, the pain was gone, I saw my direction clearly, and was returned to peace again about my own walk and direction for this ministry.

Not only that, the relationship with these people and ministry was restored to a correct relationship. What I was doing and what they were doing were both great things, yet independent of each other. See I wanted to "belong." But God was trying to get through to me was that I did belong, He had a plan, and I didn't need approval of man to do it.

A scripture comes to mind along these lines. Jesus was talking with the disciples one day when one of the disciples brought to his attention that they heard of a man teaching in Jesus name! Yet he was not with them. Jesus said, let the man alone, if he is for us, he's not against us. I realized after recalling that story that that person is me. I don't have to belong to an "organization" to be effective in the lives of people. I don't have to belong to an "organized religion" to follow the Lord Jesus.

Relationship:

In order to replace the need for religion (methodology, program) we need to go after what true religion is really about. Pure religion is relationship! To visit those who are in need. To love the fatherless. To help those who cannot help themselves. To stay free from the bondage of this world. And we do that by building our relationship with God, our Heavenly Father, as our Father, relationship with Jesus, who is our Savior, Lord, brother, and King, and the Holy Ghost who has sealed us and is now keeping us secure. Then to build relationships with ourselves, and with others.

Until we have the relationships with God, we cannot possibly have good relationships with others. As married couples, the first thing the wife wants to do (in some cases) is change their husband. But the truth is, only God can change someone. Our role is to seek God, receive His love, power, and all the fruit to live a godly life, and He will change your spouse. A religious spirit causes us to want others to be like us. But the truth is, some of you don't even like yourselves, so why would you want someone to be like you? We have to love and accept each other where they are now, and if things needs to change, take it to the Lord in prayer.

On a personal note, this has been Tom and my daily petition to the Lord. We know we can't change each other, so we take our thoughts and requests to the Lord. It's amazing how many times the other changes, just from a prayer! And then there are times when we don't, because that wasn't a good change. If we would simply trust God with our children, spouse, boss, and even ourselves, we would walk in more peace. That controlling religious spirit won't have a leg to stand on, and you will enjoy your life. Not to mention, others will get to enjoy their lives too. Because from this spirit comes the need to control. Well, if you don't like being controlled, those you are trying to control don't like it either.

Ministry

After recognizing these very things I'm teaching you, I had a little talk with God and it went something like this: (Now this is not a "how to" prayer, you can pray your own way.)

"Father, I recognize that I have a religious spirit. That's the last thing I ever wanted to have, but since I do, I will admit it and ask for your forgiveness of allowing it to reign in my life. I fall out of agreement with it right now. Forgive me that I didn't think you were enough. Forgive me for desiring glory. The truth is, I can do nothing good without you, so no matter how "good" things go, it's you who allows me to do of your good pleasure. So truthfully, I cannot gain glory, so the spirit within me is desiring it. Forgive me for being controlling, fearful, respecter of persons, looking for ways to make a buck, being jealous and envious, and back-biter. Forgive me for telling Tom what to do, that is not my desire at all. Cleanse me now from all sin and unrighteousness.

Now I take authority by the power of the Holy Ghost given me to break that power of the religious spirit off my life now and cast it out now in Jesus name. Fill me with your love Lord and ground me deeper in relationship with you. . But now that I see the spirit behind it, help me to recognize those thoughts before they ever leave my mouth! Thank you for letting me see that I had a religious spirit, because now I am made free by the blood of the lamb and the word of my testimony. In Jesus name, I pray Amen."

CHAPTER THIRTY-THREE

Fasting and Praying

I don't pretend to know everything about fasting and praying, and there are many ideas about it, this is mine. We all have perceptions and revelations that could differ. So this is mine.

This revelation impacted my life. Again, these are insights and things the Lord has put on my heart for me, if they apply to you, then that's great, if not, then that's okay too... but don't throw the baby out with the bath water if you read something you don't agree with. Remember, I am also flesh and blood and still learning and growing, like you, in the things of the Lord.

As I was reading through scripture, I saw something a little different than what I'm hearing behind the pulpit.

I'll share this with you as I learned it. So let's start with Jesus. As far as I can see, He fasted one time, found in Matthew 4:1: "Then Jesus was led up of the spirit into the wilderness to be tempted of the devil. And when he had fasted forty days and forty nights, he was afterward hungry."

I don't see in this passage where Jesus fasted and "prayed" for something specific. I have a problem with pastors asking people to pray for "something" they need. I don't believe fasting is for that reason.

My husband told me something that actually gave insight regarding fasting. He said, "You know why Jesus fasted? Because He was preparing for His return home." My husband hit it on the head. Fasting is when we put aside something (including food but not limited to) that consumes us and distracts us from God. Fasting is to help you become more intimate with Him and helps us learn to be completely dependent on Him and nothing or no one else. It's a time to reflect on what the Word says. It's time to hear from God, it's time to enjoy His sweet fellowship. I don't see where we are to ask for things during the fasting time. If anything is asked, it should be for more of Him in our lives.

What I saw according to Jesus' experience was that He fasted 40 days and 40 nights in preparation of the three temptations. It was His time to get closer to the Lord, strengthened, and given power to overcome the tempter. According to how He handled the devil, it looks like He was also meditating on the "Word" because that's what He used to defeat the enemy. Because remember, Jesus was also a man. He was God, and sinless, but He still had the flesh to contend with.

As a believer when we need something, we are free to ask. There are no deals to be made with God. Sometimes people think if they fast and ask it will come faster. But I don't see that in scripture. I see that we can ask anything in His name, and we shall receive it. Now I'm not talking about personal growth things here, I'm talking about things like buying a car, which school to go to, selling something, direction for ministry, etc., Those things are our God given right to ask Him when the needs come up. Fasting for these may not necessarily move God's hand. That is why so many people seem to get discouraged because it's almost a way of trying to manipulate God into doing something. I have to say that we are setting ourselves up for disappointment with that motive and could even cause disappointment with God.

I also noticed that Jesus fasted but it didn't say fasted and prayed. I think we can assume He did, but it doesn't say it here. Perhaps because we need to understand what praying is. I heard a great message on what prayer was, and it's like this: Praying is talking with God and making requests, asking, etc. It's not communicating with God because communication involves back and forth and God doesn't pray to us. So perhaps that is why Jesus didn't "pray" because He knew what that Word meant. We know He fellowshipped with His Father in Heaven what else would He be doing for 40 days? Pure speculation but I think He was in constant fellowship with His Father in Heaven in preparation for the temptation on earth and for His journey back home. This reminds me when David spent years with sheep... did he talk to the sheep? No, he wrote songs and fellowshipped with God, which prepared him for becoming king!

When you fast, what you are praying about? Are you wanting a better job? Are you needing to be healed? Now there is a scripture that says "These things (devils) don't come out except by fasting and prayer. This is an exception to the rule because they aren't talking about getting anything for ones self, it's talking about helping others be free. And also, fasting may not be food in this instance. I believe this type of fasting is all about relationship, ministry and love as described in Isaiah 58.

Isaiah 58:6-7 *"Is not this the fast that I have chosen, to loose the bands of wickedness, to undo the heavy burdens, and to let the oppressed go free, and that ye break every yoke? Is it not to deal thy bread to the hungry, and that thou bring the poor that are cast out to thy house? When you see the naked, you cover him, and that you don't hide yourself from your own family members (flesh)?*

But if you read verses 3-4 you will see how the people were fasting, and it appears we still do it today. *"Wherefore have we fasted, say they, and thou seest not? Wherefore have we afflicted our soul; and thou takest no knowledge? Behold in the day of your fast ye find pleasure, and exact all your labors, behold, ye fast for strife and debate, and to smite with the fist of wickedness, ye shall not fast as ye do this day, to make your voice heard on high. Is it such a fast that I have chosen? For a man to afflict his soul? To bow down his head as a bulrush and to spread sackcloth and ashes under him? Will you call this a fast and an acceptable day to the Lord?"*

It appears that the people wanted recognition because it was all about them. How much affliction the can put on themselves made them feel spiritual. They fasted for things that aren't part of what God calls a fast and because of that their voice was not heard in Heaven. In other words, if we don't fast with a correct heart motive, our fasting is in vein.

Again, there are two different fasts: One that talks about food, and the other one to minister to people.

If you think about it, the disciples didn't fast because Jesus was still with them (Matthew 9:14-15). That is very clear. But it does say that when Jesus leaves to be with the Father, they will fast. So fasting is clearly about our relationship with Jesus and our Heavenly Father. So if you want to cast out an evil spirit from someone and it doesn't leave, perhaps you need to see if you have been "fasting" as it states in Isaiah 58. Casting out spirits may not have anything to do with food or fasting food, it has to do with what kind of a relationship do you have with your Heavenly Father and with others at that time. Jesus cast out the spirit when the disciples couldn't. Why? Because Jesus was continually in a "fasting" mode of loving people and setting them free, just as Isaiah 58:6-7 says.

This is just my take on it, you can continue studying this for yourself or ignore it, but I did have to share my heart on this subject. I found that once I have learned this, I actually had a sense of freedom in my heart. The burden was no longer there to get God to do this or that, fasting is a pleasure to have opportunity to fellowship closely with God, and prayer is a time of petition. We can do both together if the motive is not for selfish reasons or gain. Remember, it is your God given right as a believer to ask for whatever you need and He will give it.

Let me give you my personal testimonial on this. I realized that I had been consumed by TV for many years. I had 5 televisions in our home at one time, and one giant screen in the living room. One day as I was "vegging" in front of the television. And by the way, that's exactly what it is, not having to think. Have you ever tried to talk to someone who was so consumed by a television program? You cannot get them to listen, because they are "consumed" with the programming. I remember when my husband would walk into the room and I was involved in a movie I didn't even know he entered the room.

So for me television was something that came between not only God, but with my family. But it did comfort me, it helped me escape my current life, a way to make the day go by faster, I even made believe that those people on television were my friends and we were visiting with each other when I'd watch. But the truth was, it was still a lie and deception, I was trying to get the comfort from television instead of from what was real. So I had enough of this, I knew it was damaging my mind and I had to do something about it.

I decided to fast the TV. Recently I shared that with someone and they said you the can't fast television, fasting is only about food. But I didn't get offended because I knew in my heart that fasting was giving up something that consumed me... and at this time it was TV. So I fasted five days, and it was hard because I had a ritual for watching TV. It was like breaking a habit or something, I had withdrawals!! It was like I was getting off drugs or something - it was amazing how much hold it had on me. And during that fast I didn't ask for anything, I just fasted and waited on God. And to my surprise, He Spoke! Wow, it was awesome. I began thinking - because when you watch TV or do something that consumes you, you don't have to think! You don't have to deal with your thoughts, but during this time when I didn't watch TV I was left alone with my thoughts.

During this time I was delivered from so many issues, things I never even saw before. My heart was changing, my mind was being renewed, it was awesome to grow into a deeper relationship with God because I wasn't distracted from hearing Him!

I believe the reason we focus on food for the fasting part is because it's something that satisfies and fills us up by saying "man shall not live by bread alone but by every word that comes out of the mouth of God." So food seems to be implicated but I believe - again, this is what I believe - it's also meaning anything that we put our confidence in BESIDES God. I believe fasting is to show our love to Him indicating that He is all we need. Fasting is a way to separate ourselves from the thing that comes between us and God or acts as our comforter instead of the Holy Ghost. It's anything that we think we need to be fulfilled for our happiness. And as we give up that "thing" for a time of fasting it also helps us break habits. We are creatures of habit and it's good to stir things up in that area so that nothing controls us. When we are habitually doing something, after a long period of time it becomes a habit and a need when we are to be habitually filled with God and God alone. Paul taught us not to be controlled by anything.

Like I said, during this fast I was left alone with my thoughts. (If I just gave up food, these revelations would never have come). I didn't like what I saw. So for that whole week God and was doing some house cleaning and OHHHH... it hurt so good. I saw things there that I didn't want to see, but once I did, I didn't fall under guilt or condemnation, I was glad so that I could be purged. TV let me escape from myself for a moment but there is no escaping the truth, it's still there waiting for you. Through these past days I felt that I was kicked up a notch, but the truth was, I was kicked down a notch - in other words, my soapbox was being kicked out from under me. During this time I had a major breakthrough about the need to be needed. The Lord revealed to me that this was rooted in pride. Yikes! Having the soapbox removed was pride being removed. As a teacher it's easy to fall into this area of being needed by others, but if we don't have discernment, it can back fire and we can turn out to be the ones in need! So we need discernment in this area to remove what pride is there and to keep it from taking root again. And that's what happened to me, it was pride that was inside.

The indicators came when I got "embarrassed" about something that happened to me. I wondered who saw it, I wondered what they were thinking. I was also feeling rejection - which was interesting because I had been freed from rejection - but this was another level, which was attached to pride! This kind of pride says: "How dare they reject me" kind of pride. "Don't they know who I am?" "Don't you know you need me?" blah, blah, blah... How yucky is that! These were things that I had been thinking that laid way back in my thoughts, nothing I would say out loud (except now because I'm sharing this story) but things I would think from time to time.

Pride is at the root of striving for acceptance and approval! And that's what happens to someone who needs to be needed.

If there are needs in our lives when we do fast, God already knows what they are (Matthew 6:8). We ask when the needs arise (Matthew 7:7,11). This is our God given right as a believer to ask Him. Also remember, when asking, when we believe what we ask, we shall receive. Also, a reminder that you ask God for things by petition through Jesus Christ.

I've identified a few scriptures for you to read through. Take some time and allow the scriptures to speak to your spirit. Ask the Lord to help you understand a deeper truth about fasting. You may get a complete different take on it, but that's good.

- Matthew 8:19
- Matthew 21:22
- Luke 11:9-13
- John 15:7 (key to your receiving what you ask)
- John 14:13-14
- John 15:16
- John 16:23
- Ephesians 3:20
- James 1:6
- James 4:3
- 1 John 3:22 (another key to receiving what you ask for - we receive when we obey)
- 1 John 5:14-15

The following scriptures I found helpful in my study about fasting, I actually did a word search to see other accounts about fasting.

Judges 20:26 - *"Then all the children of Israel, and all the people went up and came to the house of God and wept (because they saw that their sin was great) and sat before the LORD, and fasted that day until the evening, and offered burnt offerings and peace offerings before the Lord."*

I believe this scripture shows two things: Fasting was a way of exposing sin in our lives because as we fast it causes us to get closer to God and as we get closer to God more sin is revealed, and 2) a way of makings offering to God, not asking for something.

1 Samuel 7:6 - indicates that fasting helped them see that they sinned against the Lord.

2 Samuel 1:12 - *And they mourned and wept, and fasted until even, for Saul, and for Jonathan his son, and for the people of the Lord, and for the house of Israel, because they were fallen by the sword."*

Isaiah 58 talks about the fast of helping people. So if you are fasting for loved ones, for their salvation or healing, etc., that is good. It's when we ask for "things" to consume upon our own lusts (I mean lives). We need to ask ourselves what our motives are of prayer during fasts.

2 Samuel 12:22 - talks about David fasting because of his son that was dying. Again, a correct fasting prayer.

Nehemiah 1:3-7 - Nehemiah fasted and prayed for the people because they were in captivity.

Acts 13:2 - As they ministered to the Lord, and fasted, the Holy Ghost said, *"Separate me, Barnabus and Saul for the work whereunto I have called them."* During the time of fasting, they ministered to the Lord. How do you do that? By ministering to others - again Isaiah 58 fasting - to help those in bondage and when we do that, during that fast we may get direction for our lives as with this scripture. But that was NOT their motive, their motive was to serve the Lord then God gave them clear direction.

Joel 2:12 sums it up: *Therefore also now, saith the Lord, turn ye even to me with all your heart and with fasting and with weeping and with mourning; and rend your heart and not your garments, and turn unto the Lord your God, for he is gracious and merciful, slow to anger, and of great kindness and repenteth him of the evil.* (I looked this up in the Amplified Bible and it actually talks about restoring relationships!)

You can continue to do a study on fasting and praying as well and I believe you will find that:

❑ Fasting can be: 1) food (Matthew 15:32); OR 2) something consuming you (1 Corinthians 7:5). If you believe it's always food, cool, if you agree with me that it's not always food, cool too, but it's not about that, it's about your heart condition WHILE fasting. I'm not trying to make a new theology, I'm just wanting to see what the scriptures say instead of what the pastors say.

❑ Our prayers during that fast should be to 1) To get closer to God; 2) Pray for people's lives - relationships.

❑ What we do while fasting - serve God. (Luke 2:37)

❑ What not to do while fasting - ask for "things."

What is the outcome - 1) Exposes sin for repentance for restoration and healing; 2) To prepare us for this life, and so we aren't tempted by Satan (1 Corinthians 7:5); 3) A changed life while experiencing the goodness of God.

Prayer for You to Pray:

"Father, thank you for your Word of truth. We can believe all we want but we need to line things up with scripture. Whether we fast food or whether we fast by loving and ministering to others, both are correct. Thank you for showing me this truth personally so that I could share it with the readers. Help us not to get caught up in some man's laws and rules and traditions, but only caught up in truth. I ask for your love and mercy to flood this person's life and give them peace. Let them know to fast whatever they believe has come between you and them. Let them know that these are idols that have to go and we can break all habits by taking the time to fast them. I ask you to give them revelation during their times of fasting, that will change them for ever. Thank you for what you are doing in us and through us, in Jesus name, Amen."

CHAPTER THIRTY-FOUR

There may be some defects/diseases that you got from your parents. When going to the doctor, the first thing he/she asks if there are any diseases in your family tree. Why? Because they know it can be passed on to you. There is a way to stop the disease or characteristic from passing on to you and to your children.

Nehemiah 9:2: *"And the Israelites separated themselves from all foreigners and stood and confessed their sins and the iniquities of their fathers."*

Exodus 20:5: *"...visiting the iniquity of the fathers upon the children to the 3rd and 4th generation of those who hate Me."*

Psalm 25:18 – *"Look upon my affliction and my pain and forgive all my sins."*

Inherited Diseases and Characteristics

It's time to STOP that curse or disease. We can stop them right now and stop them from going on to our children. And we do that by confessing our sins and the iniquities of our fathers. A disease doesn't come unless there is a cause (Proverbs 26:2). As described in Deuteronomy 26, you will find all types of diseases known to mankind, even today. And we discovered that disease is a curse and curses come from sins. (Not all disease comes from sin, but a majority does.) It may not be YOUR sin but could be a sin from three generations before falling on you and your children.

Not only can physical disease be passed down, but emotional as well. Do you have any mental problems in your family? Has anyone ever committed suicide or ended up in a mental ward? What about anger? Molestation? Alcoholism? Gluttony? Do you have fear? All these things CAN be passed on. Do you believe that lying can be hereditary? Let's take a look at a character in the Bible and see if this isn't true.

Let's look the story of Abraham. He was known as our founding father but he was a liar. He lied to a king about his wife being his sister. He did it twice! Did you know he had a son – Isaac - who told the same lie to the same king 40 years later about his own wife? This same son had sons and they were all liars. They lied to their father by telling him Joseph was eaten by animals, yet what they really did was sold him into slavery. Here are three generational liars! Yes, sin can be inherited.

So how do you break the curse?

First, I have to address individuals who say that we are no longer under a curse, and so we don't have to do this. So let me ask a question. Are Christians dying of diseases? Are diseases a blessing or a curse? When we read in Deuteronomy 28:15 through the end of the chapter, it lists all kinds of diseases known to mankind, including in the believer's life. If they are no longer under the curse, then why are just as many Christians in doctor's offices as non-Christians? We have a part to play in our sanctification process. But, if you don't believe in what i'm sharing, that's okay too. To the degree you believe is the degree you are restored and healed. It's entirely up to you. If you don't believe in healing for today, then just count on not being healed. If you don't believe there are curses on lives today, then remain in your suffering. But what if the things I'm sharing with you is true?

Exercise to Identify your Family Inherited Diseases

Make a list that includes not only physical sickness and disease but mental and emotional characteristics as well. If you do not manifest them now, you need to still stop the curse from one-day manifesting or going to the next generation. Some disease skip generations and fall onto the 3rd and 4th. Why do you think God orchestrated that? I believe it's because He wanted to give the other generations the chance to break that curse off the family. But if they didn't turn to serve God and love Him with all their heart, soul and mind, then those sins/sicknesses would pass on.

The inherited characteristics can be fear, anxiety, drivenness, anger, prejudice, hate, lust, alcoholism, control, perversion, abuse, etc. Indicate which family member you believe it came through by using a W for wife, H for husband, F for Father, M for Mother, G for Grandmother, or GF for Grandfather after the disease or characteristic.

Then write down your sins. You may have done this earlier, so if you did, use that list, otherwise make a new one.

Now take your lists to God and prayer this prayer. (This is not a formula; it is a sample prayer. You can pray your own.)

"Lord, I bring my sins and the iniquities of my fathers to your throne. I ask you to forgive my fathers for not loving you. These curses only came upon those who didn't love You with all their heart, soul and mind and strength. Help me to love you like that Lord all the days of my life. I trust you to help me I believe that I have the power through the Holy Ghost to break the curse of these diseases so that they will not come upon me, nor my children, nor my children's children. So I confess the sins of my fathers and ask for forgiveness for those sins. (Name the sins one-by-one). And I now I ask you to break the curse of (NAME THE DISEASES AND CHARACTERISTICS ONE BY ONE). I trust you to cleanse me and my family from these diseases now and forever. I stand in faith believing you have done what I have asked. I will not fear disease any longer and I trust you with my life. Thank you Lord, in Jesus' Name. Amen."

You are standing in the gap for all your generations to follow. We have seen adult children's lives changed when a father and/or mother take that step of faith and pray! The scriptures say that when we love God and obey His commands, we will bless to a thousand generations!

CHAPTER THIRTY-FIVE

Is Disease from a Spiritual Condition?

Please note that dealing with dis-ease is different from dealing with tribulations and persecutions. The Bible says that we will suffer persecution and that we will endure hardships. (Matthew 5:11-12) But I found that by dealing with our own heart condition and developing a strong and intimate relationship with God, it will increase our faith and build a trust that says, *"Though He slay me, yet will I trust Him"* (Job 13:15). We will be victorious "in" our trials, and once we have come out of them (because the Lord says he delivers us out of all our troubles (Psalm 34:17) and we won't even smell like smoke! (Daniel 3:23-27)

Many believe that their disease is their cross to bear. I have to argue that point. The cross is not about sickness, because Jesus bore all our sickness on the cross so we won't have to. It may be our "thorn" but it's not our cross. Our cross is to deny ourselves daily, love the Lord with all our heart, soul and strength, to love and serve others (Matthew 16:24). God never intended disease to be our burden to carry.

I have a friend who is blind. She told me one day that her blindness is her cross to bear. It gave her comfort believing that was her lot in life from the Lord. My heart goes out to her because being blind is one of the hardest things to have to live with. But I have to ask, how can blindness be from the Lord? God is a God who only gives good things, and I don't believe being blind is good, do you? I shared the truth with her that her blindness may be a "thorn" but it's not her cross. When we believe it's our cross, we are making ourselves hang on it. That is the right only given to Jesus. We need to understand the "cross" of Calvary and what it means and it will help us understand how to bear it. We need to find truth, not be deceived in the smallest matter because one drop no matter how small the drop can sew deceit, discord and fear.

I discovered that behind most health issues and emotional or spiritual problems reside the "Spirit of Fear." The Spirit of Fear is the Devil's faith working in people by using lies to control them. And if we dwell on those lies long enough, we will begin to believe them, thus resulting in responding to them which can lead to all kinds of problems. We need to discover the root behind our problems. The things that we experience may be a manifestation of a root. But thank God, we have an advocate, Jesus Christ, who is our Savior and the Truth that makes us free! (Romans 7:24-25, 8:2) He gives us His mind (1 Corinthians 2:16). He gives us the power to cast down all imaginations and lies (2 Corinthians 10:5). We need to discover what our weapons are to cast out the lies from our minds (Ephesians 6:14). The Bible says that the Devil is the father of lies (John 8:44). So we need to learn more about truth so we can discern the lies and get rid of them. As we get closer to our Heavenly Father through His Son Jesus, we shall "know" the truth that makes us free. If we stay in fear, we are not made perfect in love, and it's the love that casts out all fear - God's love (1 John 4:18). When we aren't living in truth (faith) we are living in fear, and if long-term it could manifest in all sorts of problems - physically, mentally and spiritually (Proverbs 26:2).

Restoring you to our Heavenly Father is our main concern. It's vital to every believer whether have a dis-ease or not. Revelation 2:4-5 tells us of a church that did so many wonderful things but they lacked in one area – loving God. Having our relationship restored to God is the first step that opens to us the truth that makes us free. The closer we get to our Heavenly Father the more light is shed in our heart, and the more light that is shed in our heart the more "junk" is exposed that are not of Him. People don't understand their part in all this. Jeremiah 5:25 says it's our sins and iniquities that prevent good things from happening to us. Hosea 4:6 says that God's people perish for lack of knowledge. Isaiah 59:1-2 says to Behold, the Lord's hand is not shortened that it cannot save, neither his ear heavy, that it cannot hear; but our iniquities have separated between us and our God, and our sins have hid His face from us, that He will not hear. God can do anything, but He doesn't go against His own Word. If He sees something in us that has to go, He will cause it to be brought out into the light, and only does this for our good. Not to make us feel bad, but to show us what he wants purged. Then as it's brought out into the light, we confess it to Him through Jesus who has carried all our sins on the cross and washes us clean. When we are clean, then we can have fellowship with God. He demands holiness, and He sees us through the Blood that Jesus gave on the cross for us. This happens immediately when we receive Christ as Savior, however, many believers forget that and live as though they haven't been forgiven. (2 Peter 1:9). This ministry is here to help you remember so that you can find your peace and freedom - again.

Many of our dis-eases are being used by God to bring to surface what is in our hearts. *But let me say this very clearly, God did not give you a dis-ease.* The dis-ease is the manifestation from a heart condition. Just as a fever is an indication that something is amiss in our bodies. These are warning signs. And we can either cooperate with God and deal with what was exposed or fight Him all the way. "Come let us reason together says the Lord, though your sins be as scarlet they shall be white as snow, though they be red like crimson, they shall be as wool" (Isaiah 1:18). God already knows our heart, it's no surprise what is there. We're the ones who are surprised by what is there, and sometimes shocked! But as they come to the surface, don't run, or don't hide in the bushes like Adam did. Come to Him as a child comes to their father, and tell Him all about it. Confess what you did wrong and receive forgiveness, for in so doing you are being made clean and transparent before Him. David sinned, but he was known as a man after God's own heart. Why? Because he was truthful with God, He came to Him and confessed his sin before Him. The Lord delights in those who walk in truth (2 John 1:4).

We have designed this teaching to impart knowledge so that you have what you need to "know" the Love of Christ, you will be filled with all the fullness of God (Ephesians 3:19). We start in the area of Relationships. Even the 10 commandments reflect this. The first 5 commandments are about relationship with God, the last 5 are relationship with others. Jesus summed it up in Matthew 22:38-40. "We are to love the Lord our God with all our heart, soul and mind...

and love others as we love ourself." As we get in line with the Word of God about relationships, the chemicals in our bodies begin to balance out resulting in homeostasis (balanced chemicals in the body). It's the unbalanced chemicals in the body that make us sick. We even say that today, "My chemicals are out of balance." And that is very true. But the real truth is our bodies have the correct amount of chemicals to produce perfect health, it's our belief system that is out of balance.

Diseases that are incurable, etiology unknown or there is no cure, may constitute a spiritually rooted disease - a disease that comes from our heart condition. As shared earlier, some dis-eases are passed down through the generations, and those dis-eases derived from someone in your generations that had spiritual issues. Dis-eases start at a breakdown with someone in relationship. If you have a dis-ease, ask God where your relationship breach is. You may even have a relationship breach with yourself! Matthew 22:38-40 states that we are to love the Lord our God with all our heart, soul and mind and love our neighbor as ourself. Upon this hang all the laws and the prophets. In other words, when we keep this commandment we fulfill all the law! If we restore those areas of relationship that are not perfected in love, I can guarantee you, you will find your peace. Peace produces homeostasis that can produce good health. You do not need to know the "root" of a disease to find peace. Restoring our relationships with God, self and others, produces better health to deal with the dis-ease you may have.

The following are things I found in the Bible that actually affect our health. As you read the Bible yourself, if you are looking, you will find these and many more. This is only an example; the Bible is full of health related scriptures:

Scripture	Reference	Produces
Hope deferred makes the heart sick	Proverbs 13:12	Depression, self-pity, doubt and unbelief, heart problems, anxiety and stress, Parkinson's
A merry heart does good like a medicine	Proverbs 17:22	Joy, peace, health
A broken spirit dries up the bones	Proverbs 17:22	Brittle bones, allergies, fear
Shame to a husband is rottenness to his bones	Proverbs 12:4	When women shame their husbands, it can produce health issues in a husbands bones
A curse causeless shall not come	Proverbs 26:2	There is a reason to everything that happens. Take a look at Deuteronomy 28 to see the list of diseases - these are listed as curses.

Envy is rottenness to the bones	Proverbs 14:30	Another bone disease
Critical and perverse lips	Proverbs 4:24	Bitterness, strive and every evil thing.
God has not given us the spirit of fear	2 Timothy 1:7	Fear is a spirit that God has not given. Many roots to dis-ease start with fear.
He that hates reproof shall die	Proverbs 12:1	Not much clearer than that. The body begins dying at the cellular level. We have time to get things right in our heart long before final death happens.
He that trusts in the Lord happy is he	Proverbs 16:20	When we truly trust God, we will have peace and peace produces health and health produces happiness
Death and life are in the power of the tongue	Proverbs 18:21	Our words do matter, it can cause others to feel good or to feel terrible which can, if long term, produce illness.

The following helping terms may help you to see so you gain discernment and understanding when dealing with them in your own life.

Term	Description
Arguing	Can arguing make you sick? Where strife is, is every evil thing. (James 3:16)
Anxiety Disorder	Fear. Many have opted to use the word "stress, or Anxiety" when describing this. But these are nice ways of saying we have fear - but no one wants to admit that.
Bitterness (Unforgiveness)	Bitterness is a root that can breed other problems such as unforgiveness, resentment, retaliation, rage and anger, etc. Bitterness (offense toward someone) has to be dealt with through forgiveness.
Controller	Rooted in fear and anxiety of losing control. If a woman, can be rooted in matriarchal witchcraft.

Driven ness	The need to perform to gain attention, love and acceptance. Fear of being rejected. It's a form of control. Manipulation brought on by an unloving spirit and fear. The room may come from wanting to please a parent in a home of rejection, strife, anger, unaccepted, unloved and unrest.
Fear	Fear is a spirit. "God has not given us the spirit of fear, but power love and a sound mind." (2 Tim. 1:7) Fear is the devil's faith and anytime evil is present, fear is always. Fear is the direct opposite of love. Receive God's perfect love for you, it will cast out any fear there. Fear and love cannot reside at the same time. If you are fearing, you are not being made perfect in love. It's not our love that we need, it's God's perfect love in us. If you have difficulty receiving God's love personally, or even know how to do so, refer back to the teachings found under "blocks" in the 6 basic principles. The battle is in our minds. A fear thought comes, we begin to dwell on it, it becomes real, we become one with it, and it's taken root, now manifests in our body through sweat, anxiety, shaking, all kinds of body symptoms. The spirit needs to be cast out and replaced with the Word of God and His love. When fear is present it causes secretion of liquid into the body. A hormone called ACTH is released by the hypothalamus gland, which produces us to want to fight or run.
Hopelessness and Despair	Is a result of not knowing your identity, who you are, where you are going. Psalm 139 says to search me and know me. 2 Corinthians 10:6, 2 Corinthians 10:5. The battle begins in the mind. We need to take every thought captive and cast out the wrong thoughts of who we are and replace them with what the Bible says we are in God. Doubt and unbelief also causes hopelessness - not believing God loves you or is really there.
Inherited disease	When you have a genetic code defect it's something that is passed on to you by "familiar spirits" in the family tree. The bloodline curse is to be stopped. It can be stopped by you.

Idolatry	Putting anything before God, including yourself and your needs. Fear and worry comes by trying to do things yourself, not trusting God. You are putting yourself between you and God.
Insecurity	Rooted in fear. Feeling vulnerable and unprotected. This comes from not trusting God loves you nor receiving that love for yourself. If someone received God's love the way we were created to, this person would never feel insecure. It has nothing to do with the people around you because nothing is for certain in this world. We need to put our confidence in God not in man. (Psalm 118:8) FYI: This scripture is the center most scripture in the Bible, go figure!
Occultism	Making itself to be real when it is fake.
Pharmaceuticals	Pharmakia is the definition of the word - and Pharmakia is defined as sorcery.
Rage and Anger	Rooted in bitterness against a parent or guardian. Presumably a male figure mate. Found that men who have rage and anger stems from a mother figure who has rejected or abandoned or abused them.
Self-pity	Idolatry - putting self above God. Self-pity keeps us tied to the past hurts and disappointments, causing us to become self-consumed.
Strife	The Bible says that where ever strife is, is every evil thing. Strife is not the same as "strive." Strife is where there is an undercurrent of unrest, though no one says so. You just "feel" the tension in the air. Anger comes from strife, it starts from within with feelings of discontentment, judgment, etc.
Self-hatred, Self-bitterness, any self problems	You don't know how much God loves you, you have not accepted His unconditional love, and you have not accepted that you are righteous in Jesus Christ. A revelation of this love has to take root for you to love and accept yourself. Be sure to study the teaching on God's love.
Anti-Christ Spirit (loveless ness)	Comes from generations in family tree. "Familiar Spirit" that has been assigned to the family and is passed down from your fathers. It is not happy unless it is trashing others or self. Out of it then comes the inability to love, producing guilty complex.
Witchcraft - control nature	Stubbornness to the Word of God. Someone who makes up their own words and creates their own kingdom.

There are so many more to reference in the Word, but this gives you an idea that God knows about all these things even before we were born! He also gives us instruction on each one and more. I used to say, "How can all the answers of this world be found in the Bible?" Well, it took 20 years, but I found that it's true. Everything we need is in the Word of God. We just have to be willing to look.

5 R's (gleaned from the book "A More Excellent Way" by Pastor Henry Wright.)

And if you recognized any of these things in your life that is NOT a blessing, then it's time to do something about it. There is an insight called, "The 5 R's to freedom." When you:

- #1) Recognize. When you see what is happening, the actual truth, you are well on your way to finding your freedom. Recognizing is the #1 step in any recovery program, because until you recognize what you need to be freed from, how can you get free. Or when you recognize you need to change, how can you change?

- #2) Take Responsibility. In other words, decide today to stop blaming everyone for your life, choices and situation. Choose today to point the finger at yourself, and face the truth in every situation.

- #3) Then Repent for what you see that does not line up with God's nature and character. Just confess it to the Lord. Don't be afraid of what you see, don't run and hide. Don't get mad at yourself, just repent.

- #4) Receive. Once you repent, you now need to receive forgiveness. Many repent, repent, repent, but never "receive" forgiveness of what they are repenting for. Once you start receiving from the Lord his love and forgiveness, that's when our lives change.

- #5) Rejoice. Now be thankful. Share with others what God has done for you. You may lead someone to the Lord for salvation!

Practicing these 5 R's is something we can do everyday to help keep us and give us victory.

Ministry Prayer for You:

"Father, thank you for this insightful teaching. I ask you to help each person retain what needs to be retained so they can grow in every area they desire. Bless them with truth Lord. Open them up to seeing within their heart. Let them not be afraid of what they see, but rejoice that they see it, as it's the first step to finding freedom. Help them to remember the 5 R's, and apply it to their daily lives. In Jesus name, Amen."

CHAPTER THIRTY-SIX

BUTTONS

Let me ask you something, "Does anybody push your buttons? It results in you getting all upset, frustrated at what they did and you can feel it. This is what I call the "Buttons" principle.

We are going to talk about what those buttons are and why they are there and how to get rid of those buttons. People need to be able to do whatever they want, be however they want to be, and it doesn't push any buttons in me. I should just be able to look at them and have pity for them if they start acting weird. Love them if they need a little bit of love without feeling like it's all about me. If you are thinned skinned—in other words you feel touchy-feely all the time—that means you have a lot of buttons. Button, buttons, who's got the buttons? So when anybody touches you, you say, "Ouch, eech, ouch, eech."

Now there is a scripture in Luke 8 that talks about the things that are within me. It's not what goes into my mouth but what comes out of my mouth that is the problem. Again, if someone pushes your buttons, what comes out of YOUR mouth? Where does this stuff come from? It comes out of our heart. What I found is a lot of people have little buttons in their heart. Those are the things that people push. They say things like, "they hurt my feelings. Or, "they did it again." You can actually feel the hurt come into your spirit or your chest and you feel - UGH!

It feels like a knife stabbed you in the chest. Somebody is pushing your buttons and every time you take an offense of something you received another button. You don't want anymore buttons. Let's get rid of the buttons.

It's interesting to know that each button represents a sinful reaction. For example if somebody pushes a button, it can cause anger to come up. Somebody might push another button that causes me to become confused. So these are all little buttons, stress, anxiety, fear, jealousy, envy, denial and abuse.

All these are things in our heart. You may be watching a TV show and all of a sudden you start crying. It's because something in you related (buttons) to what was going on in the show. It's not a bad thing, but it does show you want may still be in your heart that needs healing.

We need to get rid of these buttons. We need to get rid of these things because God wants to purge from you so that you can have a clean heart. So if somebody comes along that normally makes you angry you can just say, "Oh poor little thing, I forgive you and I love you." And you are at peace. That's where we need to get to; we need to get to the place of peace. But as long as we still have all those buttons in there we're going to continue bouncing around in our life.

I was giving a teaching right after the September 11th attack. I was talking about buttons and so forth. She said, "I was never suspicious until September 11th." "I was never suspicious about Islam or the people who were blamed for the attack. Now I am suspicious and I run from them." I said to her, "Honey, that button of suspicion was in there but it just took this event to bring it to the surface." Nothing that happens to me just happens to me, or jumps on me. It has to start inside my heart. It has to already be there. I can be tempted to eat a chocolate cake but I can't be tempted to go rob a bank because is not in me.

There is something with Jesus I want to share with you. It is found in Matthew chapter 4: It is when He was led up into the wilderness to be tempted of the Devil. When He had fasted and so forth the Devil came to Him and said, "If You be the Son of God command that these stones be made of bread." "And He answered and Jesus said, *"It is written, man should not live by bread alone, but by every word that proceeds out of the mouth of God."*

Then the Devil took Him again to another place and Jesus said to him, *"Thy shall not tempt the Lord thy God."* And he tempts him again and Jesus said to him, *"Get thee hence Satan for it is written thou shall worship the Lord thy God and Him only shall thy serve."* Then the Devil left. It says, "Man shall not live by bread alone but by every words that proceeds out of the mouth of God."

The reason Jesus was able to say these things to the Devil is because He didn't have any buttons in Him. He didn't have anything in Him to cause Him. Again, these buttons represent sin. Jesus had no sin in him. There was nothing in him to be tempted. He was tempted like us but He had nothing in Him to re-act upon it. Like I said I could be tempted to eat chocolate or maybe even gossip from time to time, but I am not tempted to drink alcohol, it is not in me. I never had a problem with it and it isn't anything that tempts me. You can drink around me and it doesn't bother me. I'm not tempted to rob a bank because it's not in me to do it. I bet you can find things you that tempt you. Maybe you have addictions or other things in your life you are tempted to do. Those are the buttons; those are the buttons God wants out. The way that they come out is through forgiveness and confession.

The tempter can come and tempt you to fear. How? For example. You were going to a place when the last time you went there something uncomfortable happened to you. So now you are tempted to fear that place. You start agreeing with what the tempter is saying and pretty soon you are responding with your body and you start saying, "Oh I can't go to that place because I remember what happened last time." Now you are back in a box and the tempter is laughing at you saying, "Ha...I got them again." You want to get rid of that fear.

How you get rid of fear is to first recognize that fear is a spirit. The Bible says, *"God has not given us a spirit of fear but of power, love and a sound mind."* So we can say, "I see that this is fear working here and I choose not to agree any longer, so fear GO in Jesus name." (If you need some help putting that in prayer, I will be happy to do that with you.)

The second thing is fear is a sin. By fearing we are sinning because we am not trusting God's love. The Bible says that perfect love cast out all fear. If I don't have God's love in me I am going to have that fear in me. We operate in one or the other at ALL times... fear or faith (which is God's love). So I have to confess to God, "Father, forgive me for having fear in my heart." The Bible says in I John 1:9 that, *"If I confess my sins He is faithful and just to cleanse me from all unrighteousness."* So what He does is He removes that fearful button out of your heart. Then when the tempter tries to come and tempt you with fear you will say, "Huh, well you are a liar. God loves me and there is no fear in love." That is how we walk out of those kinds of things.

So, forgiveness is the key to not adding MORE buttons. Because when you forgive someone a button will not plant in your heart. However, if you take the bait and allow it in your heart and it stays there, then you are going to have problems, more buttons on top of buttons. You are going to be loaded down, you are going to feel heavy, you are going to feel depressed. All of these buttons cause strife, anxiety and that is what we want freedom from the anxiety and the fear. Until you do you won't find the peace you need to live the life God wants you to live a full and abundant life. But we won't be able to if we are FULL of other stuff.

The Bible says that God wishes we all walked in peace and peaceable among all men. We can only do that if we do not have all those buttons in us. I am going to push your buttons; your kids are going to push your buttons, we have to get rid of the buttons. I am trying to make it as easy and as simple as I can here.

All we do is simply take our buttons to the Lord. You can even get a piece of paper and write down your buttons. Say, "Okay Lord what are my buttons?" Every time I get upset what button is being pushed? I bet if you look at that list again you are going to see that those are all sins. So you can take your sin list to the Lord and repent and receive forgiveness. Every time it starts to come back again, receive forgiveness for it. The Bible even says how many times we are to forgive our neighbor or brother, seventy times seventy. So if we need to forgive that many times, how many times does God forgive? It is infinite.

Every button is a temptation ready to happen and we don't need anymore temptation in this world do we, if they are in us let's just get rid of them. If I am walking down the street and pass by a store that has a big sale sign in the window, I am not going to run in there buy if I don't have any money. I am going to say, "wow, cool, I hope somebody gets blessed by that sale." We need to get rid of those things that pull at us and make us do things we don't want to do, those are buttons.

So I hope this helped to minister a little bit of truth to you. Get that paper out, identify all your buttons and take it to the Lord. He wants to remove the buttons so that you have the peace you need to live yourself and with others every single day.

Prayer:

Father, I ask for every heart listen that they would be able to recognize the own things in their own heart. Not in other people's hearts but their own heart and make a list and take them to you and receive forgiveness for every button that is in their heart so they will not be so sensitive and touchy and feely and easily offended. They will know how to forgive themselves and others and forgive them quickly so that new buttons do not come in. I thank You Father for Your love, I thank You for power. I ask You that You put a whole dose of Your love right now in every person reading this book right now. I pray that they would experience what it is really like to be loved by You. I ask You that, that truth that You want to teach them frees their heart, because it is that truth that sets them free. I thank You Lord in Jesus name, Amen!

Further Resources

Pick up my book called "Buttons of Self-Worth." It dives into specific details on getting rid of buttons because they actually push your worth. Let's get free today.

CHAPTER THIRTY-SEVEN

We have addressed the area of truth when we were in the "blocks" teaching. But it's important that we also share the scriptures that pertain to speaking and walking in truth. It's the Word that heals and changes people, not mine. So as you read each scripture, ponder on it for a moment allowing God time to speak to your heart. We are still in the "recognizing" stages of life, so it's always good to stay open and alert to anything the Lord wants us to see.

The following is broken down in several categories:

Speaking Truth

Psalms 145:18 - The LORD is nigh unto all them that call upon him, to all that call upon him in **truth**.

Psalms 15:2 - He that walketh uprightly, and worketh righteousness, and speaketh the **truth** in his heart.

2 Chronicles 18:15 - And the king said to him, How many times shall I adjure thee that thou say nothing but the **truth** to me in the name of the LORD?

Psalms 51:6 - Behold, thou desirest **truth** in the inward parts: and in the hidden part thou shalt make me to know wisdom.

Psalms 145:18 - The LORD is nigh unto all them that call upon him, to all that call upon him in **truth.**

Proverbs 8:7 - For my mouth shall speak **truth**; and wickedness is an abomination to my lips.

Proverbs 12:17 - He that speaketh **truth** sheweth forth righteousness: but a false witness deceit.

Proverbs 12:19 - The lip of **truth** shall be established for ever: but a lying tongue is but for a moment.

Proverbs 16:6 - By mercy and **truth** iniquity is purged: and by the fear of the LORD men depart from evil.

Zechariah 8:16 - These are the things that ye shall do; Speak ye every man the **truth** to his neighbor; execute the judgment of **truth** and peace in your gates.

Malachi 2:6 - The law of **truth** was in his mouth, and iniquity was not found in his lips: he walked with me in peace and equity, and did turn many away from iniquity.

Mark 5:33 - But the woman fearing and trembling, knowing what was done in her, came and fell down before him, and told him all the **truth**.

John 17:19 - And for their sakes I sanctify myself, that they also might be sanctified through the **truth**.

2 Corinthians 4:2 - But have renounced the hidden things of dishonesty, not walking in craftiness, nor handling the word of God deceitfully; but by manifestation of the **truth** commending ourselves to every man's conscience in the sight of God.

2 Corinthians 7:14 - For if I have boasted any thing to him of you, I am not ashamed; but as we spake all things to you in **truth**, even so our boasting, which I made before Titus, is found a **truth**.

Ephesians 4:15 - But speaking the **truth** in love, may grow up into him in all things, which is the head, even Christ.

Ephesians 4:25 - Wherefore putting away lying, speak every man **truth** with his neighbour: for we are members one of another.

Ephesians 6:14 - Stand therefore, having your loins girt about with **truth**, and having on the breastplate of righteousness.

2 Timothy 2:25 - In meekness instructing those that oppose themselves; if God peradventure will give them repentance to the acknowledging of the **truth**.

James 3:14 - But if ye have bitter envying and strife in your hearts, glory not, and lie not against the **truth**.

Knowing Truth:

Titus 1:1 - Paul, a servant of God, and an apostle of Jesus Christ, according to the faith of God's elect, and the acknowledging of the **truth** which is after godliness.

Psalms 119:142 - Thy righteousness is an everlasting righteousness, and thy law is the **truth**.

John 1:17 - For the law was given by Moses, but grace and **truth** came by Jesus Christ.

John 8:32 - And ye shall know the **truth**, and the **truth** shall make you free.

John 14:6 - Jesus saith unto him, I am the way, the **truth**, and the life: no man cometh unto the Father, but by me.

John 14:17 - Even the Spirit of **truth**; whom the world cannot receive, because it seeth him not, neither knoweth him: but ye know him; for he dwelleth with you, and shall be in you.

1 Timothy 6:5 - Perverse disputings of men of corrupt minds, and destitute of the **truth**, supposing that gain is godliness: from such withdraw thyself.

1 Timothy 4:3 - Forbidding to marry, and commanding to abstain from meats, which God hath created to be received with thanksgiving of them which believe and know the **truth.**

2 Timothy 3:7 - Ever learning, and never able to come to the knowledge of the **truth.**

1 Peter 1:22 - Seeing ye have purified your souls in obeying the **truth** through the Spirit unto unfeigned love of the brethren, see that ye love one another with a pure heart fervently.

1 John 1:8 - If we say that we have no sin, we deceive ourselves, and the **truth** is not in us.

1 John 2:4 - He that saith, I know him, and keepeth not his commandments, is a liar, and the **truth** is not in him.

1 John 3:18 - My little children, let us not love in word, neither in tongue; but in deed and in **truth**.

3 John 1:8 - We therefore ought to receive such, that we might be fellow helpers to the **truth**.

James 5:19 - Brethren, if any of you do err from the **truth**, and one convert him; let him know, that he which converteth the sinner from the error of his way shall save a soul from death, and shall hide a multitude of sins.

Result of Living Truth

John 17:17 - Sanctify them through thy **truth**: thy word is truth.

1 Corinthians 5:8 - Therefore let us keep the feast, not with old leaven, neither with the leaven of malice and wickedness; but with the unleavened bread of sincerity and **truth.**

Psalms 40:11 - Withhold not thou thy tender mercies from me, O LORD: let thy loving kindness and thy **truth** continually preserve me.

Psalms 91:4 - He shall cover thee with his feathers, and under his wings shalt thou trust: his **truth** shall be thy shield and buckler

Proverbs 3:3 - Let not mercy and **truth** forsake thee: bind them about thy neck; write them upon the table of thine heart.

Isaiah 26:2 - Open ye the gates, that the righteous nation which keepeth the **truth** may enter in.

Isaiah 38:3 - And said, Remember now, O LORD, I beseech thee, how I have walked before thee in **truth** and with a perfect heart, and have done that which is good in thy sight.

Isaiah 59:4 - None calleth for justice, nor any pleadeth for **truth**: they trust in vanity, and speak lies; they conceive mischief, and bring forth iniquity.

Jeremiah 33:6 - Behold, I will bring it health and cure, and I will cure them, and will reveal unto them the abundance of peace and **truth**.

Hosea 4:1 - Hear the word of the LORD, ye children of Israel: for the LORD hath a controversy with the inhabitants of the land, because there is no **truth**, nor mercy, nor knowledge of God in the land.

John 3:21 - But he that doeth **truth** cometh to the light, that his deeds may be made manifest, that they are wrought in God.

John 4:23 - But the hour cometh, and now is, when the true worshippers shall worship the Father in spirit and in **truth**: for the Father seeketh such to worship him.

John 4:24 - God is a Spirit: and they that worship him must worship him in spirit and in **truth**.

John 8:44 - Ye are of your father the devil, and the lusts of your father ye will do. He was a murderer from the beginning, and abode not in the **truth**, because there is no **truth** in him. When he speaketh a lie, he speaketh of his own: for he is a liar, and the father of it.

2 Thessalonians 2:10 - And with all deceivableness of unrighteousness in them that perish; because they received not the love of the **truth**, that they might be saved.

CHAPTER THIRTY-EIGHT

Work Out

Philippians 2:12 *Wherefore, my beloved, as ye have always obeyed, not as in my presence only, but now much more in my absence, work out your own salvation with fear and trembling.*

You have gone through a lot of teaching now allow yourself time to absorb it and allow the Holy Spirit to work it in you - this is what it means to work out your own salvation with fear and trembling. This takes a bit of time, this is the sanctification process. So give yourself permission to take it slow. Yes, many of you want it now... go back over the teaching on patience. Every thing taught in this web site has been personally applied by me. These are all areas that the Lord used to help me in my life to grow in strength, courage, boldness, peace, joy and the righteousness of Christ. This was my journey, you have one too. Let God take the lead and you'll experience things you never thought could ever happen.

These teachings do not teach about everything, nor do we presume to have everything figured out. By sharing this site with you is our part - but only a "part." You have a part too and when you do your part and I do my part, we will see the whole picture. He may show you the same things in the same way He showed me or in another way, but we will all end up in the same place - discovering truth. God isn't in a box and will do what He pleases by carefully choose His methods for every life. We may never figure out "His ways" but we can trust Him nonetheless. Isaiah 55:9 says that His ways and thoughts are higher than our ways and thoughts so no one will have it **all** figured out but these teachings are provided to help you on your journey to "see" what is inside you that is not of God so that you can cooperate with Him for your freedom. Remember, your job is to recognize, take responsibility, repent and God will do the healing, restoring, cleansing, purging, and delivering. When we do our part God can do His.

What does the Bible say about God's work?

- ❑ Philippians 2:13 *"For it is God which worketh in you both to will and to do of his good pleasure."*

- ❑ Isaiah 1:17 *"Come let us reason together says the Lord, though your sins be as scarlet, they shall be white as snow, though they be as crimson, they shall be as wool."*

- ❑ Genesis 27:20 *But Isaac said to his son, "How did you ever find it so quickly, my son?" He replied, "Because the LORD your God worked it out for me."*

- ❑ Psalm 92:4-5 *"For thou, Lord, hast made me glad through thy work: I will triumph in the works of thy hands. O Lord, how great are thy works and thy thoughts are very deep."*

- ❏ Isaiah 61:8 *"For I the LORD love judgment, I hate robbery for burnt offering; and I will direct their work in truth, and I will make an everlasting covenant with them."*

- ❏ Acts 13:41 *"Behold, ye despisers, and wonder, and perish: for I work a work in your days, a work which ye shall in no wise believe, though a man declare it unto you."*

- ❏ Romans 8:28 *"And we know that all things work together for good to them that love God, to them who are the called according to his purpose."*

- ❏ 1 Corinthians 12:6 *"And there are diversities of operations, but it is the same God which worketh all in all."*

- ❏ 1 Corinthians 12:11 *"But all these worketh that one and the selfsame Spirit, dividing to every man severally as he will."*

- ❏ Philippians 1:6 *"Being confident of this very thing, that he which hath begun a good work in you will perform it until the day of Jesus Christ:"*

- ❏ Hebrews 1:10 *"And, Thou, Lord, in the beginning hast laid the foundation of the earth; and the heavens are the works of thine hands:"*

- ❏ Romans 16:20 *"And the God of peace shall bruise Satan under your feet shortly. The grace of our Lord Jesus Christ be with you. Amen."*

It is clear by looking up the scriptures of Work, that most of the work is done by God. So what is our work?

What does the Bible say about Jesus' work?

- ❏ John 14:10 *"Believest thou not that I am in the Father, and the Father in me? the words that I speak unto you I speak not of myself: but the Father that dwelleth in me, He doeth the works."*

(There are several scriptures of the work Jesus did, but the bottom line is that Jesus never did anything or say anything that He didn't see His Father in heaven say and do!)

What does the Scriptures say about our work?

- ❏ John 6:28 - *"Then said they to him, what shall we do that we might work the works of God? Jesus answered and said unto them, this is the work of God, that ye believe on him who he hath sent."*

  1. This is a vital truth for your life. Whatever you "do" is it from a motive of love?

  2. The work we are to do is believe - believe God's love, believe Jesus and all he offered, and receive these truths personally.

Romans 3:27 - *"Does it say that we work for God's love? Does it say we work to gain recognition? Do we work to keep our salvation?"* No. It's a heart matter. The work we are asked to do by Jesus is believe. Believe the gospel of Peace. Believe God loves you, believe you are forgiven, believe Jesus paid for all your sins so you don't need to suffer them, believe, believe, believe is the work we are to do (John 6:29).

❑ Romans 11:6 "And if by grace, then is it no more of works: otherwise grace is no more grace. But if it be of works, then it is no more grace: otherwise work is no more work."

❑ Romans 2:10 "But glory, honor, and peace, to every man that worketh good, to the Jew first, and also to the Gentile."

❑ Romans 3:27 and Romans 4:2 "Where is boasting then? It is excluded. By what law? of works? Nay: but by the law of faith"- As Abraham, we are also not justified by works! It is a gift from God and let no man boast thinking he did anything. For all good things come from God, and anything that we do that IS Good is God doing it through us. If we have a special gift, it's the gift given you by God. You are a vessel, that is it. But what you hold in your vessel is what manifests in your life. As a matter of fact, your life isn't even yours, you have been bought.

So our work is simple - cleave to that which is good, abhor that which is evil. And this is the "work out" - learning which is which - this is discernment (Hebrews 5:14)

❑ 1 Corinthians 15:58 "Therefore, my beloved brethren, be ye steadfast, unmovable, always abounding in the work of the Lord, forasmuch as ye know that your labor is not in vain in the Lord."

❑ Galatians 2:16 "Knowing that a man is not justified by the works of the law, but by the faith of Jesus Christ, even we have believed in Jesus Christ, that we might be justified by the faith of Christ, and not by the works of the law: for by the works of the law shall no flesh be justified."

❑ Galatians 3:10 "For as many as are of the works of the law are under the curse: for it is written, Cursed is every one that continueth not in all things which are written in the book of the law to do them."

❑ 1 Thessalonians 1:3 "Remembering without ceasing your work of faith, and labor of love, and patience of hope in our Lord Jesus Christ, in the sight of God and our Father."

❑ 2 Timothy 2:15 "Study to shew thyself approved unto God, a workman that needeth not to be ashamed, rightly dividing the word of truth."

❑ 2 Timothy 4:5 "But watch thou in all things, endure afflictions, do the work of an evangelist, make full proof of thy ministry."

❑ Titus 3:5 "Not by works of righteousness which we have done, but according to his mercy he saved us, by the washing of regeneration, and renewing of the Holy Ghost;"

❑ James 1:27 "Pure religion and undefiled before God and the Father is this, To visit the fatherless and widows in their affliction, and to keep himself unspotted from the world." (This is faith at work - it's love at work - Because faith - love - without works is dead. - James 2:20)

What is worked out of us or into us?

- ❑ Romans 5:3 "And not only so, but we glory in tribulations also: knowing that tribulation **worketh** patience; and patience experience and experience hope; and hope maketh not ashamed, because the love of God is shed abroad in our hearts by the Holy Ghost which is given unto us."

- ❑ Patience is to be worked in us. In one of the sessions we addressed patience. Be sure to go over it again because without patience you will never obtain the peace you desire - and it's clear that patience also removes all shame because we finally believe God's love for us is true and real.

- ❑ 2 Thessalonians 1:11 "Wherefore also we pray always for you, that our God would count you worthy of this calling, and fulfill all the good pleasure of his goodness, and the work of faith with power."

- ❑ 1 Corinthians 3:13 "Every man's work shall be made manifest: for the day shall declare it, because it shall be revealed by fire; and the fire shall try every man's work of what sort it is."

- ❑ 2 Corinthians 4:17 "For our light affliction, which is but for a moment, worketh for us a far more exceeding and eternal weight of glory."

- ❑ Ephesians 3:7 "Whereof I was made a minister, according to the gift of the grace of God given unto me by the effectual working of his power."

- ❑ Ephesians 4:16 "From whom the whole body fitly joined together and compacted by that which every joint supplieth, according to the effectual working in the measure of every part, maketh increase of the body unto the edifying of itself in love."

- ❑ Colossians 1:29 "Whereunto I also labor, striving according to his working, which worketh in me mightily."

- ❑ Ephesians 4:28 "Let him that stole steal no more: but rather let him labor, working with his hands the thing which is good, that he may have to give to him that needeth."

- ❑ 1 Thessalonians 1:3 "Remembering without ceasing your work of faith, and labor of love, and patience of hope in our Lord Jesus Christ, in the sight of God and our Father."

- ❑ 1 Thessalonians 5:13 "And to esteem them very highly in love for their work's sake. And be at peace among yourselves.."

- ❑ 2 Timothy 2:21 "If a man therefore purge himself from these, he shall be a vessel unto honor, sanctified, and meet for the master's use, and prepared unto every good work."

- ❑ 2 Timothy 4:18 "And the Lord shall deliver me from every evil work, and will preserve me unto his heavenly kingdom: to whom be glory for ever and ever, Amen."

- ❑ James 1:3-4 "...knowing this, that the trying of your faith worketh patience. But let patience have her perfect work, that ye may be perfect and entire, wanting nothing.

- ❑ James 1:25 "But whoso looketh into the perfect law of liberty, and continueth therein, he being not a forgetful hearer, but a doer of the work, this man shall be blessed in his deed."

- ❑ John 14:12 "Verily, verily, I say unto you, He that believeth on me, the works that I do shall he do also; and greater works than these shall he do; because I go unto my Father.

- ❑ Ephesians 1:19 "And what is the exceeding greatness of his power to us-ward who believe, according to the working of his mighty power."

- ❑ 1 Thessalonians 2:13 "For this cause also thank we God without ceasing, because, when ye received the word of God which ye heard of us, ye received it not as the word of men, but as it is in truth, the word of God, which effectually worketh also in you that believe."

- ❑ Hebrews 4:3 "For we which have believed do enter into rest, as he said, As I have sworn in my wrath, if they shall enter into my rest: although the works were finished from the foundation of the world."

- ❑ Hebrews 4:10 "For he that is entered into his rest, he also hath ceased from his own works, as God did from his."

- ❑ Acts 26:18 "To open their eyes, and to turn them from darkness to light, and from the power of Satan unto God, that they may receive forgiveness of sins, and inheritance among them which are sanctified by faith that is in me.

What does the Scripture say about the Enemy's work?

- ❑ Romans 13:12 "The night is far spent, the day is at hand: let us therefore cast off the works of darkness, and let us put on the armour of light."

- ❑ Ephesians 5:11 "And have no fellowship with the unfruitful works of darkness, but rather reprove them."

- ❑ Ephesians 2:2 "Wherein in time past ye walked according to the course of this world, according to the prince of the power of the air, the spirit that now worketh in the children of disobedience:"

- ❑ John 10:10: "The thief comes to kill, steal and destroy..."

- ❑ 1 Chronicles 21:1 "And Satan stood up against Israel, and provoked David to number Israel."

- ❑ Psalm 109:6 "Set thou a wicked man over him: and let Satan stand at his right hand."

- ❑ Matthew 4:10 "Then saith Jesus unto him, Get thee hence, Satan: for it is written, Thou shalt worship the Lord thy God, and him only shalt thou serve."

- ❑ Mark 8:33 "But when he had turned about and looked on his disciples, he rebuked Peter, saying, Get thee behind me, Satan: for thou savourest not the things that be of God, but the things that be of men."

- ❑ Luke 13:16 "And ought not this woman, being a daughter of Abraham, whom Satan hath bound, lo, these eighteen years, be loosed from this bond on the Sabbath day?"

- ❑ Luke 22:31 "And the Lord said, Simon, Simon, behold, Satan hath desired to have you, that he may sift you as wheat:"

- ❑ Acts 5:3 "But Peter said, Ananias, why hath Satan filled thine heart to lie to the Holy Ghost, and to keep back part of the price of the land?"

- ❑ Romans 8:38 "For I am persuaded, that neither death, nor life, nor angels, nor principalities, nor powers, nor things present, nor things to come..."

- ❑ 2 Corinthians 2:11 "Lest Satan should get an advantage of us: for we are not ignorant of his devices."

- ❑ 2 Corinthians 11:14 "And don't marvel; for Satan himself is transformed into an angel of light."

- ❑ 2 Corinthians 12:7 "And lest I should be exalted above measure through the abundance of the revelations, there was given to me a thorn in the flesh, the messenger of Satan to buffet me, lest I should be exalted above measure."

- ❑ 2 Thessalonians 2:9 "Even him, whose coming is after the working of Satan with all power and signs and lying wonders."

- ❑ Ephesians 6:12 "For we wrestle not against flesh and blood, but against principalities, against powers, against the rulers of the darkness of this world, against spiritual wickedness in high places."

- ❑ It is clear that the enemy can only gain access to you when you let him. And he comes in due to the sin within us. He cannot tempt you to do anything unless it's already an issue in your life yet to overcome.

Ministry:

(2 Timothy 3:14) *"But continue in the things which you have learned and hast been assured of, knowing of whom you have learned them. And that from a child thou hast known the holy scriptures, which are able to make thee wise unto salvation through faith which is in Christ Jesus. All scripture is given by inspiration of God, and is profitable for doctrine, for reproof, for correction, for instruction in righteousness, that the man of God may be perfect, thoroughly furnished unto all good works."*

Remember you have been made free by the blood of the Lamb (Revelation 12:11) and you have forgotten you are cleansed from your old sins (2 Peter 1:9). We have victory in this. Not to be sin conscious all the time but to be well-balanced in our thinking so that when we see deceitfulness in our thoughts, we can address it immediately. This ministry is for people who have been unbelieving believers, to help you get back into fellowship with the Lord, with yourself and with others to complete the work God has for you to complete. But if we are continually dealing with our same issues, we are going to stay incomplete and not fulfill the call on our life.

So to get past all this and into the new things God has for you, take all those things that you saw in your life that are not of God (rap sheet) and confess them to the Lord. As you went through the teachings, you had opportunity to do it at that time, so whatever you didn't do, do it now. You can have others help in this if desired. James 5:16 says "If we confess our faults one to another and pray one for another, we shall be healed." It's good to talk to someone you trust, or someone in ministry to pray with you about these things.

You can also minister to yourself. As you recognized the things from this workbook in your own life, you may have experienced pain, sadness, discomfort, and perhaps intensifying your current illness. 1 Peter 4:1 says: " Forasmuch then as Christ hath suffered for us in the flesh, arm yourselves likewise with the same mind: for he that hath suffered in the flesh hath ceased from sin." This is ALL GOOD! It means that the enemy has been stirred up and is going to put up a fight to leave.

As you recognize these things, you have the power and authority of the Holy Spirit (As a Child of God) to cast them out. You have had many opportunities during this workshop to identify those things that have to go. It's your turn to take back your life.

Following is a sample prayer for confession.

"Heavenly Father, I recognize that I have allowed these sins to dwell in me long enough. I do not want them there any longer. I confess to you my sin(s) of _____(name each one), and receive forgiveness now in Jesus Name. I ask for your love to flood my soul and I pray for your healing and restoration to manifest in my life in Jesus Name."

Following is a sample prayer for deliverance of evil spirits:

"Heavenly Father, I recognize that I have allowed the spirit of _____ (name them) to dwell in my life and live through me. I ask for your forgiveness for allowing it to be there and not seeing it before. I now take authority over this spirit in Jesus Name and command it to leave. I am no longer giving it permission to dwell in my life. I have fallen out of agreement with it's thoughts and intents. So now I speak to you spirit of _____. Go now, in Jesus name. Go to a dry place and do not return. Father, I ask for your love to flood me right now in every area of my life that the spirit had control. Fill me with your presence, peace, love and joy. I receive your love now in Jesus name, Amen."

Working Out what you have learned

- ❏ Be Thankful!! In everything by prayer and supplication with thanksgiving.... ask God for things you want or need. But first come to Him with thanksgiving. A thankful heart is a "receiving" heart. When we thank God for His love, at that moment we are receiving it. If you want to receive more grace, thank Him for it first. If you want to receive more provision, thank Him for it first.

- ❏ Rejoice! (Luke 10:20) Rejoice that your name is written in the lambs book of life, not that we have the ability to cast out devils. Because the Bible says that in the judgment day of Christ, even those that cast out devils was told He never knew them (Luke 13:26-27).

- ❏ Develop a clear understanding of Salvation and forgiveness of sins. If you have problems believing you are saved, perhaps you need to talk with God about that. When you have problems, it means you are still feeling guilty about them. We need to understand all our guilt and sins are forgiven. Pray for revelation in this area. You have been forgiven of all your sins today yesterday and forever - once and for all time.

- ❏ Keep our thoughts captive under truth. (II Corinthians 10:5) Casting down all imaginations that exalts itself against the knowledge of God. If we let anything hinder our relationship with God, that is IDOLATRY. It could be anything.

- ❏ We are to KNOW Satan's Devices! (Ephesians 6:11-18) "Put on the whole armor of God so that we can stand against the wiles of the devil..." Now that you have gained discernment in these things, you can resist the enemy at his attacks!

- ❏ (Revelations 12:11) We overcome him (the devil) by the blood of the lamb and the word of our testimony. It's important to share with others what God is doing in your life. Not only are you re-enforcing the truth in your own life, by sharing the goodness of God, you will win others to the Lord.

- ❏ As you are purged, there are "spaces" inside you that need to be filled. It's very vital to fill that "space" with the things of God. Read the Word; visit with Him, Praise Him, and Thank Him. You will soon find that void will be gone and your life is even more full than ever before. By filling that void with God, there is no room for the enemy to return. (Matthew 12:43-45)

- ❏ Be transformed in our minds to God's thoughts, not conformed to the thoughts of this world. (Romans 12:2) Everything begins with our mind. Choose for your life what will help you establish good thoughts, and rid yourself of things that may be tempting and cause you to think wrongly.

- ❏ Continue building your relationship with God the Father, God the Son and God the Holy Ghost. Become thankful for them. Continue receiving Love from God to love yourself and others. Don't TRY just RECEIVE. "We are called to freedom - serve one another in love" (Galatians 5:13-14)

❑ Read the Word. You cannot trust WHOM you do not know. Jesus is the "word come in the flesh" (John 1:14). When we get to know Jesus, you get to know the Father (John 10:30).

❑ Get to know your own heart and you will not be judged. (1 Peter 4:7) "For the time is come that judgment must begin at the house of God: and if it first begins with us, what shall the end be of them that obey not the gospel of God." Don't be afraid of what you see, the more you see that does not belong, the more free you will become when addressing those issues in your life. When we know who we are, where we've been, or where we are going, it brings stability in our lives.

❑ Put all your confidence in God, not man. (Psalm 118:8) By growing in faith in God you will allow men to live freely because you trust God "with" man.

❑ Resist the attacks of the enemy. Especially when you have a chance to be offended. Forgive QUICKLY or else roots will grow that will cause another layer to be added to your onion skin. (James 4:7) This also means to remove things from your life that allow the enemy access to your life.

❑ When you begin feeling bad or experiencing things you learned to discern in your life, simply take them to God in confession. They are sins! They are from the enemy. Discernment knows good and evil and which is which! Now you see those things and can resist them by the Word of God. Run to God NOT from Him when you begin manifesting these things. Repent! Repent means to be sorry for your sin, and confess them so God can cleanse you.

❑ If you find yourself in a battle, it may be with a spirit. If it is, such as fear or anger, you can say, "I will not fear and I will not be angry. Those things are NOT from God, and I will not entertain them any longer. You will need to leave me, you have no rights to me. Lord, Forgive me for even letting those thoughts into my mind and stop any thing from rooting in my spirit." Then go on with your day forgetting those things.

❑ Whatever you have experienced to become free, you will need to continue to stay free. Everyone doesn't have the same needs and same problems, so do NOT compare yourself with others. If you worked at getting free, then you may have to work at staying free. But I found that when I discovered my problem, repented, God made me free. He sustains me, I don't sustain myself. He keeps me, I don't keep myself (Psalm 121). The more excellent way is to choose Him, then He will do the work. He will fight your battles and He will "make" you to lie down beside green pastures (Psalm 23). He will make your feet like Hinds' feet (Habakkuk 3:18-20).

❑ Separate yourself from those that are contrary to the Word (Romans 16:17). You can also learn to separate them from their sin so that you can love the sinner but hate the sin (Romans 7).

❑ Choose to stop sinning today lest a worse thing come upon you. (John 5:14) And when you do sin, take it immediately to the Lord and you will stay clean! By staying transparent before God, walking in truth, you will remain free.

- Walking in Love is spiritual warfare. (1 Corinthians 13). How hard is it to love and forgive? Look around the world. Wars and fights always come from offense, lack of love, and unforgiveness. It is spiritual warfare to love one another. There is no enemy that can conquer love. A soft answer turns away wrath (Proverbs 15:1).

- Acknowledge God in all your ways and He will direct your paths. Include God in every area of your life, from mowing the lawn to changing baby diapers or leading worship at Church. In ALL your ways... in everything you do! Many think that He has better things to do with His time than to help you cut the lawn, but that is further from the truth. We don't understand how God can be involved in every person's life on this planet, but He is. We have to take that by faith. You ARE special! You ARE important. Bring everything to the Lord. The Bible says, "You have not because you ask not, and when you ask, you ask for something to consume upon your own lust." We need to acknowledge Him even in our asking because when we ask according to His will (and in order to know His will, we need to know his character and nature) then we will have it!

- (John 14:27) - Jesus left us his peace. He bequeathed it to us as an inheritance upon his going to be with His Father in Heaven. That means we have access to it. "Take your peace" is action. How to walk in peace when things aren't so peaceful. "Blessed are the peacemakers for they shall be called the children of God. (Matthew 5).

- (Galatians 5:1-3) "Being justified by faith, we have peace with God through Jesus.

- James 1: Tribulations work patience - patience produces peace.

- Psalm 23 - "You are what I need so I won't need. The Lord is my shepherd I shall not want."

Ministry Prayer for You:

"Father, there is a lot of teaching in this book, including this chapter. I pray that the Holy Spirit hold onto things that pertain to this individuals life, and have it come up when they need it. Let them know that all they are to do is love You, love others and love themselves. Help them not to be confused or think this is too hard, because we can do ALL THINGS through Christ's power in us. Help them to find peace by trusting You in all areas. In Jesus name, Amen."

BOOK Resources

Written by Linda Lange

A Matter of the Mind - Linda's autobiography of freedom from anxiety and stress that began her ministry in helping others overcome.

A Matter of the Heart - Linda shares revelations and insights as the Lord brought her out of fear and into faith. A journey of the heart!

Abandonment and Rejection - You can be restored and never feel rejection again! Linda shares the truth that will make you free.

Aha Moments - Daily Devotional comprised of biblical insights and Linda's personal experiences.

Buttons of Self-Worth - Has anyone ever pushed your buttons? Get free today!

Believe Journal - A journal that helps activate your faith to believe for prayers to be answered.

Bitterness and Unforgiveness - "the deadly duo." Bitterness can result in various illnesses. We need to get rid of all unforgiveness and bitterness today.

Discovering God - Workbook - Learn how to have a relationship with the Father, Son and Holy Ghost, yourself and others. (Matthew 22:38-40). We dive into a bit of it in this book, but for the fullness of the teaching and audio access to the teachings, you will develop a more intimate relationship with the godhead. This is also the workbook I use when teaching at seminars and conferences. Everything you need to know about God is in this workbook.

Do You Have an UnBiblical Cord? - freeing yourself from soul-ties and co-dependencies.

Envy and Jealousy - Many don't even know they operate in this. And others don't know how to stay free from other's toxicity. This book will help you see the truth that will make you free.

Forgiving from Your Heart - a study and exercise on how to truly forgive from your heart, not just with lip service but with a heart change.

Fearless Living Workbook - Learn to live fearlessly!! This is a great study for personal growth or group. We also provide the teaching guide in audio, upon request.

Freedom from Guilt and Condemnation - as we referenced in this book, but for the complete teaching pick up the book.

Grieving Loss without the Bitter Pain - I wrote this book after my sister's death. What God showed me and freed me from was remarkable, to the extent when others read this book they say it's the best book on grieving they have ever read.

Holes - stop the leak - How many wonder why you aren't being blessed? Maybe there is a hole somewhere in your life? Let's get that fixed!

How to Walk in the Spirit of God - as referenced in this book. But for the complete teaching plus on-line guide, pick it up at our book store.

Loving God and workbook - This is a must! To really know how to love God with all of your heart, soul, mind and strength is key to living a whole and healthy life.

Life Lessons for Children - Filled with a study for every Sunday of the week, to help children grow in the things of the Lord. It has scriptures, studies, and craft items to do.

Nothing but the Truth so Help me God! - We all need help from the Lord to see the truth. But we also need to know how to share the truth without having to walk on egg shells. Learn how.

Prayer Guide - this is a great resource for helping with a variety of prayer topics.

Position Yourself to Receive - In order to receive from God, we need to be in position to catch the blessings. This book gives great insights and practical application for a victorious Christ-filled life.

Root - Learn the roots to your issues. It's the truth that makes us free.

Stopping the Accuser - we have the power to stop the words of accusations from messing with our lives. Learn how today.

Trauma and Post Traumatic Stress Disorder - My husband is a Vietnam Veteran and wounded in action. He is very familiar with the ramifications of war. This book shared some about my husband and how he was made free.

Toms' Tidbits - A fun loving book! Filled with one-liners that Tom has shared with me over the years in discussions. I would explain a huge revelation in many words, and he would sum it all up with one line! Many have used these as a daily devotional.

Understanding Manipulation and Control - Once we understand what is going on, we can find our freedom.

What Was I Thinking? This book was also referenced, but you can get the full version, and upon request, the student guide to help deeper study. If you are a teacher, pick up the teacher's guide. It can be used in personal study or in a class setting.

Why Do We Get Sick? This is a study workbook answering this and many other questions about health and the Bible. It also comes with a guided audio version upon request.

These are the books that Linda has written over the years that has impacted her lives and the lives of those who read them. Again, she does not teach anything she has not received victory in. If God can do it for her, He can certainly do it for you. Once we have ALL THE FACTS about specific topics, you will have what you need to become free.

John 8:32 *"You shall know the truth, and the truth shall make you free."*

More Resources:

Access Linda's website at: www.truthfrees.org to order your books today. They are also found on amazon.com. Some are ebooks, so be sure to check that out.

We also offer teachings on the website freely. So visit us today at:

www.truthfrees.org.

CONTACT US

I am open to speak to you on your issues and needs. Please connect with me at: linda@truthfrees.org or www.truthfrees.org.

Our motto is, "Helping people one heart at a time."

Call:

(530) 620-4641

Or Write:

LAM
P.O. Box 165
Mt. Aukum, CA 95656

Life Applications Ministry Church

Join us every Sunday at 10:30 AM (PST) via Telephone at:

712-775-8968 access code: 742492
(Connect with us as this number may change)

We are a home based church reaching people locally and around the world, sharing things we have talked about in this book, Holy Spirit driven.

www.ingramcontent.com/pod-product-compliance
Lightning Source LLC
Chambersburg PA
CBHW081227090426
42738CB00016B/3209